LONDON THE PROMISED LAND REVISITED

Studies in Migration and Diaspora

Series Editor:
Anne J. Kershen, Queen Mary University of London, UK

Studies in Migration and Diaspora is a series designed to showcase the interdisciplinary and multidisciplinary nature of research in this important field. Volumes in the series cover local, national and global issues and engage with both historical and contemporary events. The books will appeal to scholars, students and all those engaged in the study of migration and diaspora. Amongst the topics covered are minority ethnic relations, transnational movements and the cultural, social and political implications of moving from 'over there', to 'over here'.

Also in the series:

Migration Across Boundaries
Linking Research to Practice and Experience
Edited by Parvati Nair and Tendayi Bloom
ISBN 978-1-4724-4049-5

Human Exhibitions
Race, Gender and Sexuality in Ethnic Displays
Rikke Andreassen
ISBN 978-1-4724-2245-3

The Somatechnics of Whiteness and Race
Colonialism and Mestiza *Privilege*
Elaine Marie Carbonell Laforteza
ISBN 978-1-4724-5307-5

Antisemitism and Anti-Zionism
Representation, Cognition and Everyday Talk
Rusi Jaspal
ISBN 978-1-4094-5437-3

Heritage, Diaspora and the Consumption of Culture
Movements in Irish Landscapes
Edited by Diane Sabenacio Nititham and Rebecca Boyd
ISBN 978-1-4724-2509-6

London the Promised Land Revisited

The Changing Face of the London Migrant Landscape in the Early 21st Century

Edited by
ANNE J. KERSHEN
Queen Mary University of London, UK

ASHGATE

Published by
Ashgate Publishing Limited
Wey Court East
Union Road
Farnham
Surrey, GU9 7PT
England

Ashgate Publishing Company
110 Cherry Street
Suite 3-1
Burlington, VT 05401-3818
USA

www.ashgate.com

British Library Cataloguing in Publication Data
A catalogue record for this book is available from the British Library

The Library of Congress has cataloged the printed edition as follows:
London the promised land revisited : the changing face of the London migrant landscape
  in the early 21st century / [edited] by Anne J. Kershen.
    pages cm. – (Studies in migration and diaspora)
  Includes bibliographical references and index.
  ISBN 978-1-4724-4727-2 (hardback) – ISBN 978-1-4724-4728-9 (ebook) –
  ISBN 978-1-4724-4729-6 (ePub) 1. London (England) – Ethnic relations. 2. London
(England) – Emigration and immigration – Social aspects. 3. Minorities – England –
London – Social conditions – 21st century. 4. Immigrants – England – London – Social
conditions – 21st century. 5. London (England) – Social conditions – 21st century.
    I. Kershen, Anne J. II. London, the promised land?

  DA676.9.A1L66 2015
  305.9'0691209421–dc23

                                                                          2015014511

ISBN 9781472447272 (hbk)
ISBN 9781472447289 (ebk – PDF)
ISBN 9781472447296 (ebk – ePUB)

Printed in the United Kingdom by Henry Ling Limited,
at the Dorset Press, Dorchester, DT1 1HD

Contents

List of Figures

Notes on Contributors

Professor Jane Anderson (Homerton University Hospital NHS Foundation Trust) has been involved in the clinical care of people with HIV since the beginning of the epidemic and currently works as a clinician and researcher in HIV medicine in East London. Her work focuses on the needs of ethnic minority and migrant populations in relation to HIV in the UK, with a particular focus on HIV care for women and families. She is a consultant physician and Director of the Centre of Sexual Health and HIV. She holds honorary academic appointments at Barts and the London School of Medicine and Dentistry and at University College London. Jane is the immediate past Chair of the British HIV Association and is currently seconded to Public Health England as an advisor on HIV and sexual health.

Dr Tendayi Bloom is a political theorist who has taught and published in the fields of Political Theory, Ethics and Politics. Her publications include; 'Asylum seekers: subjects or objects of research?' in the *American Journal of Bioethics* in 2010; 'Contradictions in Formal Commonwealth Citizenship Rights' in *The Round Table* in 2011, and 'Just open borders?', published in the *Journal of Global Ethics* in 2009. She has also co-authored work in this area, including 'European Union and Commonwealth Free Movement', with Katherine Tonkiss, published in the *Journal of Ethnic and Migration Studies* in 2013 and 'Migration and Citizenship: Rights and Exclusions', with Rayah Feldman, published in 2011 in *Migration and Social Protection*, edited by Rayah Feldman and Rachel Sabates-Wheeler. She is a contributing co-editor with Parvati Nair of *Migration Across Boundaries* (2015). She is interested in the nature of non-citizenship, and how existing systems can be used to improve rights-acquisition for non-citizens. She obtained her PhD in Political Theory from the School of Law at Queen Mary University of London, during which time she acted as a Research Associate at the Centre for the Study of Migration. She is currently Research Fellow at the United Nations University Institute on Globalization, Culture and Mobility in Barcelona.

Professor John Eade is Professor of Sociology and Anthropology at the University of Roehampton, a member of the Migration Research Unit at UCL and Visiting Professor at the University of Toronto. He has studied urban ethnicity and identity politics in the context of Bangladeshi settlement since the 1980s. He has published extensively and relevant publications include *The Politics of Community* (1989) and *Placing London* (2000) as well as the single-edited *Living the Global City* (1997) and the co-edited *Understanding the City: Contemporary and Future Perspectives* (2002), *Transnational Ties* (2008) and *Accession and Migration:*

Changing Policy, Society, and Culture in an Enlarged Europe (2009). His recent publications include, 'Religious place-making and migration across a globalising city: Responding to mobility in London' in *Culture and Religion* (2012); 'Crossing Boundaries and Identification Processes' in *Integrative Psychological and Behavioral Science* (2013); 'Representing British Bangladeshis in the global city: Authenticity, text and performance' in S. McLoughlin et al. (eds), *Writing the City in British Asian Diasporas* (2014); 'Bengalis in Britain: Migration, State Controls and Settlement' in J. Chatterji and D. Washbrook (eds), *Routledge Handbook of the South Asian Diaspora* (2013) and 'Identitarian Pilgrimage and Multicultural Society' in A. Pazos (ed.), *Pilgrims and Pilgrimages as Peacemakers in Christianity, Judaism and Islam* (2013).

Dr Michał Garapich is a social anthropologist, Lecturer at the University of Roehampton and Research Fellow at CROMM (Centre for Research on Migration and Multiculturalism) specialising in the issues of migration, ethnicity, nationalism, multiculturalism, substance misuse, homelessness and migration from Poland. Since 2005 Michał has conducted numerous research projects using both quantitative as well as ethnographic methods exploring various aspects of life of migrants from Accession States (EU10) in the UK, as well as migrants from Africa. His research has been funded by local government in London including Hammersmith & Fulham, Redbridge, Lewisham, Waltham Forest, Greenwich, the European Commission, Research Council (ESRC), media (BBC Newsnight, Channel 4), think tanks (IPPR) and the charitable trust, Southlands Methodist Trust. His work currently focuses on homelessness, Eastern and Central Europeans' participation in British politics and constructions of race among migrants from EU10. Besides academic work published in four languages, he is a regular contributor to the media in Poland and is a co-editor of *Przeglad Polonijny-Studia Migracyjne*, a peer-reviewed journal published by the Polish Academy of Sciences. He has been recently appointed to a panel of migration experts advising the Polish Senate.

Michael Keating has wide experience researching and understanding sensitive and controversial diversity and equality issues gained from a range of roles in local government, the health service and higher education. Since June 2012, Michael has worked as a freelance adviser for the London Boroughs of Brent, Enfield and Hackney, Hertfordshire County Council and East London Foundation Trust. In 2014 he produced a guide to the Fundamental Rights Agency's human rights toolkit for local government across Europe. From 2003 until May 2012, Michael was the corporate lead for equality, cohesion and partnerships at the London Borough of Tower Hamlets. Between January 2010 and March 2011 he was seconded to the Local Government Association (formerly IDeA) as the National Adviser for Equalities and Cohesion, working not only with all English councils but the wider public sector as well. Michael was also a local councillor between 1994 and 2002. With Kevan Collins, Chief Executive of the Education

Endowment Foundation, Michael co-authored 'An East End Tale', in Peter Marshall (ed.), *The Tail: How Britain's Schools Fail One Child in Five – and What Can be Done* (Profile Books, February 2013). Based on understanding how Tower Hamlets has sustained ongoing improvement in education standards, this argues that schools working with strong and ambitious local communities can achieve more than schools working alone.

Dr Anne J. Kershen was Barnet Shine Senior Research Fellow in the Department of Politics (now the School of Politics and International Relations) at Queen Mary University of London from 1990 until her (semi)retirement in 2010. She is now Honorary Senior Research Fellow at the Centre for the Study of Migration at QMUL and Honorary Senior Research Associate at the Bartlett School of Graduate Studies, UCL. In 1995 she founded the Centre for the Study of Migration and became its Director, a position she held until 2010. In 1997 she edited the first book – *London the Promised Land? The Migrant Experience in a Capital City* (published by Avebury) – in what was to become a distinguished series; she edited three further books in the series and continues to be Series Editor for what is now the Migration and Diaspora list for Ashgate. She has published widely, appeared on television and radio and acted as a consultant to the media on migration in London. Her recent publications include: 'Food in the Migrant Experience', in *Crossings: Journal of Migration and Culture* (2014); 'Afterword' in M. Tromp, M. Bachman and H. Kaufman (eds) *Fear and Loathing and Victorian Xenophobia* (2013); with Laura Vaughan, 'There was a Priest, a rabbi and an imam ...; Religious continuity and discontinuity in East London', *Material Religion* (2013); 'Married Jewish and Muslim Women Don't Work', *Home Cultures* (2011); 'Synagogues and Mosques: Bagels and Curries', *Jewish Culture and History* (2011). Her single authored books include: *Strangers, Aliens and Asians: Huguenots, Jews and Bangladeshis in Spitalfields 1666–2000*, (2005): *Uniting the Tailors: Trade Unionism amongst the tailoring workers of London and Leeds 1870–1939* (1995) and jointly with Jonathan Romain, *Tradition and Change: History of Reform Judaism in Britain 1840– 1995* (1995). Together with Colin Holmes, she is currently editing *East End and Beyond: Essays in Memory of Bill Fishman* to be published in 2016.

Professor Cathy McIlwaine is Professor of Geography at Queen Mary, University of London. Her early research focused on gender, civil society and urban violence in the Global South, but more recent work has examined low-paid migrant labour and transnational migration in the UK with a specific focus on Latin Americans from the perspective of gender, livelihoods and transnational voting. Cathy has published nine books with the most recent including *Cross-Border Migration among Latin Americans* (edited, Palgrave Macmillan, 2011) and *Global Cities at Work* (co-authored, Pluto, London, 2010). Recent journal contributions include, 'Legal Latins: Creating Webs and Practices of Immigration Status among Latin American Migrants in London', *Journal of Ethnic and Migration Studies*

(2015); 'Ambivalent citizenship and extra-territorial voting among Colombians in London and Madrid', *Global Networks* (2015) (co-authored) and 'Everyday Urban Violence and Transnational Displacement of Colombian Urban Migrants to London, UK'.

Professor Parvati Nair is the Founding Director of the United Nations University Institute in Barcelona, which focuses on globalisation, culture and mobility. She was previously Professor of Hispanic, Cultural and Migration Studies and Director of the Centre for the Study of Migration at Queen Mary University of London. Her research focuses on migration, ethnicity and gender. She combines the study of photography, music and film with ethnography in order to study these fields. Her research and writing centre around, but are not limited to, Hispanic contexts and her concern is primarily with the cultural and political displacements and mobilities of globalisation and questions of cultural representation. She is the author of *Configuring Community: Theories, Narratives and Practices of Community Identities in Contemporary Spain* (MHRA, 2004) and of *Rumbo al norte: inmigración y movimientos culturales entre el Magreb y España* (Edicions Bellaterra, 2006). She is the founder and Principal Editor of the refereed journal *Crossings: Journal of Migration and Culture* and the co-editor of *Gender and Spanish Cinema* (Berg, 2004) and of *Hispanic and Lusophone Women Filmmakers: Critical Discourses and Cinematic Practices* (Manchester University Press, 2015). Her latest book is *A Different Light: The Photography of Sebastião Salgado* (Duke University Press, 2012). Among other projects that she is currently working on is a monograph entitled *Flamenco Rhythms: People, Place, Performance* on the global travels and dissemination of flamenco, she has also recently co-edited *Migration Across Boundaries* (2015) with Tendayi Bloom. She also writes a blog on flamenco: www.flamencorhythms.com

Professor Philip Ogden is Professor of Human Geography at QMUL. He was Senior Vice-Principal of Queen Mary from 2005–2011, serving as Acting Principal from 2009–2010, and a Vice-Principal from 1996–2005. He was elected to the Academy of Social Sciences in 2009, and is an Adviser to the London Chamber Orchestra. His research interests include demographic change and migration. He has published widely, his key recent publications including; with S. Buzar, A. Haase, R. Hall, S. Kabisch, 'Household Structure, migration trends and residential preferences in inner-city Leon, Spain', *Urban Geography* (2010); with A. Haase, S. Kabisch, S. Steinfuhrer, S. Bouzarovski, R. Hall, 'Emergent Spaces of reurbanisation', *Urban Geography* (2010), with S. Buzar, R. Hall, A. Haase, S. Kabisch and S. Steinfurher, 'Splintering Urban Populations: emergent landscapes of re-urbanisation in four European cities', *Urban Studies* (2007).

Professor Laura Vaughan is Professor of Urban Form and Society and Director of the Space Syntax Laboratory at the UCL Bartlett School of Architecture, where she teaches on the MSc in Spatial Design: Architecture and Cities. She studied

Environmental Design at the Bezalel Academy of Art and Design, Jerusalem and she has an MSc Advanced Architectural Studies and PhD in Architecture from UCL. Since joining UCL in 2001, Laura has used space syntax in a series of multi-disciplinary research projects to study the relationship between micro- and macro-scales of urban form and society, focusing on a range of critical aspects of urbanism today, such as town centre adaptability and socio-spatial segregation, addressing the inherent complexity of the urban environment both theoretically and methodologically. Her key publications include: Kershen, A.J. and L. Vaughan (2013), 'There was a Priest, a Rabbi and an Imam ...; an analysis of urban space and religious practice in London's East End, 1685–2010'; *Material Religion*; Vaughan, L. (2007). 'The spatial foundations of community construction: the future of pluralism in Britain's 'multi-cultural' society', *Global Built Environment Review* 6; Vaughan, L. and S. Arbaci (2011), 'The Challenges of Understanding Urban Segregation', *Built Environment* 37; Vaughan, L., D.C. Clark, et al. (2005), 'Space and Exclusion: Does urban morphology play a part in social deprivation?', *Area* 37; Vaughan, L. and A. Penn (2006). 'Jewish Immigrant Settlement Patterns in Manchester and Leeds 1881', *Urban Studies* 43; forthcoming in 2015/16, *Suburban Urbanities: Studies in the Socio-spatial Complexity of Historical Town Centres* (UCL Press).

Professor Bronwen Walter is Professor of Irish Diaspora Studies at Anglia Ruskin University. She has published widely on Irish migration to Britain and Irish women in the diaspora. She is co-author of the CRE Report *Discrimination and the Irish Community in Britain* (1997) and her book *Outsiders Inside: Whiteness, Place and Irish Women* was published by Routledge in 2001. She directed the ESRC Major Grant '*The second-generation Irish: a hidden population in multi-ethnic Britain*' (2000–2002) and the international research team which produced an academic study to inform the Task Force on Policy Regarding Emigrants, Office of the Minister for Foreign Affairs, Dublin (2002). Her current research explores multi-generational Irish identities in Britain, New Zealand and Newfoundland.

Dr Veronica L.C. White BSc MBBS MSc MD FRCP is a Consultant Respiratory Physician and TB Clinical Lead Barts Health NHS London. Her MD was on 'Barriers to the Effective Management of Tuberculosis in the Bangladeshi Community of East London', and she has published widely in her field.

Acknowledgements

Firstly, in my capacity as editor of *London the Promised Land Revisited*, I should like to thank all those who have contributed essays to this volume. They are people I have known and had the pleasure to work with in the past and it has been a delight to have been able to combine academe with friendship and put this book together. All are very busy individuals and I do appreciate the time taken out of demanding professional lives in order to research and write the chapters which follow. Many thanks also to Laura who, in addition to contributing her chapter, agreed to be the 'editor's editor', and read so carefully through my contributions – though, of course, any errors are solely mine! Special thanks to my husband Martin for his patience and tolerance whilst I was working on this book.

Secondly, in my role as both this book's editor and series editor for Studies in Migration and Diaspora, I wish to express my most sincere gratitude to Ashgate's Senior Commissioning Editor, Neil Jordan for his support and help with this volume and all the others that have appeared in the series. It is a pleasure to work with someone who shows such concern and interest in the manuscripts that travel across his desk and I look forward to continuing to work with him in the future. Many thanks also to Pam Bertram, Senior Editor, for her help with the editing of this book.

Anne J. Kershen
July 2015

Foreword

There can be no doubt about the continuing importance and relevance of studying the impact of migration on London. The capital has long been a global city, attracting migrants from all over the world who have transformed its neighbourhoods and landscapes. This has never been more clearly the case than in the last two decades, since the launch of the Centre for Migration Studies at Queen Mary University of London. This was marked by the publication of *London the Promised Land? The Migrant Experience in the Capital City*, the first of almost 40 volumes in a series devoted to migration. In those twenty years, the trends that were so evident in the second half of the 20th century have been magnified still further, both by the continued arrival of diverse migrant streams and by the effects of previous migrations on the demography, economy and culture of the city.

London both as a whole and in the inner city has returned to a phase of strong population growth. By early 2015, the population had reached 8.6 million, almost reaching the peak of 1939, confounding expectations at the start of the new century that the capital would probably stabilise at around 7 million people. Further growth is forecast and in inner London, long associated with population decline, the population increased by a quarter between the censuses of 1991 and 2011. The vitality of the city is inextricably linked to its attraction to migrants. London is now characterised by a 'super-diversity' of migrant groups, spanning barriers of income, social class and geographical location. A few statistics help to summarise the revolution that has taken place in London's population composition. In 1951, one in twenty Londoners was born outside the UK, by 1991 one in five and by 2011 more than one in three. In just the decade 2001–11, the non-UK born population increased by 1 million, or 54 per cent. Forty per cent of all the overseas-born population of England and Wales is to be found in the capital. The longer-term effects of migration are everywhere apparent: some 80 per cent of children in primary schools in inner London are from ethnic minority communities and 50 per cent do not have English as a first language. The top five spoken first languages in the capital besides English are Polish, Bengali, Gujarati, French and Urdu, eloquent testimony to the diversity of migration trends. In London as a whole by 2015, 44 per cent of the population are of black or minority ethnicity, with several boroughs exceeding 50 per cent.

These trends throw up a mass of research questions, many of which are addressed in this volume. Three strike me as of particular significance. Though segregation of some migrant groups is still apparent, it is remarkable how far migration affects almost all of the city, suburbs as well as the central boroughs; and that relatively new migrant groups (for example, Latin Americans) vie for attention alongside the more well established (for example, the Irish). Secondly, understanding of causality remains crucial, with undocumented migrants and refugee and asylum seekers providing the sharpest possible contrasts with those attracted by secure employment at a variety of levels. Thirdly, there is much to be learnt about the ways in which institutions react to, and interact with, migrants, for example, local authorities, health services and schools; and about ways in which migrants and their descendants are represented, for example in literature, films, theatre or oral history. This volume is timely indeed.

Philip E. Ogden
Queen Mary University of London
February 2015

Chapter 1

Introduction: London the Promised Land Revisited: The Migrant Landscape in the 21st Century

Anne J. Kershen

The Centre for the Study of Migration at Queen Mary University of London was launched in November 1995 with a conference entitled 'London the Promised Land? The Migrant Experience in a Capital City'. Two years later an edited volume of the same name was published which consisted of selected papers from that conference together with others specially commissioned. They were a mixture of the historical and the contemporary and were a clear pronouncement of the Centre's intention to highlight and encourage the growing interdisciplinary nature of migration studies. For many years migration had been a theme which formed part of the academic discourse but was not regarded as a subject in itself. However, from the 1970s onwards, migration began to emerge as a specific topic – though not then, and still not even today, an independent discipline – focused on and claimed by many, but not able to stand alone. By the mid-1990s work on migration was burgeoning, undertaken by academics and practitioners in an ever expanding range of research projects and professions. Much has been written, in a variety of disciplines and contexts about migration and migrants, yet only a small number of books have focused solely on London, one of the early few being *London the Promised Land? The Immigrant Experience in a Capital City* (Kershen, 1997) published in 1997. That collection of essays, the outcome of the 1995 conference, became the first in a series now known as *Studies in Migration and Diaspora*, which currently (early 2015), has a published list of 38 titles, with still more in the pipeline for the coming years.[1] A read-through of that list will confirm how migration studies have proliferated; globally and locally, thematically, theoretically and methodologically.

The decades following the publication of that first volume in the series have been ones in which the migrant demography of the capital has become even more varied, resulting in its immigrant population now being categorised as

---

1   Though of that only a very small number are London-centric, see <http://www.ashgate.com/default.aspx?page=1249&calcTitle=1&forthcoming=1&pagecount=0&series_id=77> for the full series list.

'super-diverse'.[2] Without exception all the London boroughs can lay claim to an immigrant presence; these ranging from billionaire Russian oligarchs in Westminster, Knightsbridge and Chelsea to unemployed ethnic minorities in Tower Hamlets and Newham.[3] Twenty years on from that inaugural conference debates about immigration feature prominently on the United Kingdom's political agenda and on the national landscape. Significantly, where once the critical focus was on migrants from the New Commonwealth, the spotlight has now moved on to those coming from Eastern Europe, both within and outside the EU.

This book explores the impact and implications of the migrant presence in London in the early 21st century. It underlines the diverse nature of contemporary migration studies and the themes and issues which are emerging from current research. The contributors to this book are leaders in their fields; the range of topics covered more than satisfying the original interdisciplinary requirements of the series in which this book appears. Without exception the chapters underline the ways in which the migrant presence touches all those in the capital and, tangentially, the country as a whole.

Whilst the contributors may seem to have little in common – being medical consultants, a national adviser on equality and diversity and academics in the fields of anthropology, geography, history, language and culture, political theory, sociology and space syntax – all the chapters are linked by themes which envelop modern day migration issues. These include: migrant visibility and invisibility; location and housing; transnationalism, gender and age, legal status, ethnicity and nationality and the post-multi-cultural society and its responses to integration and separation. However, it should not be forgotten that the heart of the book is London, its arteries the way in which migrants are perceived and the means by which those migrants are coming to terms with their lives in this early 21st century 'promised land'.

---

2   See chapters within this volume and work by Steven Vertovec, for example: S. Vertovec (2006), *The Emergence of Super-Diversity in Britain*, Centre on Migration, Policy and Society, Working Paper No. 25, COMPAS, The Centre on Migration, Policy and Society, Oxford.

3   Statistics produced in 2011 showed that in Newham only 49 per cent of its BAME population were in employment; see <http://www.aston-mansfield.org.uk/wp-content/uploads/2012/09/newham-key-statistics.pdf> accessed 20 February 2015. A draft consultation document published by Tower Hamlets in 2011, revealed that the highest proportion of those on Job Seekers Allowance (JSA) were from the Bangladeshi community; other minorities claiming JSA were listed as 'other' Asians and members of the Black community; see www.whatdotheyknow.com/request/81800/response/205985/attach/3/Draft%20Tower%20Hamlets%20Employment%20Strategy%202011%201.pdf accessed 20/02/2015.

Super-Diversity

The above inventory of this book's authors and topics provides an introduction to the concept of super-diversity which is a recurring theme throughout all the chapters in this volume; the concept was first introduced by Steven Vertovec in 2006.[4] As Vertovec points out, the diverse nature of immigrant demography in early 21st century London is of a more complex nature than the capital has previously known. And, as I recount in Chapter 2, while the migrant presence in the capital is nothing new, it is the coming together in time and space of so many variations of ethnic and national background, together with the gamut of legal/illegal status, an extensive range of employable skills, of not only different religions but the variation of sects within those religions and an assortment of dialectics within an array of languages plus gender and the span of migrant ages, that makes London a perfect template for super-diversity. The chapter provides an overview of the migrant presence in London in recent decades, demonstrating the ways in which diversity has metamorphosed into super-diversity; the chapters that follow serve to reinforce the recognition of the intricate composition of the capital's 21st century migrant landscape.

This book enables us to take into account the varied courses migration and migrant life take in London; in addition it highlights the diversity of those engaged in researching and recording the migrant experience. As becomes apparent from the chapters that follow, super-diversity is not only the lens through which migration is being examined; it is also a description of those carrying out the examination. The following paragraphs consider some of the core elements of super-diversity that emerge from the chapters in this book.

Visibility and Invisibility

Migrant visibility and invisibility is a theme which features in a number of chapters in this volume. However, when examining the different perspectives taken by the contributors, there is a need to take account of the context in which the descriptions are applied and to ask whether the nouns are being used in a tangible sense, that is, to suggest that migrant (in)conspicuousness is due to colour, racial or physiognomical otherness – for example, as I note in Chapter 2, recent research in Central London revealed that Black African hotel workers were rarely employed front of house, where they might be visible, but rather in the kitchens where they were not on view to the general public (McDowell et al., 2007); or whether the nouns are being applied in the context of institutional or state recognition, thereby intimating that visibility is dependent on formal documentation – he/she is on record therefore he/she exists? For example, when

4   Vertovec, S. (2006). This work subsequently appeared as 'Super-diversity and its implications' in *Ethnic and Racial Studies* (2007), 30(6): 1024–54.

carrying out research into the new immigrant experience in Nashville, USA, James Winders discovered that if immigrants were 'invisible' then their presence could have no influence – for good or ill – on the political system or on local or national policy making (Winders, 2012). In other words undocumented migrants would be excluded from the dominant habitus. Whilst the focal epicentre of research in this volume is a capital city on the other side of the Atlantic, the issues are not dissimilar. Michael Keating's account of the way in which certain London borough councils accommodate ethnic difference in the provision of a range of local services, highlights the need for resident visibility. In order to satisfactorily provide for the minority migrant/ethnic presence the provider needs to be informed, and have documented, *all* those living within borough council boundaries. In her chapter Tendayi Bloom highlights the negative effect of migrant invisibility, describing how London's 'ghosts', as she calls refused asylum seekers who remain in the capital, suffer the fate of falling below the parapet of authoritative recognition, becoming as she explains, 'victims of the policy of destitution'. However, lack of documentation, or the interpretation of migrant status as illegal or irregular[5] is not always indicative of penury or invisibility. As Michał Garapich, Cathy McIlwaine and Parvati Nair all describe, a number of London's migrant workers fall within the category of illegal or irregular even though many are gainfully employed, in some instances paying income tax and national insurance, and making their contribution to the capital's economic expansion and leading global status.

Invisibility is often applied to a group, even if its individual members are formally recorded and, accordingly, above the radar. Carrying out ethnographic research in the London Borough of Hackney, Susanne Wessendorf was told by a primary school teacher that the local Vietnamese community was invisible (Wessendorf, 2013, 415–16), though the children were being educated and thus formally recorded. In her chapter in this volume, McIlwaine highlights the ways in which group visibility can be a double edged sword. For undocumented Latin Americans attending social and/or cultural events in London, there is the opportunity to openly interact with fellow nationals; to purchase the provisions of home, reinforce their national identity and send money back through transnational 'donkeys'.[6] However, by being in the public arena, albeit one which is so reflective of their place of origin, there is a risk of being identified by Home Office officials, who attend such gatherings on the lookout for undocumented migrants who will subsequently be deported.

In her chapter Bronwen Walter focuses on White Irish migrants – a category which she notes 'is extremely complex to interpret' and one that has become further confused by the nomenclatures used in the 2011 Census. For while there are high-flying visible young Irish people, migrants who have negotiated the

---

5   See Kershen, Chapter 2, for definitions legal, illegal and irregular migrant status.

6   'Donkey' is the term used to describe unofficial carriers of remittance money – either carrying the money personally or by sending it through informal routes.

rise and fall of the Celtic Tiger, and who have developed survival strategies on both the mainland and in Eire, there are those Irish immigrants, particularly amongst the older population, that have been transformed from the visible to the invisible – some having fallen under the radar as a result of neglect by care providers – becoming destitute and even homeless. Others have been let down by the Irish Republic government which has not kept its promise of support to emigrants. And there are other Irish invisibles, impoverished Irish travellers[7] whose presence has not been recorded and as a result have been excluded from any benefit entitlement in the UK that may be available. Elsewhere, in a previous essay, Walter points out that in the context of the racialised 'visible' minorities, in contrast with those who are non-white, the Irish in Britain are low down the scale, however, they are almost at the top when it comes to racialised audibility; when they open their mouths the Irish become the 'black whites', adopting strategies of silence in order to avoid discrimination (Walter, 2000, p. 65).

For some migrants, invisibility or visibility is a condition of choice, determined by what is considered most rewarding economically and socially at the time. As Garapich illustrates, some Polish migrants moved between visibility and invisibility, at times even adopting another (false) identity, in order to manipulate and overcome pre-2004 EU accession border controls. In his chapter, John Eade describes how visible status is not always the choice of the individual migrant. Through the mediums of film, literature, art and oral history, the voices of the migrant subalterns have become visible and audible. Eade highlights the way in which the lenses through which the migrants are reflected have, more recently, widened. On occasions this has led to criticism by those being observed and recorded. Some groups have objected to the manner in which they have been taken out of the shadows and misrepresented by their new found visibility. He uses the examples of Salman Rushdie's *The Satanic Verses* and Monica Ali's *Brick Lane* to illustrate the fact that these insider 'cultural mediators' can become the targets of their own subaltern groups that previously have been marginalised and obscure. Parvati Nair reminds us that the undocumented and 'invisible' migrant work force of London includes, not only those who have left home in pursuit of the economic dream, in order to return home as 'rich men of high status'[8] but, in addition, those

---

7 Walter's notes that Irish traveller numbers were far more than those recorded in the 2011 Census of England and Wales.

8 Many of the early Bangladeshi immigrants came to London, only in order to make sufficient money to return home and gain respect because of their wealth – often manifest in the purchase of land upon which stone houses were built from the remittance monies sent home. Villages where such houses were built became known as 'Londoni'. In reality few of the migrants made enough money to retire to their homeland and their dream of doing so became known as the 'myth of return', a term coined by Anwar in his book of that name. See Anwar, M., 1979.

seeking refuge from the cruelty and ravages of war and – what is often lethal – state discrimination.[9]

Integration and Interaction: Separation and Segregation

Any discussion of the integration and separation of migrants within British society must be located within the broader context of debates about the failure of multi-culturalism to create a cohesive yet ethnically diverse society. In an essay which appeared in 2010, Steven Vertovec first provides a global view of multi-culturalism and then proceeds to examine the imposition of policies which supported parallel cultures rather than encouraging group interaction and cohesion. He illustrates the way in which, on both sides of the political spectrum, there has been a growing acceptance of the manner by which these policies have created communal separation and distrust, to a point where they have been blamed for the increase in the numbers of home grown terrorists, such as those responsible for the London bombings of 2005 (Vertovec, 2010, p. 86). In contrast, Heath and Demireva, in an article published in 2014, argue that multi-culturalism cannot be put forward as the only cause of segregation and separation between different ethnic groups and from the host society. They suggest that powerful factors such as discrimination, in-group marriage and intergenerational difference play their part in determining the way in which super-diverse societies do, or do not, coalesce, stating that their report paints 'rather an optimistic picture of multi-ethnic Britain' (Heath and Demivera, 2014, pp. 177–8).

The achievement of a fully integrated yet diverse society is, at the time of writing, an aim rather than a reality. It requires a populace free from discrimination and racism, a society in which all its members are equal and desegregated. It need not necessarily imply a landscape free from ethnic, religious or national clustering, but rather one in which interaction and interconnectivity are the order of the day. A space where individuals can move freely between states of difference. An example of where this takes place is provided by Laura Vaughan in Chapter 3. She focuses on the ethnic marketplace, demonstrating that in spaces where migrants initially set out to reproduce the taste and products of home for their group members, the marketplace gradually becomes a place of connectivity and interactivity as outsiders, eager to experience difference, experiment with the unknown, and discover that the other, in a variety of senses, is not threatening but instead can be included as part of us, rather than being part of them. And yet, are we asking too much of minority groups by demanding that they become part of the mainstream and by so doing surrender their cultural identities. Whilst the era of multi-culturalism may be past, is it right to substitute this with mono-culturalism? Equality of all within society, one that is

---

9   Nair is someone who has explored migration through the lens of photography. Her latest publication demonstrates the ways in which, through documentary photography, undertaken by both insiders and outsiders, invisibility and inequity of status are exposed, and the invisible made visible. See Nair, 2015.

without segregation or discrimination is a utopian ideal to aim for, but surely not a utopia which is devoid of the rich tapestry and history of cultural diversity.

Location, Location, Location ...

The chapters in this book all are written within the spatial context of London, a city with a migrant population which is spread across the capital and which is composed of a multiplicity of ethnic and racial groups from all continents speaking more than 300 languages. Although there is pronounced clustering in certain areas and boroughs, for example Bangladeshis in Tower Hamlets; Polish immigrants in Ealing; Latin Americans in Elephant and Castle and Seven Sisters, North London and a preponderance of people of Indian origin in Hounslow and Newham, a recent mapping of the capital by James Cheshire and Oliver Uberti (Cheshire and Uberti 2014) shows that London's migrant population is distributed across the boroughs – only thinning out at the very edges of Bromley to the south east, Havering to the north east and to the north and south of the western borough of Hillingdon.[10] The complexity of the map produced by Cheshire and Uberti highlights in technicolour the super-diversity that is London's immigrant landscape. The essays that appear here, which explore both the general and the particular in terms of the geography and demography of the capital, go some way towards putting meat on the bones of the map's coloured dots that represent the migrant population of London.

It must be noticeable from reading the foregoing paragraphs that two of this book's contributors have not been referenced directly when the themes which run through its chapters are explored. This is not because they are not relevant but rather that the work of Veronica White and Jane Anderson falls into a very specialist and a complex science – medicine. They are both at the coalface of interacting and interconnecting with members of the migrant population of London, at a time when the migrant, as patient, is most in need of compassion and professional expertise and understanding. Their chapters underscore the increasing diversity, or rather super-diversity, of the ethnic patient community in London, and the need for the practitioner to be not only an expert clinician, but in addition, be one that has the ability to comprehend the problems of patients who have little or no English and are from cultures which have very different approaches to the treatment of ill health and disease. Veronica White explains how, when diagnosing and treating Bangladeshi patients who have tuberculosis, she has to appreciate that often the patient will use western and traditional healing treatments in tandem. At the same time, as Jane Anderson points out, the medical practitioner, particularly in areas which have experienced the recent changes in patterns of migrant arrival – as for example the growth in incomers from Eastern Europe – has to acknowledge the 'altered profile of infectious conditions in the capital' together with the responses from the National Health Service at a

---

10   See the scatter map on '12 data maps that sum up London', BBC News Magazine, 12 November 2014, <http://www.bbc.co.uk/news/magazine-29915801>

time when it is under surveillance and extreme pressure. As she notes, new Health and Social care legislation is having an impact on immigrant sufferers from HIV, particularly those who come within the category of the irregular or illegal.

Structure of London the Promised Land Revisited

The order of chapters in this book begins by focusing on migrants and migration in general and then proceeds to studies of particular groups. As mentioned above, all carry with them the themes that weave the tapestry of London's contemporary migrant panorama. In Chapter 2, I provide an overview of the London migrant landscape in the 21st century and, by spotlighting place, economy, language and religion highlight the changing face of recent migration and settlement in the capital and set the scene for the essays that follow. In Chapter 3, Laura Vaughan takes the reader through the complex stages of the transformation from the singular of migrant diversity to the many layers of super-diversity. She describes the ways in which public space allows interconnectivity and inter-communal action to take place, enabling the building of bridges between them and us; gradually transforming the local into the glocal. Next, Michael Keating examines the way in which national debates on immigration have filtered down into local politics. He takes us through the workings of three London borough councils – Enfield, Hackney and Tower Hamlets – to demonstrate how they have delivered 'equality' in boroughs where diversity is morphing into super diversity.

The 'ghosts' of London's migrant community are persons that Tendayi Bloom in Chapter 5, says, 'the state would rather ignore'. These spectres are of multi-ethnic, multi-national origin, their only crime having been made destitute by the state itself as a result of their appeals for asylum having been rejected. Parvati Nair continues with the theme of the invisible yet, rather than concentrate on the impecunious and rejected, she examines the vital role that undocumented workers, from multifarious backgrounds, play in keeping the capital moving and, as she describes it, 'forging new borderlands'. Cultural diversity and its representation provide the foci for John Eade's exploration of the mediums through which migrants in London, in both the colonial and postcolonial period, have been portrayed in literature, film and through oral histories. He notes the responses to their representation by those who have been thrust from the shadows into the limelight and by those who view the immigrant colonialist and postcolonialist through the lens of the outsider.

The following three chapters take on a more specific focus. Bronwen Walter explores the Irish community, which though their roots in London can be traced back centuries, are still classified, and perceived, as outsiders. Significantly she asks, 'who are the Irish Londoners' and how do they construct their identity, one which combines a British and 'Irish' ancestry? Perhaps the most talked about migrants of the early 21st century are those that originate from Eastern Europe, and more particularly, from Poland. Michał Garapich takes an original approach to this much referenced group by considering 'the political significance of transnational action from the perspective of the individual migrant'. He reveals the ways in which Polish migrants have developed strategies which have enabled them to overcome state regulations – both in the UK and in Poland – in order to exercise control on their mobility and lives in London. In contrast with the spotlighting of migrants from Poland, Romania, Bulgaria and other Eastern European states, in her essay, Cathy McIlwaine introduces the reader to the 'ramifications of the growing presence of Latin Americans', in London. Though often ignored in the accounts of both visible and invisible migrant labour, these immigrants play a vital role in keeping the capital running. However, McIlwaine believes that, whilst it is preferable for these migrants to be recognised and recorded, it is often in their best personal interests not to be.

The two final chapters are devoted to the ways in which the health of London's migrant population impacts on the migrant individual, on the physicians and on the state. Both Veronica White and Jane Anderson highlight the ways in which recent migration has emphasised the need for the capital's new migrant presence to be taken into account by health providers, particularly in the cases of HIV and TB. White highlights the impact of the migrant patient on the capital's medical landscape by focusing on East London, a traditional place of settlement for migrants, whilst Anderson puts the spotlight on the capital as a whole in order to reveal the inequities that have arisen in the provision of healthcare for – particularly the invisible – migrants in London.

Though the geographic focus of the book is London, the topics covered and questions raised have relevance for the United Kingdom as a whole, particularly as a number of the chapters illustrate, in the context of political action and reaction. At the time of writing, the 2015 election approaches and immigration, both overtly and covertly, is high on the list of public concerns, either as an issue by itself or as it impacts on the nation's health, housing and jobs. Finally, it must be said that though this book does not cover every migrant group that is resident in the capital, or all the debates that their presence gives rise to, the chapters that follow do provide a starting point from which to put the early 21st century migrant landscape of London under the microscope. As such it is of significant value and importance to all those working in the field of migration studies.

References

Anwar, M. (1979), *The Myth of Return: Pakistanis in Britain*. London: Heinemann.

Cheshire, J. and Uberti, O. (2014), *London the Information Capital: 100 maps and graphics that will change how you view the city*. London: Particular Books (Penguin Books).

Heath, A. and Demireva, N. (2014), 'Has multiculturalism failed in Britain?', *Ethnic and Racial Studies*, 37(1): 161–80.

Kershen, A.J. (1997), *London the Promised Land? The Migrant Experience in a Capital City*. Aldershot: Ashgate.

McDowell, L., Batnitzky, A. and S. Dyer, (2007) 'Division, Segmentation and Interpellation: The Embodied Labours of Migrant Workers in a Greater London Hotel', *Economic Geography*, 83(1): 15.

Nair, P. (2015), *Migration Across Boundaries*. Aldershot: Ashgate.

Vertovec, S. (2006), 'The Emergence of Super-Diversity in Britain', Working Paper, No. 25, COMPAS, The Centre on Migration, Policy and Society, Oxford.

Vertovec, S. (2007), 'Super Diversity and its implications', *Ethnic and Racial Studies*, 30(6): 1024–54.

Vertovec, S. (2010), 'Towards post-multiculturalism: Changing communities, conditions and contexts of diversity', *International Science Journal*, 61(199), pp. 83–95.

Walter, B. (2000), 'Shamrocks Growing out of their Mouths: Language and the Racialisation of the Irish in Britain', in Kershen, A., *Language, Labour and Migration*. Aldershot: Ashgate, pp. 57–73.

Wessendorf, S. (2013), 'Commonplace diversity and the 'ethos of mixing': perceptions of difference in a London neighbourhood', *Identities: Global Studies in Culture and Power*, 20(4): 407–22.

Winders, J. (2012), 'Seeing Immigrants Institutional Visibility and Immigrant Incorporation in New Immigrant Destinations', *Annals*, AMPSS, 641, May, pp. 58–78.

Chapter 2

London's Migrant Landscape in the 21st Century

Anne J. Kershen

This chapter provides the context for those that follow. It is an overview of the way in which late 20th century and early 21st century migration into the capital has tinted its landscape. Within the limitations of a chapter it is impossible to cover all the diverse aspects of the migrant experience in London, the multiplicity of incomers who have arrived for both the long and short term and the varied outcomes of that migrant presence. The themes selected are those deemed most central to the lives of all residents in a capital city; space and place, interaction by means of language and cultural connection, economic activity, and religion, particularly the freedom to observe, or not, at will. As is mentioned below the immigrant place in British society is currently (January 2015) an impassioned topic and one that is being debated at all levels. It is hoped that this chapter may help dispel some of the myths that surround the migrant landscape in early 21st century London.

For centuries London has been a magnet for migrants. Long before the arrival of the telegraph, telephone, email, mobile phone, skype and, what is now, a myriad of social networks, the information that the capital city offered significant economic opportunities was transmitted through, and even beyond, Europe. A glance at a London street directory provides an insight into the way in which early migrants became embedded in the landscape. Old Jewry, Lombard Street and Petty France, are place names that were part of London's topography long before the end of the 17th century (Weinreb and Hibbert, 1983). They are a reminder of the early entrepreneurs who recognised the potential of an expanding mercantile metropolis. Jewish moneylenders,[1] Italian bankers, Dutch beer brewers and tile makers, Hanseatic, French, and Italian merchants, sowed the seeds for those who would follow. By the mid-17th century the capital was a vibrant, cosmopolitan, and increasingly tolerant, city. In 1656, with the agreement of Oliver Cromwell, the practice of Judaism was again permitted. Following the revocation of the Edict of Nantes in 1685, French Calvinists (the Huguenots), denied religious freedom in

---

1   The Jews arrived in England in the wake of William the Conqueror, many taking up the role of moneylenders. In 1290, in the era of the Crusades and as they were no longer of financial benefit, they were expelled from the country. For an account of the events leading up to the expulsion, see Julius, 2010.

France, found sanctuary in London. In the centuries that followed, metaphorically and literally, successive waves of immigrants made their imprint on the London landscape and on the social and political discourses of the nation.

In recent decades, a burgeoning number of publications and commentaries have highlighted the multidisciplinary nature of migration studies[2] and the diversity – now 'super-diversity' – of the migrant presence in one of the world's leading global cities. In the immediate postwar period the nature of immigration was predominantly New Commonwealth.[3] As the 20th century drew to its close refugees from the Middle East and Africa swelled the numbers.[4] Concerns over the impact of immigration resulted in a raft of new immigration controls. Whereas the legislation of the postwar period had been a direct reaction to the influx of New Commonwealth migrants, from the 1990s onwards controls were in response to the wider spectrum of incomers. Eight new immigration laws were passed between 1993 and 2009, with a new law coming onto the Statute book in October 2014.[5] The word 'refugee', originating with the arrival of the Huguenots in the 17th century, has taken on a new meaning. No longer a condition of persecution and fear to be assuaged in a tolerant land, it has become a nomenclature to be applied for and *possibly* (rather than definitely) awarded and celebrated; the alternative being refusal, rejection and either forced repatriation or recourse to illegality or irregularity.[6]

The past three decades have seen a sea change in the origin, character and clustering of 21st century migrants in London. As mentioned in the Introduction to this volume, the major migrant influx to Britain since the beginning of this century has been from Eastern Europe, from both within and outside the European Union. The accession of eight Eastern European countries to the EU in 2004 and

---

2   For example, the series under which this book appears – *Studies in Migration and Diaspora* – has an extensive list with contributors from the fields of sociology, anthropology, cultural studies, gender studies, archaeology, history, geography, linguistics and education to name just a few. Though the spatial foci are global, a significant number spotlight the migrant experience in London.

3   The earliest postwar arrivals were survivors of the Holocaust and European Voluntary Workers. The coincidence of the 1948 British Nationality Act and the arrival of the *Empire Windrush* from the Caribbean in June of that year heralded the start of immigration from the Caribbean and the New Commonwealth. See Anwar (1979); Fryer (2010, ed.); Gilroy (2002, ed.).

4   Included in these are refugees from Afghanistan, Iran, Iraq, Zimbabwe.

5   The main revisions are: criminals not allowed to use family life to delay deportation; no appeal on decision that deportation is conducive to the public good; reform of appeals system for students; restrictions on housing rental by illegal immigrants; Tier One threshold raised to £2,000,000; limit to repeated bail applications. See: <https://www.gov. uk/government/speeches/immigration-act-commencement-and-statement-of-changes-in-immigration-rules>

6   For a discussion on the application of these terms, see below, this chapter.

a further two in 2007[7] resulted in an unanticipated large scale entry which has, as will be shown below, changed the capital's migrant landscape and the nature of the immigration debate. The migrant population of the capital is as diverse as one would expect from one of the world's leading global cities. One in which more than 300 languages are spoken, more than 14 faiths worshipped and one which has a migrant population that manifests significant variations in economic and legal status; from builders to bankers, from legals to illegals/irregulars and all shades in between. Writing in the *Guardian* in 2005, Leo Benedictus called London, 'the world in one city'. The combination of a multiplicity of races, nationalities, religions, skills, languages, places of residence and immigrant status has taken diversity to a new level, that of super-diversity. In 2006, Steven Vertovec defined this as:

> [A] notion intended to underline a level and kind of complexity surpassing anything the country has previously experienced. Such a condition is distinguished by a dynamic interplay of variables among an increased number of new, small and scattered, multiple-origin, transnationally connected, socio-economically differentiated and legally stratified immigrants who have arrived over the last decade. (Vertovec, 2006, p. 1)

Taking that definition and applying it specifically to London, makes it clear that the capital is now host to a super-diverse immigrant population. The following sets out to illustrate the super-diversity of the London migrant population by exploring their place, language, religion, economic activity and integration in the London landscape of the early decades of the 21st century.

London's Migrant Population: An Overview

People and Place

The 2011 Decennial Census revealed that almost three million out of the capital's total population of eight million, were born outside of the United Kingdom (Census 2011, Table QSZ03EW);[8] an increase of almost one million since the 2001 census, when the number of non-UK born residents was recorded as 1,785,619 (Census 2001, Table KS05). The most influential factor in that decennial growth was the accession of the ten Eastern European countries and the migratory movement that

---

7 The 2004 Eastern European accession countries were: Czech Republic, Estonia, Hungary, Latvia, Lithuania, Poland, Slovakia and Slovenia. In 2007 Romania and Bulgaria were admitted though with harsher restrictions imposed regarding freedom of employment than those of 2004.

8 The approximate figures were, total population 8,173,941, UK born 5,175,671. The non-UK born figure included the Republic of Ireland.

Figure 2.1   Map showing London Boroughs with Irish population of more than 4,500

Source: Census 2011, Table QS203EW.

resulted. For many London became an accessible 'promised land'. For example, the Polish born population of the London Borough of Ealing grew from 3,695 in 2001 to 21,507 in 2011; in the Borough of Haringey the number rose from 868 to 10,865 and in Hounslow from 841 to 10,355. Whilst the percentage figures vary, there were significant increases in the Polish migrant communities of all the London boroughs; the overall growth in numbers of Polish born migrants in London from 2001 to 2011, was 136,064 (Census 2001, KS05 and Census 2011, QSZ03EW).

There were also – though overall less sizeable – increases in the Nigerian, Indian, Pakistani and Bengali born populations. By contrast there was a noticeable decrease in the number of Irish (both Republic of Ireland and Northern Ireland) non-UK mainland 'born' residents in the capital, which fell by 32,278, from 194,859 in 2001 to 162,581 in 2011 (Census 2001, KS05 and Census 2011, QSZ03EW). There are several reasons for this, the return to the Republic in the first half of the 'noughties' of those pulled by the Celtic Tiger economy as well as the variations in self-identity by those resident in London. In spite of the reduction, there are still a number of London boroughs where there are communities of more than 4,500 of Irish origin (see Figure 2.1), whilst there is not one borough in which the 'Irish' are not represented. In her chapter in this volume, Bronwen Walter explores the diverse nature of the Irish population and its rootedness in the capital.

One of the most discussed, though least accurately recorded, migrant communities in London, is that of those originating from what is now Russia, or more formally, the Russian Federation. Whilst the 2011 Decennial Census did not separately categorise those of Russian nationality, data from the Estimated Country of Birth and Nationality Data Sheet published in 2012, records the figure as being in the region of 22,500 (Population by country of birth and nationality data sheet, 2012).[9] The 2011 Decennial Census 'Major or Preferred Languages' table, presents the figure of 26,603 Russian speakers in London (Census 2011, QS204EW). However this figure should be viewed with caution as it may well include those whose country of origin is now one of the nine, Commonwealth of Independent States, a group formed after the break-up of the Soviet Union.[10] Whatever the exact number there is no denying that *Londongrad*, with its couture shops, high flying interior designers and top public schools, has been attracting an increasing number of Russian Tier One visa applicants.[11] Between June 2013 and June 2014 there were 180 investor visas issued to rich Russians, a 50 per cent increase on the previous year. However, most users of the Tier One scheme in that period were the Chinese with 295 visas being awarded, an increase of 71 per cent on the previous year and 275 more than the number awarded in 2010. (*The Times*, 6 November 2014). An article in the *Daily Mail*, published in September 2013, suggested that there were as many as 300,000 Russians living in the capital, many occupying super-high priced properties in Knightsbridge, Chelsea and Notting Hill. While this is clearly a gross exaggeration, there are smaller clusters – of over 1,000 – in Newham, Tower Hamlets, Camden and in Outer London in Barnet, Ealing and Waltham Forest. In fact, there are 'Russian Speakers' recorded in each of the Greater London boroughs (Census 2011, Table QS24EW). A survey carried out by a leading UK estate agent reported that between 2010 and 2013 the highest percentage of million pound plus properties sold in the capital – with the exception of UK born purchasers – were bought by Russians (Knight Frank, 2014), though in the first half of 2014, the Russian place at the top of the table was taken by Italy, with Russia falling to third place behind France. A report published at the end of 2014 revealed a 70 per cent fall in the number of Russians buying homes in London, the market having divided into the super rich Russians who are still

---

9   The figures are in quantities of 1,000 and allow for a variance of 1,000 where accurate statistics were not available.

10   Prior to independence, for some, their main language would have been Russian, accordingly the figure for country of birth/nationality will differ from major or preferred language.

11   The Tier 1 applicants from Russia were 'Investors' who had upwards of £1,000,000 – this threshold has now been raised to £2,000,000 – to invest in the UK. For these wealthy incomers all restrictions are waived, including the English Language requirement.

purchasing £20 million plus properties, and 'the others'[12] adversely affected by the collapse of the Russian currency. At the time of writing, the super rich still see London as a safe haven, particularly while the value of the rouble is falling (*The Times*, 22 December 2014). However, whether the number is 30,000 or 300,000, the Russian presence in London is a notable one and, as in the case of the Accession migrants, very much a phenomenon of the 21st century.

At the other end of the migrant housing scale is Newham, one of London's most ethnically diverse and overcrowded boroughs. Unlike its neighbour Tower Hamlets, which houses the largest number of Bangladeshis outside of Bangladesh, as well as smaller clusters of other immigrant groups, Newham is host to a multiplicity of immigrant communities of moderate size, more than half the population having being born outside the UK. The largest group being the 26,807 from India (Census 2011, Table QS203EW). Those claiming Indian ethnicity in the Borough was recorded as 42,484 (Census 2011, Table KS201EW). The Borough's migrant population is burgeoning. Earlier arrived relatives who have found themselves at the receiving end of the migrant chain have had to resort to constructing breeze block sheds and wooden outhouses in their rear gardens to accommodate the inflow. The Borough is a living manifestation of migrant overcrowding, the worst recorded example, according to the Council, being 38 immigrants found living in one property (*Economist*, 2012). The reality of the super-diverse migrant housing landscape in London is that of extreme opulence and extreme poverty existing almost cheek by jowl. For example, in the east of the capital, within a radius of just over three miles, there are new migrants living in conditions of excessive overcrowding in the London Borough of Newham, while European and North American bankers occupy multi-million pound apartments in Canary Wharf, in the London Borough of Tower Hamlets.

There has been some discussion around the issues of migrant clustering and diffusion (Graff and Nijkamp, 2010). Whilst certain ethnic groups are noticeable by their predilection to cluster in tightly knit communities, it has seemed that the recent Eastern European incomers are more widely spread. Whilst this might be correct when taking a national view, an examination of the location of non UK nationals as located across the London boroughs reveals that specific nationalities are contiguously linked both north and south of the River Thames. The boroughs of Hounslow, Ealing, Brent, Barnet, Enfield, Haringey, Waltham Forest and Newham – contiguous north of the Thames – and to the south of the river, the neighbouring boroughs of Wandsworth, Merton, Croydon and Lambeth, all record Polish born communities of more than 5,000. Thus, as Figure 2.2 below demonstrates, whilst it has been suggested that the Polish migrants disperse rather than cluster, the map highlights the way in which the communities have spread out, yet remain

---

12 Many of the 'others' are Russians in the employ of Russian owned companies in London who are paid in roubles which have to be changed into UK currency and, as the value of the rouble falls, so does their income (*The Times*, 22 December 2014).

Figure 2.2   Map showing boroughs in London with more than 5,000 Polish born residents

Source: Census 2011, Table QS203EW.

connected.[13] As Figure 2.3 below illustrates, the larger Indian communities present an interesting comparison, whilst there is a cluster of more than 5,000 Indian born people in each of the following west London boroughs: Hillingdon, Hounslow, Ealing, Harrow, Brent, and Barnet, to the east of London the link is restricted to Redbridge and Newham, whilst South of the River the larger Indian community is just to be found in Croydon. Croydon too, provides the base for the largest south of the Thames Pakistani born community, with close by Wandsworth home to a community of more than 5,000. North of the river communities of over 5,000 immigrants from Pakistan are to be found in Hounslow, Ealing and Brent and to the east in Redbridge, Newham and Waltham Forest. The third migrant group originating from South East Asia is that from Bangladesh. Bangladeshi born migrants are to be found mainly to the east of the capital; 20,945 in Newham and 7,225 in Redbridge with smaller numbers in other boroughs. However, the largest Bangladeshi community in London – indeed the largest clustered group outside of Bangladesh – is located in Tower Hamlets. According to the 2011 Census, 81,377

---

13   Only those boroughs with more than 5,000 Polish nationals have been selected, but other boroughs have smaller Polish communities.

**Figure 2.3   Map showing boroughs in London with more than 5,000
            Indian born residents**

Source: Census 2011, Table QS203EW.

people in the Borough claimed Bangladeshi ethnicity; of that number, 38,877 were
born in Bangladesh.[14] The third largest Bangladeshi community in London is more
centrally located in Camden, well known for the Bengali restaurants and provision
stores in Drummond Street, close by Euston Station.[15]

It should not be thought that the London migrant population is restricted to
Eastern European and New Commonwealth arrivals. All seven continents and
their nationalities are represented in London, and indeed, there is not one borough
in the capital that is not home to a potpourri of migrant communities (Census
2011, Table QS203EW). Taking the capital as a whole, according to the 2011

---

14   For the purposes of this chapter – with the exception of the Irish immigrant
communities where the threshold is 4,500 – I have highlighted instances where the specific
migrant communities in a specific borough number more than 5,000. However, it must be
noted that a) there are other national communities whose numbers exceed 5,000 in any
one borough, for example Turkish nationals in Hackney, and b) that there are other smaller
national communities for example Polish immigrants, in most boroughs in the capital.

15   The 2011 Census recorded the size of the community as 5,947.

Census, the top five UK non national groups in London are those from: India, Poland, Bangladesh, Pakistan and the Republic of Ireland.[16]

Language

The super-diversity of London's immigrant population is clearly exemplified by the range of languages other than English recorded in the 2011 Census, as 'Main or Preferred Language'. There are over 300 different languages spoken in London. Ancillaries to this are the different levels of English fluency and the dialects that are sub factors in the language table. For example, under the heading of Bengali – for the Bangladeshi population – we must include the dialects of Sylheti and Chatgaga; members of the Chinese community/ies are recorded as speaking, Mandarin, Cantonese and 'all other Chinese' dialects. And whilst the official language of India might be Hindi, of which there are at least 21,503 speakers in the capital, the 2011 Census also lists speakers of Gujarati, Marathi, Telugu, Tamil and Malayalam as living in the London. Similar first language differences are to be found within the Pakistani population of London and, as noted above, migrants from countries that were part of the Soviet Union may well have the choice of Russian or, Armenian, Romanian, Azerbaijani and a range of other languages (Census 2011, Table QS24EW).

What are the implications of this linguistic super-diversity? There are issues here for both children and adults. For example, in the London Borough of Newham, 42 per cent of the population recorded a language other than English as their first language; of that number 21 per cent said they could not speak English well – or not at all. Not only does this have repercussions for the integration of adult migrants, it also impacts on the children of those families. In the context of young immigrants who are at school, the diversity of languages and the fact that some parents speak little or no English, creates problems for educationalists, who sometimes have to accommodate a broad range of languages in one school and pupils for whom entry to school is the first time they hear English spoken as a means of communication. A report published at the end of the first decade of the 21st century showed that at least 40 different languages were spoken by more than one thousand pupils in the state system in the capital. As the authors of the report stated, this is 'An example of remarkable diversity' (Ahn, et al., 2010, p. 1). Confronting linguistic diversity in schools requires an awareness of the changing nature of the local migrant population and the needs of its children of school going age. For example, in a report produced

---

16   Mention needs to be made of the way in which official records can determine, for some, migrant visibility. For example, the 2011 Decennial Census table for 'Detailed Country of Birth', broken down into local authorities (Table QS203EW), has a number of country omissions. For instance, Russia does not appear on the table. For a more comprehensive list of places of birth, one which is composed of 201 places/countries, referral should be made to the Labour Force Survey, Population by Country of Birth data sheet, published annually by the Office of National Statistics: see www.ons.gov.uk.

by Baker and Eversley in 2000, only 17 per cent of London's schoolchildren were recorded as having Polish as their home language, Polish being positioned 25 in their list of 40 home languages – with English at the top (Baker and Eversley, 2000, p. 5). In a follow up report, which appeared in 2008 (Eversley et al., 2008) in a list which excluded English, the position of Polish speakers had risen to 12, coming below French and Portuguese; it also noted that the number of Somali speakers had doubled in under a decade. Romanian and Bulgarian appear neither in the 2000, nor 2008 school language list, yet by 2011 there were 40,000 Romanian and 23,000 Bulgarian speakers living in London (Ahn, et al., 2010, p. 3), yet another manifestation of the impact of the 2004 and 2007 accessions.

The 2008 report records the presence of 10,991 Polish children in the London state school system – both primary and secondary – yet the 2011 Census recorded 147,816 individuals who put Polish as their main or preferred language – next to English the most widely spoken language in the capital, and indeed in the country. Discounting those under school going age, there remains a sizeable difference between the number of Polish speaking schoolchildren and the total number of Polish speakers in the capital, suggestive of the adult nature of the Polish migrant population of London, many of whom wait until they have secured their financial position, either in Poland or the UK, before starting a family or bringing their families over to join them (Coyle, 2007).

So far the discussion on linguistic diversity has focused on the way in which the immigrant's native tongue impacts on his/her, or children's, way of life. However, in recent research, Jenny Cheshire and fellow researchers have highlighted the way in which a new, creolised, language has emerged in multi-ethnic areas of London. They refer to this language as, 'Multicultural London English'.[17] Cheshire and her fellow researchers have shown how young people, whose home languages have their roots in different countries and continents, for example, the Caribbean, Africa, India and Bangladesh, have created a creolised way of speech, one which heralds a 'distinct and important type of community language change'(Cheshire et al., 2011). These youth are coming to the host language through a new, secondary, route and by so doing are adding yet another layer to the super-diversity of the language scene in the capital.

Religion

The face, and diversity, of immigrant religion has long been a facet of the London landscape, both architecturally and figuratively. By the middle of the 16th century, immigrants from France and Holland had established their own churches in the City

---

17   A recent article in *The Economist* highlighted the fact that the fastest growing ethnic minority group was that of those from a mixed-ethnic background. However in the context of the London migrant landscape the article also revealed that in the second decade of the 21st century this phenomenon was far greater beyond, rather than within, the capital. (*The Economist*, 2014).

of London. By the early 18th century there were Huguenot (Calvinist) chapels and two Jewish synagogues in the East of the capital. Two centuries later, London's East End was flooded with *chevrot* (small synagogues) established by immigrants from Eastern Europe – some located in what previously had been Huguenot churches – later some of these would become mosques. As the 19th century drew to its close, the wide-ranging nature of provision for foreign Christian worshippers was highlighted by the presence of Greek Orthodox, Russian, Spanish and Italian churches on the streets of London.[18]

By the close of the first decade of the 21st century the six main religions, as identified by the 2011 Decennial Census, as well as all of the listed minor religions, had an acknowledged presence in the capital.[19] The first purpose built mosque in the capital was erected and opened in 1926, in South West London. The magnificent golden-domed Central London Mosque was opened in Regent's Park in 1978; whilst the East London Mosque in Whitechapel Road – one of the largest in Europe, was (re)-opened in its present form in 1985. The earliest dedicated Hindu temple in the capital dates from 1970, whilst the largest Hindu temple outside of India – the Swaminarayan Mandir and Haveli – was opened in Neasden, North West London, in 1995. A Sikh Gurdwara (temple) was established in London in 1911 and a Buddhist temple in 1926.

Yet, though the impressive range of religious choice suggests that migrants could, and thus would, automatically continue to follow their home religion, finding comfort in the familiar and thus a means of building bridges between 'over there' and 'over here', this is not always the case. For some, the freedom and variety on offer in the global city has presented an opportunity to experiment with other branches of their religion or, in some cases, make the move towards secularity. This has been shown to be true of diasporic Iranians who have come from a Muslim background and who have chosen to lead a secular, that is non-Islamic, life in London. They have embraced the freedom of the capital in order to eschew the strict Islamic identity that is now a part of the Iranian state. Members of the Persian/Iranian migrant community have chosen to identify themselves as 'Persian' in order to choose how they fashion their cultural, political, religious and sexual lives, in a state of what Reza Gholami has called 'non-Islamiosity' (Gholami, 2015).

Secularity was not the obvious, or majority, option for immigrants coming from Eastern Europe after Accession. Choice – or perhaps for some confusion – was what they found amongst the Roman Catholic Churches in London. For whilst spatially there were churches ready and waiting to accommodate new arrivals

---

18   A Greek orthodox church was first opened in 1670; a Russian embassy church was available for worshippers in 1716, a Spanish chapel was opened in 1791 and an Italian Church in 1863.

19   In addition to the six, Christianity, Buddhism, Hinduism, Judaism, Islam and Sikhism, another 40 religions were recorded as well as a number of 'non-religions', See Decennial Census 2011, Table QS210EW.

when Poland entered Europe in 2004, for Polish Catholic migrants in London, their choice of specific place of worship was complicated by the structure of the Polish churches.

> There is a dual or triple institutional structure of the Polish churches here – churches run by the Polish Church answerable to the Polish bishop in Poland, congregations run by English church with a Polish-speaking priest hired independently by the English hierarchy, and congregations run by the religious orders answerable to the Vatican. (Garapich, 2014)

Thus, when in 2008, the Cardinal Archbishop of Westminster expressed his desire to see the new Polish immigrants integrate into the British Catholic Church, once they had learned English, Polish priests in the capital felt their flocks were threatened (Eade, 2011). The result was a drive to recruit priests directly from Poland with whom the new arrivals could relate – the 'Easyjet Priests'(Trzebiatowsha, 2010). Though many of the Polish Catholic migrants found attendance at a Polish Catholic Church an enjoyable and worthwhile experience, one which reinforced both their national and religious identity, it had become evident that the liturgy in the British and older Polish Catholic churches did not fulfil the needs of all the newly arrived worshippers (Grymalamoszczynska, and Krotofil, 2011).[20] However, in spite of the various attempts to keep the newcomers within the fold, others have taken the opportunity to sample the variety of non-Catholic churches in the capital and there are even those who have been drawn to churches which have a more evangelical dimension. Others still have eschewed religion in favour of a more secular, less constrained life style. The tolerant nature of London has even enabled Polish Jehovah's Witnesses – who experience discrimination in their own country – an opportunity to seek to proselytise their fellow expatriates (Garapich, 2014). As Eade points out, under communism, religion was muted, if non-existent (Eade, 2011). Children brought up by parents who lacked a religious background have taken one of two paths, either that of exploring their national, or an alternative, religion or embracing the freedom that non-observance allows.

It is not only Polish Catholicism that is present on the London immigrant religious landscape. It is estimated that there are between 57,343 (Census 2011, QS203EW) and 113,500 (McIlwaine, 2011, p. 7) South Americans – predominately from Brazil, Colombia, Ecuador, Bolivia and Peru – living in London. The numerical discrepancy lying in the fact that the greater figure includes regular/irregular and second generation rather than solely those legal residents who answered the question 'country of birth' in the 2011 Census. For many of these migrants the churches, particularly the Roman Catholic Church, provide not only services taken by Latin American priests and pastors, speaking either Spanish or Portuguese, but in addition facilities which include 'a free GP for people, and

---

20   Some of the older Polish churches were established in the late 19th century. See Grymalamoszczynska, H. and Krotofil, J. (2011 p. 207, ff 4).

a lawyer in Spanish who comes every Thursday night for free ... we also have a group of doctors who can help people who can't visit doctors and they give prescriptions'. For both the religious and the non-believer these churches provide a support network which not only enables the migrants to retain pride in their identity, they are also guardians of respectability, helping those who attend to avoid, 'drugs, prostitution, sometimes robbery'(McIlwaine, 2011, pp 105–6).

An echo of the religiously liberating impact of arrival in London is also to be found in the pattern of behaviour manifested by the early arrivals from Bangladesh. Having lived under the strictures of Islam in their home countries, on first arriving in the 1960s and 1970s, the young men, though not fully eschewing their religion, put it on hold, enjoying the pleasures of white women, alcohol, gambling and, rather than eating halal, just avoiding pork (Kershen and Vaughan, 2013). However as bachelor enclaves turned into family communities the men returned to religion and began to establish a range of mosques that today is estimated to number somewhere between 364 and 411.[21] Because there is no legal requirement for the registration of a mosque, unless it is also a charity, it is impossible to accurately quantify or locate the rooms, flats, houses, sheds – and in one case a car park – that provide facilities for the Muslims in London to worship. The worship of Islam is yet another exemplification of the super-diversity of religion in the capital. In addition to the main branches of Sunni, Shia and Sufi on offer, worshippers can find mosques which accommodate a variety of themes including Dawoodi, Deobandi, Maudoodi, Salafi and Wahabi. What is significant, is the increased religiosity of the Bengali Muslim youth, as compared to that of their parents, the original migrants. As one Bengali, who migrated to London 45 years ago explained, 'my son is much more religious than I ever was' (Kershen, 2013). This move towards, rather than away from, religion amongst young Muslims may provide a reason for the increased number of mosques that have appeared on the London landscape over the past thirty years.

Whilst the desire for proximity for a place of prayer, close to home and work, is seen almost as a necessity for observant Muslims, as for example in Tower Hamlets, for others, particularly Pentecostal worshippers, it is the desire to join together and pray with co-religionists from similar cultural and religious backgrounds, in 'gathered communities' that, is making a spatial imprint on other parts of the capital. A report published in June 2013 revealed that there were over 240 Black Majority Churches (BMC) in the London Borough of Southwark, accommodating at times more than 20,000 worshippers drawn from all over the capital and its outer suburbs, the worshippers being mainly African or African-Caribbean. At a time when attendance at traditional Anglican and Catholic churches is decreasing the reverse is seen to be true of BMC, 'There are twice as many BMC churches in Southwark as there are others' (Rogers, 2013). The researchers highlight the

---

21   There is clearly variance in the recorded number of mosques in London as <http://mosques-map.muslimsinbritain.org/maps.php#/town/London> records 364 while <http://www.mosquedirectory.co.uk/mosques/england/london> records 411.

fact that the growth in the number of churches – many in buildings which were only licensed for industrial use and thus did not meet with Council approval '... is in the present tense; the reality is of the present moment, actual and constantly developing' (Rogers, 2013). The more shadowy religious buildings in current usage for services enable an invisibility which reduces the impact of the dominant presence of the BMC in the Borough; many BMC churches only in evidence when their congregants attend prayers.

In contrast, visibility was the determining factor in the refusal by the local councils for planning permission applied for by the Kingsway International Christian Church (KICC) to build large scale, community gathering, Pentecostal churches in the London suburbs of Rainham and Crystal Palace. Eade shows how, in the case of the former, Rainham Council considered an 8,000-seater house of worship totally inappropriate for the area, whilst the KICC's plans to convert a local cinema in Crystal Palace into a church were considered unacceptable (Eade, 2012). These are two clear examples of instances where concerns about the migrant's imprint on the architectural landscape received an overwhelmingly negative reception.

There is no doubt that in the context of both religiosity and secularisation, over the past 30 years the migrant presence in London has made a significant impression on the religious panorama of London. Globalisation has forced the capital's churches and mosques to respond, as have Hindu and Sikh Temples – though perhaps less so synagogues, as recent Jewish immigrants to the UK are either accommodated by existing Jewish religious movements or are non-observant (see Staetsky and Boyd, 2014). What we can learn from studying the arrival of new migrants into the capital's religious environment is that London offers multiple choices for worshippers of all religions and, for those previously under religious and regime restraints, that choose to follow a secular, agnostic or atheistic pathway, the freedom to live their lives as they wish.

Economic Activity

The reaction to immigrant workers in London ranges from the centuries old, 'they are taking the jobs of Englishmen' (Kershen, 2005) to the, though albeit unattributable, belief that if all the immigrant workers were removed from the capital, it would grind to a halt. What is undeniable is that the super-diversity of London's early 21st century migrant population is clearly apparent in the capital's workforce, which includes migrant workers from more than 63 different countries (Wills et al., 2010).[22] The diversity is manifest not only in nationality, but also in levels of skill, job type and, significantly, in worker status, which may be legal, illegal or irregular. There is a degree of confusion, and debate, over the designations 'illegal' immigrant and 'irregular' immigrant. Illegal migrants are those who

---

22   These 63 countries were located in Africa, North and South America, the Caribbean, Asia, Australasia and Eastern, Central and Western Europe. See J. Wills, et al., (2010).

have entered a country clandestinely and have no legal right of residence, an irregular migrant may have had a legal right of entry but then may have violated the restrictions placed on entry (Vollmer, 2011), for example, by overstaying, or breaking the provisions of his/her visa. Without official documentation, illegal and irregular migrant workers would seemingly all be invisible members of the labour force. And yet, the invisible can become legitimately visible, either by registration for National Insurance (see below) or, as has been the case for many Eastern Europeans following the 2004 and 2007 Accessions, when their countries entered the European Union and access to the UK became freely available.

One of the main criticisms of migrant workers, both legal and illegal/irregular is their cost to the UK in terms of health, housing and education. However, research has shown that, irrespective of legal status, some workers pay National Insurance and Income Tax. Many having purchased – as opposite to having been granted – legitimate or forged National Insurance numbers. Speaking in 2010, Professor Ian Gordon stated that he believed that two-thirds of illegal migrants (European and non-European) paid National Insurance and Income Tax (BBC Radio 4, 2010). The contribution made to the UK by EU migrants was further highlighted by research carried at the University College London Centre for Research and Analysis of Migration (CReAM), which was published in an article which appeared in *The Economic Journal* at the beginning of November 2014. This revealed that since the year 2000, EU workers had contributed more to, and taken less, benefits and transfers than had their indigenous counterparts. In a press release which accompanied the article's publication, the lead researchers, Professor Christian Dustmann and Dr Tommaso Frattin, stated that:

> [W]e performed extensive sensitivity analysis, which does not alter our main conclusions: immigration to the UK since 2000 has been of substantial net fiscal benefit, with immigrants contributing more than they have received in benefits and transfers. This is true for immigrants from Central and Eastern Europe as well as the rest of the EU.

> When we additionally consider that immigrants bring their own educational qualifications whose costs are borne by other countries and that they contribute to financing fixed public services such as defence, these contributions are even larger.

> European immigrants, particularly, both from the new accession countries and the rest of the European Union, make the most substantial contributions. This is mainly down to their higher average labour market participation compared with natives and their lower receipt of welfare benefits. (CReAM, 2014)

In contrast the same report showed that migrants from outside the European Economic Area had made a negative contribution to the economy of £117.9 billion as a result of their consuming more in public expenditure than they contributed in taxes. Bearing in mind the high proportion of immigrants in London, the migrant presence cannot be said to have made only a positive economic impact on the capital's economy.

London has been a global labour market for centuries, but never more so than in the 21st century, with nearly all sectors employing workers from within and beyond the European Union; levels of skill ranging from top professionals in banking – for example Mark Carney, the current Governor of the Bank of England – academe, industry and medicine, through to unskilled cleaners, carers and construction workers. In 2012, 36 per cent of all employed foreign-born workers and 45 per cent of all self-employed foreign workers in the UK were working in London (Migration Observatory, 2013). A look at recent non-UK born NINo (National Insurance Number) registration figures provides an insight into the 'visible' scale of migrant workers in the capital. In 2004, the year of the first EU accessions, the number of non-British citizens applying for NINos in the capital was 169,204. The total number of those registered between 2004 and 2013 was 24,421,924 with the largest number being in 2011, when 286,895 non UK born workers in London applied for NINos (NINo registrations, 2014). These statistics do not provide a breakdown of nationalities, nor do they record whether those migrants given a National Insurance number have since left the capital or indeed the country, what they do illustrate is the magnetism of London as a source of employment for immigrants from overseas.

Recent research has highlighted the fact that there is a pattern of clustering in specific labour sectors. For example, three-quarters of cleaners on the London Underground are Black African; one-quarter of office cleaners Latin American; one-quarter of those working in hospitality Eastern European and those engaged in the construction industry mostly Polish and Brazilian (Wills et al., 2010). The hospitality industry, in which 69 per cent of migrant workers find employment, provides a good example of the hierarchy which operates in the migrant workforce; it also enables us to understand the value to migrant workers of imported cultural capital. Language, the ability to speak good English, is a vital tool, for whilst good English is not necessary in the kitchens of restaurants and hotels when washing up or scrubbing floors, it is when interacting with customers, in restaurants, front of house and even when cleaning their rooms. The same can be said of a clean and neat appearance. However, the latter does not always guarantee a job, as colour/racial prejudice has been found to play its part in determining the hospitality employment pecking order. One researcher found that whilst Asians were employed in both front and back of house in London hotels, Black Africans were very rarely found working directly with the public (McDowell et.al., 2007). In contrast to this finding, a Rowntree Report published in 2014, quoted an African Caribbean worker who, though he lived outside the capital, worked in London because he found it had a less 'racialised labour market'(Barnard, 2014).

Hospitality is a transient industry, used by migrants as a stepping stone – particularly by those from Eastern Europe, some of whom arrive with diplomas and qualifications that are not recognised in the UK. Thus young men and women accept downward labour mobility in order to acquire the linguistic and vocational capital that will enable them to ascend the employment skill ladder. For example, in one central London hotel, where there had been a (predominantly) female Polish housekeeping workforce it had become noticeable that Polish workers were, in the summer of 2014, moving on to 'better' jobs. Having been pushed into emigrating by the high Spanish unemployment rate, which at the time of writing stands at 23.7, (*Trading Economics*, 2014), Spanish replacements are now being brought in by recruitment agencies.[23] Hotels are amongst the highest employers of newly arrived migrant workers and whilst some may operate strict control over those who are working under their roofs, ensuring payment of the minimum wage and acceptable working conditions, others are less concerned, content to provide jobs irrespective of workers' legal status (Alberti, 2014). In addition to recruitment by the multiplicity of specialist employment agencies based both in London and overseas, there also operates a manager and supervisor migrant worker employment chain, which ensures that workers of the same nationality or ethnicity are given preferential treatment, in many instances creating a virtual closed shop.

At the time of writing the tensions surrounding migration and migrant workers is palpable, with politicians from all parties promising some form of control. Yet, it is clear that migrant workers are doing the jobs that many members of the indigenous population will not undertake, either because the work is distasteful or because, even if the basic minimum wage is offered, the take home pay is too low. Thus, the question arises, if controls are imposed on EU immigrants and incomers from Europe are deterred, who will do the jobs that 'Englishmen' would rather not do'?[24]

Integration or Separation?

With a multiplicity of nationalities and ethnicities to be found across London, one is led to ask whether these disparities are integrated or separated, assimilated or segregated. Do different peoples mingle, or rather remain within their own tight

---

23   The author in conversation with Guest Relations Manager of 5* Central London Hotel, 17 July 2014.

24   In a speech made on 28 November 2014, David Cameron put forward proposals as to how he envisaged migrant numbers might be controlled. He was no longer advocating capping migrant numbers, a promise he had previously made that which, for practical and political reasons, was no longer a viable proposition. Rather, the emphasis was on discouraging EU migrants by curbing payment of benefits. The range of these included no longer paying child benefit for children living overseas and the withholding of certain benefits – particularly tax credits, and social and council housing benefits – until migrants have been resident in the UK for four years. In addition he was proposing that migrants be sent back to their home country if they remained unemployed for more than six months. For the full speech, see <http://www.bbc.co.uk/news/uk-politics-30250299>. However, these new conditions would require agreement with other EU countries and thus the issue of uncontrolled migrant entry from Europe, remains at the time of writing, unresolved.

knit communities? In her research into the immigrant population of Hackney, Suzanne Wessendorf noted significant differences in the patterns of integration amongst outsiders (Wessendorf, 2013). She records how certain ethnicities eagerly and freely 'mix' in the public space, whilst others are reluctant to do so; the latter being particularly true of members of the first generation Turkish community in the Borough. According to the 2011 Census they number some 8,982 (Census 2011, Table QS203EW) and represent one of the largest non-UK national groups in Hackney; the third largest Turkish community in London. The self-sufficiency of Hackney's Turkish population, with their traditional food outlets, community based newspapers, self-help organisations, taxi services etc. has created an older generation that is inward looking, reluctant to attain proficiency in English and concerned that the younger, British born members of the community do not lose their Turkish identity, or marry outside their ethnic group. However, this sense of separateness was contradicted by the way in which Turkish parents encouraged their children's participation in school activities and celebrations and, like their Vietnamese counterparts in the Borough,[25] interacted with the mainstream – if the diverse ethnic mix in the Borough can be called such – in external activities such as shopping and children's schooling. Parental presence at children's events may have a dual role; to police the degree of 'mixing' while attempting to integrate at a low level as a means of ensuring good communal relations. Thus we find diversity in integrative behaviour, 'keeping themselves to themselves' in socialising yet intermingling in the context of their children's and their public lives.

This duality of neighbourhood engagement is notable in Tower Hamlets, where a 2012/13 Council survey reported that 81 per cent of residents, in a Borough where Bangladeshis were in the majority, considered that the local area was, 'a place where different people get on well together'. It is significant that on the questions of both satisfaction with the area in which they lived and the way in which people from different backgrounds inter-related, the percentage of positive responses to both points had risen from the low seventies to the low eighties over a period of five years (Tower Hamlets, 2012/13). However, it should also be noted that in contrast to integration in the public space, private socialising still takes place within the specific ethnic group, and that amongst the older members of the Bangladeshi community, particularly the women, there is little interaction in either the public or the private domain; a determining factor in this separation being English language deficiency. As Ahmed discovered in her research (Ahmed, 2008), older Bengali women in Tower Hamlets are very conscious of the social and cultural divide created by their lack of English. One elderly Bangladeshi woman explained, 'The English and Jamaicans in the area are very nice ... [but] I don't have a clue what they are saying.' All too often responsibility for linguistic separation lies in the hands of husbands who fear that if their wives interact too closely with non-Bengalis they may become liberated and less subservient

---

25   A primary teacher interviewed by Wessendorf considered the local Vietnamese community to be an 'invisible' community (Wessendorf, 2013, pp. 415–16).

– Nazneen, the heroine in Monica Ali's *Brick Lane* providing such an example (Ali, 2003). As another woman told Ahmed, 'My husband wouldn't let me go to [English] classes, he would tell me off and say, "why would you want to do that?" What are you going to do with English' (Ahmed, 2008). In some cases even women who were able to speak English were discouraged from doing so. As a (female) student told the author, 'My mother used to speak English, but she doesn't any more' (Kershen, 2005).

Integration between immigrant groups and the host society and interaction between different immigrant groups is dependent on a number of factors, language being just one. Cultural and educational background, that now disputed term, class, as well as gender, all create divisions; yet these can be overcome, or accommodated. As Wessendorf concludes, the binary of mixing and separateness, if balanced, does not harm interethnic relations in a space as ethnically diverse as Hackney (Wessendorf, 2013). Indeed, interaction, at whatever pace, advances understanding, and enhances tolerance. In this way super-diversity can work for the common good.

Concluding Thoughts

It has been suggested that modern technology, most particularly the internet, has lessened the desire for immigrant integration. And, that what in the past created unity no longer exists, with the result that what was once a cohesive society has become fractured (Sacks, 2014). And yet the evidence provided in this chapter suggests that this is not the complete picture. For whilst some might argue that the transnational life style of some migrants, and the marginalisation of others, has indeed weakened the desire for integration and created migrant antipathy, cultural sharing and transference is abundantly available – and visible – for both indigenes and outsiders in the capital. In some parts of London, particularly amongst young people, multi-culturalism is giving way to fusion culturalism as the more adventurous and curious journey into previously unknown cultural territories. As familiarity increases, misbeliefs and misunderstandings can evaporate and tensions ease. Sadly, this outcome is not universal but it is a beginning; fusion food, music and drama unite, creating new, shared cultures, as evidenced in the emergence of Multicultural London English, a product of ethnic diversity and youthful interaction in inner London.[26] Even in the 21st century life cannot be lived entirely in a virtual bubble. As Laura Vaughan shows in this book, materiality, in the form of the living,

---

26 One of the fastest growing multi-cultural groups is that of those of mixed-ethnic origin. However, the phenomenon is not as noticeable in London where there are large clusters of ethnic groups such as Indians, Bengalis, Pakistanis and African-Caribbeans. The partnering of people of different ethnic backgrounds is more common amongst middle-class people who are living outside of the capital, in the suburbs and commuter towns. (see *The Economist*, 2014).

vibrant marketplace – the traditional and the modern – provides a space, and a tangible place, for multi-various migrant groups and the host society to congregate and interact. Nor is ethnic social interaction solely the province of the young, as manifested by the burgeoning number of interfaith groups in the capital – the Interfaith Network lists 23 (Interfaith Network, 2014) – and in local community social clubs such as that described by Wessendorf, where different ethnic groups are brought together to learn about, and experience, each others' cultures. There would seem to be room for both the interactive and the separate. In Tower Hamlets there are *communal* clubs as well as those which cater for specific groups including Somalis, Chinese, Vietnamese, Bengalis and the dwindling, elderly Jewish community, which once was one of the largest minority groups in the Borough. Yet the speed at which the nature of British society is changing is resented by some, both indigenes and long time settled immigrants who have integrated into the mainstream; a concern that is felt more strongly at the periphery of the capital than at its heart. This was evident when the residents of Havering, a borough on the border with Essex, became one of the three Greater London boroughs to elect representatives of UKIP[27] onto the Council in the 2014 local elections (*Guardian*, 2014).

This is a book, and a chapter, about London and its migrant landscape and it would be incorrect to minimise the capital's unique, and long time cosmopolitan character, which in this second decade of the 21st century is becoming increasingly evident. However, one must question whether this is both more acceptable and more common in London than beyond the capital. It cannot be denied that there are general concerns about the changing nature of British society, but are the concerns more frequently articulated where the migrant communities have a shorter history and thus appear more threateningly other? For centuries London has housed migrant groups which, over time, have become part of the landscape, joining the ranks of those who have preceded them. Whatever else they might be, they also become Londoners. In this volume Bronwen Walter talks about Irish immigrants who, whilst finding it hard to identify as English, or British, of their own volition opt for a 'London Irish' identity. When asked how he accounted for his bravery when a bomb exploded on his Number 30 bus in Tavistock Square, on 7 July 2005, the Greek driver replied, 'because I am a Londoner', echoing the theme of the song written in 1944, to express the solidarity of those who had lived through the dark days of war in the capital. How many of the migrants living, working and worshipping in the early 21st century London landscape, whatever their ethnicity and/or nationality, see themselves as 'Londoners'? An identity which by the very nature of the city and its ever-changing migrant population is one which never stands still?

---

27 According to its website, UKIP (the United Kingdom Independence Party), 'is a patriotic party that promotes independence; from the EU, and from government interference.' It believes 'in free trade, lower taxes, personal freedom and responsibility' (http://www.ukip.org/issues). At the time of writing (January 2015) it has two members of parliament, both previously Conservative MPs who stood down and then were re-elected as members for UKIP.

References

Ahmed, N. (2008), 'Language, Gender and Citizenship: Obstacles in the Path to Learning English for Bangladeshi Women in London's East End', *Sociological Research Online*, 13(5), <http://www.socresonline.org.uk/13/5/12.html> accessed 27 October 2014.

von, Ahn, M., Lupton, R., Greenwood, C. and Wiggins, D. (2010), *Language, Ethnicity and Education in London*. ESRC/University of London.

Ali, M. (2003), *Brick Lane*. New York: Random House.

Anwar, M. (1979), *The Myth of Return: Pakistanis in Britain*. Portsmouth, NH: Heinemann.

Alberti, G. (2011), 'Transient Labour in London's Hotels: An Ethnography of Migrants' Experiences at Work and Challenges for Union Organising', paper presented at the ESRC Seminar, 'Migrant labour and Industrial Relations', on <www.business.leeds.ac.uk/about-us/faculty-staff/member> accessed 27 October 2014.

Baker, P. and Eversley, J. (eds) (2000), *Multilingual Capital: The Languages of London's Schoolchildren and their Relevance to Economic, Social and Educational Policies*. London: Battlebridge Publications.

Barnard, H. (2014), *Tackling Poverty Across All Ethnicities in the UK*. York: Joseph Rowntree Foundation.

Cheshire, J., et al. (2011), 'Contact, the feature pool and the speech community: The Emergence of Multicultural London English', *Journal of Social Linguistics*, 15(2).

Coyle, A. (2007), *Gender in Transition: Has Transition Left Women Behind? Polish Women's Labour-markets at 'Home' and 'Abroad'*, Issue 8, LSE: Development and Transition.

Daily Mail (2013), 'Meet the Russians' <http://www.dailymail.co.uk/tvshowbiz/article-2420391/Meet-Russians-Russians-buying-Britain-star-vulgar-reality-TV-show.html> accessed 13 January 2015.

Eade, J. (2011a), 'Multiculturalism and Contested Urban Space', in Beaumont, J. and Baker, C., *Postsecular Cities: Space, Theory and Practice*. London: Bloomsbury, pp. 154–67.

Eade, J. (2012b), 'Religious place-making and migration across a globalising city: Responding to mobility in London', *Culture and Religion* 13(4): 469–83.

Eversley, J., Mehmedbegović, D., Sanderson, A., Tinsley, T., von Ahn, M. and Wiggins, R.D. (2010) *Language Capital – Mapping the Languages of London's Schoolchildren*, London: CILT.

Fryer, P. (1984), *Staying Power: The History of Black People in Britain*. London: Pluto Press.

Gholami, R, (2015), *Secularism and Identity: Non-Islamiosity in the Iranian Diaspora*. Aldershot: Ashgate.

Gilroy, P. (2002 ed.), *There Ain't No Black in the Union Jack: The Cultural Politics of Race and Nation*. Oxford: Routledge.

Graff, T. de and Nijkamp, P. (2010), 'Socio-economic impacts of migrant clustering on Dutch neighbourhoods: In search of optimal migrant diversity', *Socio-Economic Planning Sciences*, 44(4): 231–9.

Grymalamoszczynska, H. and Krotofil, J. (2011) 'Holy Spirit Weekend – Charismatic Experience of Polish Catholics in the UK', in *Sudia Migracyjne –Przeglad Polonijny Apistrésci*, No 1.

Guardian (2005) 'London the World in One City', <http://www.theguardian.com/uk/2005/jan/21/britishidentity> accessed 13 January 2015.

Julius, A. (2010), *Trials of the Diaspora: A History of Anti-Semitism in England*, Oxford: Oxford University Press, Part 2, Chapter 3.

Kershen, A.J. (2005), *Strangers, Aliens and Asians: Huguenots, Jews and Bangladeshis in Spitalfields 1660–2000*. Oxford: Routledge.

Kershen, A.J and Vaughan, L, (2013), '"There was a priest, a rabbi and an imam ...": An analysis of urban space and religious practice in London's East End, 1685–2010', *Material Religion*, 9(1): 10–35.

Kershen, A.J. (2013) Unpublished report for Tower Hamlets and Shropshire Councils, 'How does Middle England compare with an inner city London borough? A Comparison of Local Government responses to the immigrant presence in Shropshire and Tower Hamlets', p. 43.

Knight Frank Residential Research Department, email to author, 26 June 2014.

McDowell, L., Batnitzky, A. and Dyer, S. (2007), 'Division, Segmentation and Interpellation: The Embodied Labours of Migrant Workers in a Greater London Hotel', *Economic Geography*, 83(1): 15.

McIlwaine, C.J. et al. (2011), *No Longer Invisible: The Latin American Community in London*. Queen Mary University of London.

Migration in the UK Labour Market: An Overview (2013), Migration Observatory, Oxford.

NINo Registrations (2014), Local area migration indicators, August 2014, tcm77-375420 (1).

Rogers, A. (2013), *Being Built Together: A story of Black Majority Churches in the London Borough of Southwark*, University of Roehampton, p. 39.

Sacks, J. (2014), *Today* Programme, BBC Radio 4, 28 October 2014.

Staetsky, L. and Boyd, J. (2014), *The Exceptional Case: Perceptions and Experiences of Antisemitism among Jews in the United Kingdom*, JPR Report, Institute for Jewish Policy Research, July.

The Times (2014), 'Changes to Tier 1', 6 November.

The Times (2014), 'Rich, Russian and Living in London', 22 December 2014.

The Economist (2014), 'Into the Melting Pot' <http://www.economist.com/news/britain/21595908-rapid-rise-mixed-race-britain-changing-neighbourhoodsand-perplexing> 8 February, accessed 20 January 2015.

Tower Hamlets Annual Residents Survey 2012/13, p. 3.

Trzebiatowsha, M. (2010), 'The Advent of the Easyjet Priest: in Dilemmas of Polish Catholic Integration in the UK', *Sociology*, 44(6): 1055–72.

Vertovec, S. (2006), *The Emergence of Super-Diversity in Britain*, Centre on Policy, Migration and Society, Working Paper No. 25, University of Oxford.

Vollmer, B. (2011), 'Irregular Immigration in the UK: Definitions, Pathways and Scale', Migration Observatory, University of Oxford.

Weinreb, B. and Hibbert, C. (eds), (1983), *The London Encyclopaedia*. London: Papermac.

Wessendorf, S. (2013), 'Commonplace diversity and the "ethos of mixing": perceptions of difference in a London neighbourhood', *Identities: Global Studies in Culture and Power*, 20(4): 407–22.

Wills, J., et al. (2010) *Global Cities at Work: New Migrants Division of Labour*. London: Pluto Press.

<http://www.cream-migration.org/files/Press_release_FiscalEJ.pdf> accessed 5 November 2014.

<http://www.theguardian.com/education/2014/oct/08/immigration-britains-changing-identity> accessed 15 November 2014.

<https://www.gov.uk/government/speeches/immigration-act-commencement-and-statement-of-changes-in-immigration-rules> accessed 26 November 2014.

<https://www.gov.uk/government/speeches/immigration-act-commencement-and-statement-of-changes-in-immigration-rules> accessed 18 November 2014.

<http://www.bbc.co.uk/news/10515057> accessed 17 October 2014.

<http://www.economist.com/node/21558572> accessed 1 November 2014.

<http://www.interfaith.org.uk/members/local-inter-faith-locator> accessed 4 November 2014.

<http://www.julyseventh.co.uk/7-7-30-bus-tavistock-square.html#psaradakis> accessed 3 November 2014.

<http://mosques-map.muslimsinbritain.org/maps.php#/town/London> accessed 17 September 2014.

<http://www.mosquedirectory.co.uk/mosques/england/london> accessed 17 September 2014.

<http://www.ukip.org/issues accessed> 26 November 2014

<http://www.bbc.co.uk/news/uk-politics-30250299> accessed 28 November 2014.

Decennial Census 2001, Table KS05.

Decennial Census 2011, Table QS203EW.

Decennial Census 2011, Table QS201EW.

Decennial Census 2011, QS204EW, Main Language, (detailed) Local Authorities, 30 January 2013.

Population by country of birth and nationality data sheets Jan12 Dec12, tcm77-324792(2). <http://www.ons.gov.uk/ons/rel/migration1/population-by-country-of-birth-and-nationality/2012/index.html> accessed 17 June 2014.

Chapter 3

The Ethnic Marketplace as Point of Transition

Laura Vaughan

Theoretical Preliminaries

Since the founding of the Centre for the Study of Migration at Queen Mary, London, London has emerged as a premier multi-cultural, or even super-diverse city, and the nature of minority cultures has shifted (Vertovec, 2007). This has involved a 'diversification of diversity', with a population characterised by multiple ethnicities, countries of origin, immigration statuses and age profiles (Hollinger, 2006). Rather than waves of discrete migration flows arriving and settling in singular areas of the city, London has experienced synchronous multiple arrivals, creating areas of first settlement that cannot be easily labelled as 'Bengali' or 'Jewish', as was the case in the past. The city itself has transformed in many ways and the aim of this chapter is to present an overview of the way in which the urban realm itself can help to shape encounters within and between immigrant and host communities in this super-diverse context. It proposes that the public realm plays an essential role in bringing together what society divides, especially in settings such as that of London, where multiplicities of identities, backgrounds, languages, religions and cultures would – on the face of it – naturally give rise to tensions or even hostilities. The very fact that London has (with the exception that proves the rule of the recent riots, which were more about poverty than ethnicity) managed to integrate successive waves of migration is indicative of its almost unique character. Some examples of this integrative role are described in the latter part of the chapter.

One of the primary means of encounter between minority and host cultures is in the ethnic marketplace and their formation and long-term persistence is a commonplace urban phenomenon, whether it is a fully-fledged Chinatown, a local centre specialising in ethnic foodstuffs, such as the middle eastern Edgware Road in London, or the countless diverse urban high streets which are as much the outcome of a process of *everyday multiculturalism*, to serve the particular needs of a minority ethnic group (Wise, 2006b). In such places, 'the banality of [the individual's] everyday needs is met together with the requirements of its diverse urban cultures' (Hall, 2012, p. 120) (Figure 3.1). At the outset, the ethnic marketplace is normally set close to areas of initial immigrant settlement. In 19th century Montreal for example the immigrant marketplace was situated so that opportunities could be maximised,

Figure 3.1   Turkish 'Food Market', Green Lanes, London

Source: Sadaf Sultan Khan, reproduced with permission.

but at the same time localised niches could be created for 'difference' to be shared
and protected (Gilliland and Olson, 2010). In a similar way the pattern of Jewish
immigrant settlement in 19th-century Manchester and Leeds allowed for cultural
co-dependence, sufficient density for important religious and communal institutions
alongside sufficient spatial accessibility to allow access to the economic heart of
the city (Vaughan, 2002). In both cases this shows the importance of residential
clustering, especially during the primary stages of minority settlements. At the same
time a correctly situated marketplace serves as a point of interaction both within
the community and without. A similar situation is true in the US context, where,
it is argued, the clustering of ethnic businesses, especially when in conjunction
with ethnic residential concentrations, can provide a resource for establishing and
maintaining a niche economy (Kaplan, 1998).

     This chapter will widen the canvas of public interaction, taking the ethnic
marketplace in its broad sense, to capture the range of economic and social
transactions that take place in the public sphere, from street market to high street to
specialist enterprise. The premise for this focus is that for the immigrant, the most
likely point of first footings in society is in public space. Of all the opportunities in
the public sphere, economic exchange is arguably the most important for contact
between migrant and host culture, since while it requires acquaintance and trust

it remains a rational transaction with little requirement of social contact. It also allows minority communities to continue to preserve their cultural exclusivity whilst integrating into general society: people can have strong commercial ties with minimal levels of intermarriage, for example.

Notably, alongside its social and economic roles in sustaining inner-group contact, the potential for the ethnic marketplace to become an 'arena of competition and cooperation' with other groups is often overlooked (Wallach, 2011). This is a complex issue. Public space, 'third places' such as cafes, bookstores and hair salons and civic institutions can create a sphere for mutual tolerance and understanding, although interaction may remain purely superficial (Oldenburg, 1997). Competition and cooperation will differ according to whether it takes place between the immigrant group and the host community or whether it is between disparate groups of 'others' co-existing and vying for the same resources and clients. The processes and rituals will differ in each case. An additional complexity arises in a context where the host culture becomes a minority, as is increasingly the case in some of London's neighbourhoods. Whilst in most instances tolerance and everyday interaction smooth out differences, some conflict can arise when more longstanding inhabitants feel that their culture has been encroached upon, which can create both tensions and opportunities (Collins, 2004).

The ethnic marketplace itself plays a variety of roles: as well as a place of interaction with the public sphere and the host society, it is also a place for others to penetrate the minority culture – whether for the newcomer from that culture or for the host society member wishing to interact with that culture. A third role that it can play is in policing or delimiting, restraining or containing the integration or acculturation of the minority culture – whether by the leaders of the minority community or the host society itself. The ethnic marketplace has an essential *spatial* role to play as well and this will be a recurring theme throughout this chapter. Its situation in relation to the domestic (private) sphere of the migrant on the one hand and in relation to the host society on the other is shaped by the environment in which it is positioned and will shape that environment in turn over time. The spatial dimension of immigrant settlement is essential to understanding the minority group's domain of exchange and interaction with the host community, whether this is through markets, niche industries or business entrepreneurship. The extended *temporal* character of all of these phenomena well beyond the first generation of settlement (so for example London's 'Jewish' Petticoat Lane market persisted well beyond the physical presence of its surrounding residential population from which it sprang) is another topic explored in this chapter.

The following sections review the various dimensions of public space in which immigrant and cross-cultural contact take place in turn, starting with an overview of the role of urban space, followed by public places and then markets, ending with conclusions about the role of the city in shaping ethnic settlement patterns and the way in which changes in London's ethnic landscape reflect these dimensions.

The Role of Urban Space

The neighbourhood of old Petticoat Lane on Sunday is one of the wonders of London, a medley of strange sights, strange sounds, and strange smells. Streets crowded so as to be thoroughfares no longer, and lined with a double or treble row of hand-barrows, set fast with empty cases, so as to assume the guise of market stalls. Here and there a cart may have been drawn in, but the horse has gone and the tilt is used as a rostrum whence the salesmen with stentorian voices cry their wares, vying with each other in introducing to the surrounding crowd their cheap garments, smart braces, sham jewellery, or patent medicines. Those who have something showy, noisily push their trade, while the modest merit of the utterly cheap makes its silent appeal from the lower stalls, on which are to be found a heterogeneous collection of such things as cotton sheeting, American cloth for furniture covers, old clothes, worn-out boots, damaged lamps, chipped china shepherdesses, rusty locks, and rubbish indescribable. Many, perhaps most, things of the silent cheap' sort are bought by the way of business; old clothes to renovate, old boots to translate, hinges and door-handles to be furbished up again. Such things cannot look too bad, for the buyer may then persuade himself that he has a bargain unsuspected by the seller. Other stalls supply daily wants – fish is sold in large quantities – vegetables and fruit – queer cakes and outlandish bread. In nearly all cases the Jew is the seller, and the Gentile the buyer; Petticoat Lane is the exchange of the Jew, but the lounge of the Christian. (Booth, 1902)

Philips notes that 'flows of people, ideas and culture associated with globalisation and growing transnational migration have brought increasing social and cultural diversity to many cities' (Phillips, 2007, p. 1138). This new multi-cultural reality is a challenge to people's sense of identity and has affected regulation of the relations among social groups which is obvious in patterns of encounter and clustering in public spaces of the city or residential clustering. She maintains that powerful determinants of identity, such as religion, intersect with race and ethnicity to produce distinctive geographies in cities. In fact, whilst in small towns and villages you might expect the public square to reflect the composition of its surrounding streets, in complex societies containing many and varied communities, public space has a different role to play. In the right circumstances, city squares will enable the encounters between different social groups, both spatial and transpatial.[1] As Hanson has shown, different social groups have different principles of solidarity, encoded into 'different daily routines and practices' that, in turn, 'lead to different modes of spatial co-presence'. These 'code differences' will naturally be 'realised in patterns of local encounter'(Hanson, 2000, p. 115). For example in 19th century London, the internal religious and charitable organisation of the Jewish community

---

1   That is, both face-to-face and across space. See Hanson and Hillier, 1987.

frequently followed the geographical origins of their founders.[2] At the same time, their economic activity took place only a couple of streets away along the main roads of the East End. A similar pattern has been shown to be the case a couple of generations later in that location: amongst the Bangladeshi immigrants and their descendants in East London (Kershen, 2004). In contrast, Ann Legeby has shown that in the Swedish city of Södertälje, where public space suffers from spatial segregation, this has contributed to the social isolation of its many immigrant inhabitants (Legeby, 2010).

Public space is not neutral. Depending on its setting, its configuration and indeed on who owns it, it may become a contested place in which to display dominance or defiance with regard to the host community, or other communities in proximity that may be vying for the same space (Shirlow and Murtagh, 2006). The notion that public space is anonymous is also debatable, especially amongst more conservative communities. As individuals leave the private domain and enter the street, they are not immediately transformed into becoming part of the urban public. Instead, as has been pointed out by Hillier, community formation is a function of the ability of the pattern of streets to bring people together or separate them out, to create intermingling of different groups, locals and strangers, that is 'dense or sparse ... continuous or sporadic' (Hillier, 1989, p. 18). It is here that movement through the city becomes a key element in creating the potential for cross-group interaction. The urban public realm contains in itself the potential for interaction between people by virtue of the flows of movement that its configuration can generate. The complex interactions between local streets and wider cross-city (as well as global) trajectories together contribute to the way in which urban spaces both acquire social meaning and have social consequences (Hillier and Vaughan, 2007). Marginal differences in neighbourhood street patterning can result in markedly different social realities. As Klinenberg showed in his study of Chicago, the spatial and physical characteristics of two adjacent neighbourhoods resulted in measurably different rates of mortality from an extreme heat-wave. Whilst both had similar proportions of poor elderly and elderly living alone, one neighbourhood incorporated lively retail, bustling sidewalks, and many more dwellings, all of which were occupied. This facilitated 'public life and informal social support for residents' (Klinenberg, 2005, p. 109). Quotidian rhythms, such as in Chicago, build up into patterns of daily encounter which foster familiarity between individuals, whilst the pattern of streets will create opportunities for chance encounters across social and ethnic divides. Indeed, Madanipour has suggested that it is necessary for a group to display itself in the public sphere in order to build group identity and communication toward others (Madanipour, 2004). Nevertheless, as Madanipour has also pointed out, this is dependent on a public space that allows diverse people to coexist. Amanda Wise has shown for example that by employing a strategy of 'non-hierarchical reciprocity', different

---

2 Synagogues were sometimes named after towns in Polish-Russia, for example. See Kershen and Vaughan, 2013.

groups can play out their cultural differences in public as a basis for an everyday smoothing over of difference. She has found that typically certain personalities emerge in local areas and use tools such as gift exchange and intercultural knowledge exchange to create 'opportunities for the production of cross-cultural embodied commensality; and the production of spaces of intercultural care and trust' (Wise, 2006, p. 4). Interestingly, Wise's research points to the fact that just as much as space is not neutral, nor do all individuals take up its potential for interaction in the same way.

Writers on this matter debate whether daily encounters in space translate into meaningful face-to-face interaction or remain superficially at the level of familiarity (Amin, 2002); (Hewstone, et al. 2005); (Valentine, 2008). They further discuss whether supposed superficial co-presence is, and of itself, of a value in creating 'community' (Legeby, 2013). Possibly a more useful approach is to see these matters as being on a continuum, from familiarity through co-presence, to encounter, to interaction and – occasionally – to actual social engagement (Lofland, 1998).[3] To dismiss the first element in this continuum as 'meaningless' is to overlook the fact that it is the first step in all the other points along the scale and indeed to overlook the fact that the opposite of co-presence is co-absence, or emptiness. Public space without public presence is unarguably dysfunctional; moreover, public space without disorder (Sennett, 1996; Watson, 2006) or without chaos (Barker, 1999) is arguably lacking an essential component of city life.

Assuming this argument is acceptable, it is useful to delve into writers on the subject to discuss how interaction works in reality. Randall Collins has a useful approach in this regard: suggesting that interaction is akin to ritual, a process in which starting with physical co-presence, a joint focus of attention can result in participants becoming entrained in each other's bodily micro-rhythms and emotions (Collins, 2004, p. 47). The micro rhythms can translate into group solidarity, a feeling of membership and ultimately, experiences of a sense of justice attached to the group (Legeby, 2013). In a similar vein, Watson has proposed the social as being on a 'continuum of limited engagement – from an exchange of glances or mutual recognition through to "thick" engagement – which may involve embodied interactions or conversation – with many dimensions in between' (Watson, 2009, p. 1581). This particular sort of engagement requires some degree of familiarity, which is why exploring the physical context in which it takes place is so important. Liebst does this, bringing together Collins' neo-Durkheimian model of interaction rituals with Hillier and Hanson's essential micro-morphological exploration of how movement patterns differ in line with spatial configuration, stating that this allows for a full understanding of 'why variations in the physical co-presence generate solidarity and social meaning'(Liebst, 2011, p. 26). Hillier and Hanson showed this, in their seminal work, *The Social Logic of Space*: space carries with it social meaning and

---

3   See further development of Lofland's ideas in the London context in Wessendorf, 2014.

shapes society as a pattern of 'encounter probabilities'; namely, that rather than space being a neutral carrier of social activity, it creates the potential for social encounter to take place at place. Space is then likely to be ordered 'in the image of' the social solidarities of the society which it contains. Not in a 1:1 relationship, but according to the differing requirements for daily/ less frequent encounter and according to the differing requirements for segregation or integration of different social groups (Hillier and Hanson, 1984).[4]

Public space thus plays an important role in bringing disparate groups together (Amin, 2008). The transformation of the individual into an urban subject is not necessarily a smooth one. Individual differences will be maintained in areas of the city where a person is known and in communities with strong social rules, this can serve to reinforce them, as shown in Sultan Khan's study of Southall (Sultan Khan, 2003). Similarly patterns of use can shift across the week, as shown in Low's study of the spatio-temporal usage of a number of Latin American squares and a recent study of public space in Nicosia. In the latter instance, Charalambous and Hadjichristos found an almost complete separation both in time and in space between the longstanding inhabitants of the old city and temporary migrant workers, the latter whom tended to use sections of the squares only in the evenings and on Sundays (Charalambous and Hadjichristos, 2011).

Spatial dynamics bring about local patterns of mutuality and cordiality. London in particular frequently features as a place where for ethnic groups such as Pakistanis and Indians, residential and economic clustering exist and 'cordial relations' are manifested between diasporic communities that were in a situation of hostility in their countries of origin (Robins and Aksoy, 2001). Similarly patterns can be found in the relationship between the Israeli and Palestinian diaspora who live on the 'Israeli' and 'Palestinian' sides of the street in lower Manhattan. Whilst in Palmers Green, London, Greek and Turkish-Cypriots find common ground in the relatively neutral environment of London's inner suburbs, although rules of endogamy continue to prevail even a generation or more after their original settlement in the 1970s. The urban setting provides a point of neutrality between supposedly 'hostile' or at least, alien communities.

In London's newly super-diverse context, the street can provide fertile ground for the vitality and economic durability of a highly diverse mix of countries of origin. Ria Thomas has shown that whilst there was co-existence of Indian and Pakistani diasporic population in two inner London suburban high streets (The Broadway, Southall and Green Street, Upton Park), the socio-spatial relationship between the two groups was more complex than originally anticipated. Despite the absence of tangible physical demarcations, distinct spatial positions were clearly manifested in the form of ethno-centric clustering of pedestrians in different sections of the high streets. These distinctions were also reflected in the ethnicity patterns of pedestrian and retail ownership, with the more spatially accessible locations owned by the more prosperous, better educated Indian population. Nevertheless,

---

4   See esp. 'Societies as encounter probabilities', p. 236 onwards.

economic advantage is not the only factor in assertion of spatial advantage, other factors to do with religious dictates, prior entrepreneurial experience, kinship ties and retail typology are shown by the author to influence the preferred location of shops in study areas (Thomas, 2010).

Despite these nuanced studies of ethnicity and space, a 'façade of solidarity' is common in the reporting of the spatialisation of ethnicity in the public sphere. This is partly a preference for the population itself, since it presents a common solidarity to the 'outside world', which can be used to assert political power, such as in the case of the 'Latino' market in Wards Corner in Tottenham, north London (which in reality is comprised of many Latin and Central American business owners and consumers). The counterpoint to this perceived uniformity in such areas, such as 'South Asian' marketplaces is simply a lack of understanding by the general population of the nuanced differences, say, between Indian, Pakistani, Bangladeshi and indeed East African-origin individuals. The emergence of London and other cities as places of 'super-diversity', means that groups that are outwardly perceived as uniform, mask an essential range of differences that is frequently overlooked, such as in the example of Greek/Turkish populations (Robins and Aksoy, 2001).

Hall's research demonstrates that the supposed intermingling of cultures in the public sphere requires detailed observations throughout the day and the week in order to capture the extent to which immigrants are interacting with members of the host culture. She shows how places such as London's Walworth Road work due to the coexistence of street spaces that are 'sufficiently small to allow for a level of self-determination and sufficiently aggregative to allow for a sense of a diverse city' (Hall, 2012, p. 125). Watson's study of a number of London markets comes to the same conclusions, showing additionally that the spatial co-presence of market traders helps reinforce strong communal ties.

The Role of Public Places

> When Lakshmi, one of my Indian research participants, moved into her house in Ashfield earlier this year, she was pleasantly surprised when Frank, her Lebanese neighbour, called over the back fence to present her with freshly picked figs from his garden in a gesture of welcome. He had seen her admiring his crop the day before. This first gift precipitated a regular exchange between them; the latest produce from their respective vegetable patches would be passed over the fence along with cooking hints to accompany unfamiliar varieties ... Bringing home a box of peaches or cucumbers or whatever, inevitably some would come Lakshmi's way ... And from the other end of the street, curry leaves from the tree in the yard of the sister of another Indian neighbour would be offered to Lakshmi whenever a new crop arrived at their place. (Wise, 2006, 5–6)

Figure 3.2   Southall Broadway – shops spilling out into the high street

Source: Sadaf Sultan Khan, reproduced with permission.

Public life takes place not only in the streets and squares of the city, but also in the market itself, the café, pub, church, cinema or library, all of which are in differing degrees public spaces and all of which allow for varying degrees of interaction between the 'guest' culture and the host community (Figure 3.2). For example Wessendorf has found in her ethnography of 'commonplace diverse' contemporary Hackney, London, that mixing in public is rarely translated into private relations. However, this is not perceived as a problem, as long as people adhere to a tacit 'ethos of mixing' (Wessendorf, 2013). This confirms Wise's findings in Sydney where 'inhabitants do not need to know their neighbours intimately or even wish to become friends, but (...) gestures of care and recognition (...) can create a feeling of connection to the diverse people who share the place' (Wise, 2005, 182). Wise reiterates the importance of local proximity and small-scale interactions. Food takes on a symbolic role of sharing as equals across cultural boundaries. This is not the same as the superficial consumption of a Chinese meal in the local town centre.

There is a gender aspect to these examples of cross communal cooperation and negotiations and Wessendorf writes about how Turkish women took the lead in cooking at school events and similar activities brought about to negotiate difference within the everyday sphere of activity. Whilst the school is not a fully public space – more of a 'parochial' space as defined by Lofland (1998) – it is one of those routine spaces where the anonymity of the truly urban street has to be discarded in order to maintain everyday parenting routines. Everyday routines create a degree of familiarity, 'familiar strangers' (Milgram, 1977). Perhaps this is unsurprising that even in the contemporary city, women take a lead on such activities. So long as the majority of childcare falls on the woman, she is more likely to be available in the local neighbourhood to create the ties with her neighbours. Indeed, Laura Ring writes of a similar mode of negotiation and diffusion of possibly volatile situations in a multi-ethnic apartment block in Karachi (Ring, 2006). Evidently social interactions in everyday locations such as schools, pubs and marketplaces facilitate cross communal cooperation.

Hall shows in her study of supposedly mundane London 'ethnic' high streets, how places such as the local café create familiar spaces 'formed out of the orientating processes of daily convenience and regularity within a local area' (p. 101), allowing for different worlds to intersect in one place, making a social space for family, friends and locals who are not necessarily from the same group, allegiance or political inclination. The café, alongside similarly semi-public spaces, provide locations for the essential 'small-scale meetings in which a public is constituted'. This has been the case for centuries, whether in the Parisian working-class cafes of the late 19th century, where social as well as political friendships were constructed, or in turn of the 20th century Warsaw (Ury, 2010). The cafe can also provide a point of transition for the immigrant into society as well as a point of entry for the host community into a supposedly 'alien' world. The film *Little Georgia*, about a Georgian cafe in Hackney illustrates this point well. The film explores notions of home, belonging, nostalgia and change told through the stories of people working in the cafe. It shows how working at a place like Little Georgia may ease some of the stresses of migration by providing a home away from home both for the workers and for Georgian immigrants who have settled in London. At the same time the aesthetics of the cafe (its Georgian-themed objects and kitsch decor) play a part in transmitting Georgian culture to the London, just as much as the supposedly 'Georgian' foods served there remain Georgian enough to provide a memory of home, but are adapted to suit the British palate (Wicki, 2010). Such multiplicity of roles provided by a small street cafe is captured in Hall's ethnography, which shows how the ethnic high street provides a realm that allows individuals 'to participate in a collection of sub-worlds that together constitute the collective public life of the multi-ethnic street' (Hall, 2012, 108).

A supposed uniformly diverse street can mask subtle spatial divisions within. As well the research by Thomas mentioned above, earlier research by Vaughan shows that, depending on the location and the way in which the street network is utilised, clustering can enable the intensification of communal activity, socialisation, networking and self-support (Vaughan, 2007; Vaughan and Penn, 2006).

A different argument about ethnic marketplaces as having shifting spatio-social roles is proposed by a study of London's Chinatown (Chung, 2009), which shows how the area shifts in its character throughout the day and the week according to the mix of Chinese, tourists and Londoners co-present in its streets. The growth of eating out as a leisure practice alongside a dramatic increase in access to formerly 'exotic' foodstuffs means that the cultural consumption of the minority food stuffs has become commonplace, to the extent that Barrett and McEvoy claim that 60 per cent of the clients in 'Indian' restaurants along Rusholme's (Manchester) Curry Mile are 'White British'. This is an example of how the ethnic marketplace has changed in its character in recent years, to become in some cases an 'ethnic destination' (Barrett and McEvoy, 2006). One feature of many of these outward facing ethnic marketplaces is their long-term persistence and there are many examples of ethnic destinations that are evidently the outcome of long-term adaptive reuse of formerly mixed use high streets. Places such as Brixton, Edgware Road and Southall, renowned for their Caribbean, Arab or South Asian businesses are clearly able to take advantage of the street centrality that made them successful high streets in the first place. Equally, their longevity as destinations may be down to their city-wide accessibility as well. Time will tell whether these ethnic marketplaces, which are characterised spatially by being incorporated into London's streetscape will withstand competition from enclosed shopping centres on the one hand and franchises and chains on the other. Whilst the former signifies a danger of interruption of the natural process of urban streets adapting to the changing nature of the cultures they contain, the latter signify a wider homogenising of the UK (and global) economy. Whilst both of these dangers are real, recent research shows that although the high street has changed and continues to do so, it still plays a role that has remained recognisable for centuries, in bringing together the rich mix of activities, flows of movement and types of people that characterise cities such as London (Bolton and Vaughan, 2014). Equally, the burgeoning of traditional street markets, such as Columbia Road, East London, to encompass vibrant and economically successful trading posts puts paid to the idea that people only wish to carry out transactions in air-conditioned anonymous boxes. The suq, market and bazaar have been with us for thousands of years. It seems unlikely that they will disappear anytime soon.

The Role of Street Markets

> Market Day means Ridley Road or Brixton Market, Dalston or Shepherd's Bush. It means finding goat's meat and greens, salt fish and ackee, bammy and breadfruit, plantains and frying bananas, and maybe even a juju talisman to ward

off unemployment or to win at the pools. Market Day means peacock plumes and combed-out Afros, corn-roll braids or straightened hair, Rasta presence and Rasta dread. It means hours spent hassling to save a few pence, and never enough money to buy never enough food. It means big, fat mamas with rags tied around their heads, babies straddled over their shoulders like a sack of just picked yams. Market Day means keeping one's stomach in tune with the Islands, at the expense of salted fish and chips, or steak and kidney pie. Market Day means a shared ritual, every Saturday morning and half the afternoon, a ritual of the gut. It means a city block full of black folk who speak the same tongues, the language of shanty-town, back-a-yard. All this and more is Saturday Market Day. (Henry Louis Gates Jr., 1976, p. 312)

As Henry Louis Gates Jr. illustrates in the quotation above, the market is not only for buying and selling. It has a vital role to play in providing a social space, as an information resource, as an opportunity for work, or as a site of 'social connections and interactions' (Watson, 2009, p. 1578). Many also maintain that the marketplace is the point of contact between otherwise disassociated groups such as immigrants and their host community. This concept of the market as a place of abstract transactions between extremes, or strangers, is proposed by Wirth who wrote of the Jewish trade relationships, that this type of relationship takes place in a situation where no other contact can take place, since trade is an abstract relationship where emotions drop into the background. Wirth maintained that the more impersonal the trader's attitude, the more efficient and successful are the transactions likely to be (Wirth, 1928, p. 25). Hence, the evident propensity for immigrants to tend towards such economic activities, whilst the dispersal of immigrants after the initial stage of settlement is enabled by successful integration into the host economy. Examples from the past, such as Leeds – where 'Don't ask the price, it's a penny' was the slogan Michael Marks used when he opened his first market stall in Leeds in 1884 – exemplify this process.[5] And an earlier study by this author suggests that the spatial correspondence between work and home plays an important role in forming immigrant niche economies too (Kaplan, 1998).

The market works in varied degrees of depth according to the individual's own background. A superficial engagement will occur for the outsider; at the other end of the scale this becomes a way in to making actual social ties. Barrett and McEvoy show how the market serves these multiple roles simultaneously: different products in the ethnic market attract different communities; whilst the co-ethnics may frequent the market for clothes, jewellery, music and food products, 'outsiders' frequent restaurants and other eateries.

Urban form has a tangible role to play once we focus in on the physical space of market transactions – in their broadest sense. As Dines showed in his

---

5   Mark's 'penny bazaar' went on in subsequent years to become one of the UK's most successful retailers – Marks and Spencer. For more on Leeds' Jewish settlement, see Vaughan, 2006.

Figure 3.3   Brixton market: 'routine, unexpected and new encounters'

Source: Sadaf Sultan Khan, reproduced with permission.

ethnography of a north London market: 'the lines of stalls, aisles and series of openings set back from the busy pavements of the adjacent Green Street – turned the market into a sort of surrogate town square that provided the setting for routine, unexpected and new encounters' (Dines, 2007, p. 8) (Figure 3.3). Similarly, Watson (op. cit.) describes a whole range of spatial interrelationships that are fundamental in creating the sorts of social connections described above, whether the seemingly trivial matter of availability of places to sit, the close proximity of market stalls, meaning that market trades build dense relationships over time, the intense physical proximity between buyer and seller which can build up into a relationship of care (looking out for the elderly in the community) and in some cases, credit. The integration of the market within the surrounding network of streets, such that it forms a continuity with the public space of the city (with no sense of constraints on behaviour as is the case with the enclosed shopping mall) is another essential feature of its spatial character. Markets with a particular ethnic 'ownership' carry these features more intensely still and the quote above from Louis Gates Jr. is just one of the many examples to be found across London or any other major city of its type.

Notably, the quote at the start of this section alludes to the role of the ethnic market in sustaining memories of home. In his journal article 'Black London' written for *The Antioch Review* in the 1970s, Louis Gates Jr. writes how reggae music along with the sights and smells of Caribbean culture helped connect people to their home. The ritual of getting kitted out in one's finest for market day is significant, illustrating the fact that the ethnic market can be a continuation of the private domain of the home. As Botticello showed in her study of a Nigerian market in contemporary London, 'practices and spatial negotiations in the public space' are comparable, in this context with the rules of behaviour in the domestic setting and where the public sphere contains specific forms of sociality common to the private sphere (Botticello, 2007). Notably this extension from the private to the public sphere may be partly due to the fact that immigrant homes are so small, that the living room extends into the city. In other instances this may be a cultural practice brought from the country of origin, such as is the case with Latin American social practices of holding celebrations in restaurants within the local neighbourhood, rather than at home (Greene, Mora, and Berrios, 2011).

An even finer spatial scale comes to play when considering the entrance of the market visitor into the inner sanctum of the market trader's domain. To receive an invitation to come to the trader's side of the stall is an important physical, as well as symbolic transition from anonymous trade to social engagement. For Botticello, such an invitation is evidently a sign of trust and familiarity. Yet more subtle rules of social control may be at play also. As Sultan Khan showed in her study of Southall's 'South Asian' high street, the very layout of the stalls, spilling out from the interiors of the shops to capture the pavement space, along with the close observations of (predominantly male) traders of the supposedly public sphere of the street creates a sense that the social rules of Karachi are being played out in London's suburbs, such that a woman walking alone is no longer anonymous. The urban experience has been transformed (Sultan Khan, 2003). In extreme situations (not necessarily the case in markets) this familiarity facilitates the policing of behaviour from within thus giving rise to the desire of younger generations of co-ethnics to move out but remain close enough to avail the conveniences of the enclave/market but far enough so as to fall outside the purview of community surveillance (Phillips, 2006).

The connection to the original place of settlement is frequently maintained for a variety of reasons: familial (as older generation still living there); religious (a desire to continue to attend a particular place of worship) and commercial (businesses are not as easy to relocate as homes are). For this reason London's 'Jewish' East End continued to be a locus of Jewish businesses at least a generation after the postwar exodus to the suburbs. The move from exclusion to integration was effected by market-activity outside of 'ghetto' area whilst maintaining foothold within it for social network purposes.

Food is also a common theme in discussions of the ethnic market. Kershen has shown that clustering can enable immigrants to 'set down roots and accommodate change in an alien society'. At the same time, linguistic sounds or 'kitchen' talks can evoke memories of home – the creation of 'a fusion of real and the imagined in the evolving myth of home' (Kershen, 2004: p. 265). As Claudia Roden has stated, 'food is that part of an immigrant culture that immigrants hold on to longest – when they have abandoned the traditional dress, the language, the music' (Roden, 1999).

Conclusions: The Role of the City in Ethnic Settlement

In the super-diverse landscape, where no single minority group stands out, the ethnic marketplace represents a new form of social integration. Wise maintains that: 'this is not integration into some normative mode of pre-existing community, but rather, represents integration as a form of open, emergent community across difference. That is, a true multi-culturalism of place-sharing' (Wise, 2005, p. 185). As London has become more diverse, it has created increasingly complex spatial and cultural juxtapositions, requiring negotiation of difference between groups at least as much as with 'host' society (Wessendorf). Research suggests that for immigrants, spatial location not only shapes processes of 'mixed-embeddedness' and economic integration, but can strengthen social networks and reciprocity, and enhances electoral power (Body-Gendrot, 2000). A fragmentation of the community can, conversely, arrest the development of political activity (and power), such as in the state of the Caribbean community of 1970s London, which according to Gates (1976) was scattered across its geography with people from Trinidad in Ladbroke Grove, from Barbados in Finsbury Park and Jamaicans in Brixton and so on.

International geography is also apparent in the ethnic marketplace. Whilst sending remittances has been a longstanding activity, for example for Bengalis in London a generation ago (Garbin, 2003), in addition to the appearance of facilities for transferring money home, ethnic high streets will frequently contain branches of local banks from the community's homeland. Possibly an indication of the volume of remittances sent home as well as the longstanding establishment of the community. Similarly, the availability of phone-cards for international telephony – providing a social glue that connects scattered communities (Vertovec, 2004) – and the presence of travel agents catering specifically to the needs of the immigrant population are an indication of a significant association to the country of origin both for and beyond the first generation of settlement. Another emerging phenomenon is the increasing presence of solicitors specialising in immigration or tax and other such facilities on the ethnic high street, turning it into a "one stop shop" of sorts where one can pick up groceries, the local gossip as well as legal/medical advice pertaining to their status as a migrant. One example of this is Brick Lane – (in fact, situated in one of London's oldest immigrant districts), where food outlets, travel agents, telephony shops, estate agents, solicitors, clothes shops and its famous mosque (originally a Huguenot church, subsequently a Methodist chapel and then a synagogue) all intermingle in this way. Interestingly, this specialisation is quite contained within the southernmost stretch of the road, whilst its character shifts dramatically from the old Truman Brewery northwards, where the infiltration of 'hipsters' to the area is evident in a proliferation of independent fashion shops, cafes and the like.

In addition to the ethnic marketplace, other urban functions such as religious buildings (see especially the work of Dwyer) serve to maintain cultural cohesion within a community as well as connections with the host community (Dwyer, Gilbert and Shah, 2013). The main point of distinction is the essential public nature of the market, square or high street.

This chapter has demonstrated the important role of urban layout in shaping the social power of the ethnic marketplace. Arguably, spatial distancing of the point of origin helps explain the shift of ethnic market to touristic destination and it is possible to identify a continuum from Walworth Road, serving a predominantly local residential population, through the South Asian examples, which serve both local and city-wide populations through to places such as Chinatown in central London's Soho quarter, which shifts during the space of the day and the week from being 'Chinese' during the dim sum Sunday lunch period to being a non-Chinese touristic destination during the remainder of the week, forming a distinct spatial and temporal pattern of occupation amongst the ethnic Chinese that differs from that of visitors to the area (Chung, 2009). Chung's analysis shows that Chinatown provides a multi-layered social spatial context for mixing and separating the various groups that occupy it. In a super-diverse landscape such as that of London, such nuanced differences are important. It is evident that in a context in which no single group predominates, shifts in spatial, temporal and ethnic mix will change the form of the ethnic marketplace in a much more dynamic fashion than the simple label of 'ethnic market' might suggest.

Acknowledgements

The author wishes to thank Sadaf Sultan Khan for her assistance in researching materials for this chapter as well as the numerous UCL Bartlett MSc Advanced Architectural Studies and MSc Spatial Design students who took it upon themselves to study the topic of ethnic markets and so enrich the content of this work. Thanks also to Susanne Wessendorf, whose close reading of this work helped enrich its content.

References

Amin, A. (2002), 'Ethnicity and the multicultural city: living with diversity', *Environment and Planning A*, 34(6): 959–80.
Amin, A. (2008), 'Collective culture and urban public space', *City*, 12(1): 5–24.
Barker, P. (1999), 'Non-Plan Revisited: Or the Real Way Cities Grow: The Tenth Reyner Banham Memorial Lecture', *Journal of Design History*, 12(2): 95–110.

Barrett, G.A. and McEvoy, D. (2006), 'The Evolution of Manchester's Curry Mile: From Suburban Shopping Street to Ethnic Destination', in D.H. Kaplan and W. Li. (eds), *Landscapes of the Ethnic Economy*. Plymouth: Rowman & Littlefield.

Body-Gendrot, S., Martiniello, M. and Centre for Research in Ethnic Relations (2000), *Minorities in European Cities: The Dynamics of Social Integration and Social Exclusion at the Neighbourhood Level*. Basingstoke: Macmillan.

Booth, C. (1902), *Life and Labour of the People in London*. 3rd series ed. 17 vols. London: Macmillan.

Botticello, J. (2007), 'Lagos in London: Finding the Space of Home', *Home Cultures*, 4: 7–23.

Charalambous, N. and Hadjichristos, C. (2011), 'Overcoming Division in Nicosia's Public Space', *Built Environment*, 37(2): 170–82.

Chung, S. (2009), 'London Chinatown: an urban artifice or authentic Chinese enclave?', paper presented at City Street International Conference – 1st International Conference on City Street, Cultural Intimacy and Global Image, 18–20 November 2009, at Notre Dame University, Louaize, Lebanon.

Collins, M. (2004), *The Likes of Us: A Biography of the White Working Class*. London: Granta.

Collins, R. (2004), *Interaction Ritual Chains*. Princeton, NJ: Princeton University Press.

Dines, N. (2007), 'The Experience of Diversity in an Era of Urban Regeneration: The Case of Queen's Market, East London', Milan, Italy: Fondazione Eni Enrico Mattei (FEEM).

Duruz, J. (2009), 'Eating at the Borders: Culinary Journeys', in A. Wise and S. Velayutham (eds), *Everyday Multiculturalism*. Basingstoke: Palgrave Macmillan.

Dwyer, C., Gilbert, D. and Shah, B. (2013), 'Faith and suburbia: secularisation, modernity and the changing geographies of religion in London's suburbs', *Transactions of the Institute of British Geographers*, 38(3): 403–19.

Garbin, D. (2003), '"Community", multi-culturalism and the diasporic negotiation of space and identity in the East End of London', in F. Eckart and D. Hassenpflug (eds), *Consumption and the Post-industrial City*, Frankfurt: Peter Lang.

Gates, H.L. (1976), 'Black London', *The Antioch Review*, 34(3): 300–317.

Gidley, B. (2013), 'Landscapes of belonging, portraits of life: researching everyday multiculture in an inner city estate', *Identities*, 20(4): 361–76.

Gilliland, J. and Olson, S. (2010), 'Residential Segregation in the Industrializing City: A Closer Look', *Urban Geography*, 31(1): 29–58.

Greene, M., Mora, R. and Berrios. E. (2011), 'Original and New Inhabitants in Three Traditional Neighbourhoods: A Case of Urban Renewal in Santiago de Chile', *Built Environment*, 37(2): 183–98.

Hall, S.M. (2012), *City, Street and Citizen: The Measure of the Ordinary*. London and New York: Routledge.

Hanson, J. (2000), 'Urban transformations: a history of design ideas', *Urban Design International*, 5: 97–122.

Hanson, J. and Hillier, B. (1987), 'The Architecture of Community: some new proposals on the social consequences of architectural and planning decisions', *Architecture et Comportement* [Architecture and Behaviour] 3(3): 251–73.

Hewstone, M., Cairns, E., Voci, A., Paolini, S., McLernon, F., Crisp, R. and Niens, U. (2005), 'Intergroup Contact in a Divided Society: Challenging Segregation in Northern Ireland', in D. Abrams, J.M. Marques and M.A. Hogg (eds), *The Social Psychology of Inclusion and Exclusion*. Philadelphia, PA: Psychology Press.

Hillier, B. (1989), 'The Architecture of the Urban Object', *Ekistics*, 334 and 335 (January/February 1989 and March/April 1989): 5–21.

Hillier, B. and Hanson, J. (1984), *The Social Logic of Space*. 1990 edn. Cambridge: Cambridge University Press.

Hillier, B. and Vaughan, L. (2007), 'The City as One Thing', in L. Vaughan (ed.) *Progress in Planning: Special Issue on The Syntax of Segregation*, 67(3): 205–30.

Hollinger, D.A. (2006), *Post-ethnic America: Beyond Multiculturalism*, New York: Basic Books.

Kaplan, D.H. (1998), 'The Spatial Structure of Urban Ethnic Economies', *Urban Geography*, 19(6): 489–501.

Kershen, A. (2004), 'The Construction of Home in a Spitalfields Landscape', *Landscape Research*, 29(3): 261–75.

Kershen, A. and Vaughan, L. (2013), '"There was a Priest, a Rabbi and an Imam ...": An analysis of urban space and religious practice in London's East End, 1685–2010', *Material Religion*, 9(1): 10–35.

Klinenberg, E. (2005), *Heat Wave: A Social Autopsy of Disaster in Chicago*. Chicago: University of Chicago Press.

Legeby, A. (2010), 'From housing segregation to integration in public space: A Space Syntax Approach Applied on the City of Södertälje', *The Journal of Space Syntax*, 1(1): 92–107.

Legeby, A. (2013), 'Patterns of co-presence: spatial configuration and social segregation', School of Architecture and the Built Environment, KTH Royal Institute of Technology, Stockholm.

Liebst, L. Suonperä (2011), Working Paper 'Useful(filling) Durkheim: Reconfiguring the Sociological Prospect of Space Syntax'. Copenhagen: University of Copenhagen.

Lofland, L.H. (1998), *The Public Realm: Exploring the City's Quintessential Social Territory*. Rutgers, NJ: Transaction Publishers.

Low, S. (2003), 'Spatializing Culture: The Social Production and Social Construction of Public Space', in *On the Plaza: The Politics of Public Space and Culture*. Austin: University of Texas Press.

Madanipour, A. (2004), 'Marginal Public Spaces in European Cities', *Journal of Urban Design*, 9(3): 267–86.

Milgram, S. (1977), 'The familiar stranger: An aspect of urban anonymity', in S. Milgram and T. Blass (eds), *The Individual in a Social World: Essays and Experiments*. London: Pinter & Martin Ltd.

Oldenburg, R. (1997), *The Great Good Place: Cafes, Coffee Shops, Bookstores, Bars, Hair Salons, and Other Hangouts at the Heart of a Community*. Boston, MA: Da Capo Press.

Phillips, D. (2006), 'Parallel lives? Challenging discourses of British Muslim self-segregation', *Environment and Planning D: Society and Space*, 24(1): 25–40.

Phillips, D. (2007), 'Ethnic and Racial Segregation: A Critical Perspective', *Geography*, 1(5): 1138–59.

Ring, L.A. (2006), *Zenana: Everyday Peace in a Karachi Apartment Building*. Bloomington: Indiana University Press.

Robins, K. and Aksoy, A. (2001), 'From spaces of identity to mental spaces: lessons from Turkish-Cypriot cultural experience in Britain', *Journal of Ethnic and Migration Studies*, 27(4): 685–711.

Roden, C. (1999), 'Food in London: The Post-Colonial City', in *London: Post-Colonial City*.

Sennett, R. (1996), *The Uses of Disorder: Personal Identity and City Life*. London: Faber & Faber.

Shirlow, P. and Murtagh, B. (2006), *Belfast: Segregation, Violence and the City*, *Contemporary Irish Studies*. London: Pluto Press.

Sultan Khan, S. (2003), 'Patterns of Settlement: The South Asian Communities in London', MSc., Bartlett School of Graduate Studies, University College London.

Thomas, R. (2010), 'South Asian Diasporas in London: clustering and cultural exchange', Bartlett School of Graduate Studies, University College London.

Ury, S. (2010), 'Common Grounds? On the Place and Role of Jewish Coffee Houses at the Turn of the Century', in François Guesnet (ed.), *Warsaw – the History of a Jewish Metropolis*. University College London.

Valentine, G. (2008), 'Living with difference: reflections on geographies of encounter', *Progress in Human Geography*, 32(3): 323–37.

Vaughan, L. (2002), 'The Unplanned "Ghetto": Immigrant work patterns in 19th century Manchester', Paper presented at 'Cities of Tomorrow', the 10th Conference of the International Planning History Society, July, 2002, at Westminster University.

Vaughan, L. (2006), 'Patterns of immigrant settlement and the construction of community', Paper presented at 'Ghettoised Perceptions versus Mainstream Constructions of English Muslims: The Future of Multicultural Built Environment', at Birmingham Institute of Art & Design, University of Central England, Birmingham.

Vaughan, L. (2007), 'The spatial foundations of community construction: the future of pluralism in Britain's "multi-cultural" society', *Global Built Environment Review*, 6(2): 3–17.

Vaughan, L. and Penn, A. (2006), 'Jewish Immigrant Settlement Patterns in Manchester and Leeds 1881', *Urban Studies*, 43(3): 653–71.

Vertovec, S. (2004), 'Cheap Calls: The Social Glue of Migrant Transnationalism', *Global Networks*, 4: 219–24.

———. (2007), 'Super-diversity and its implications', in *Ethnic and Racial Studies*. London: Routledge.

Wallach, Y. (2011), 'Shared Space in pre-1948 Jerusalem? Integration, Segregation and Urban Space through the Eyes of Justice Gad Frumkin'. Cambridge: Department of Architecture, University of Cambridge.

Watson, S. (2006), *City Publics: The (Dis)enchantments of Urban Encounters, Questioning Cities series*. Abingdon: Routledge.

Watson, S. (2009), 'The Magic of the Marketplace: Sociality in a Neglected Public Space', *Urban Studies*, 46(8): 1577–91.

Wessendorf, S. (2013), 'Commonplace diversity and the "ethos of mixing": perceptions of difference in a London neighbourhood', *Identities*, 20(4): 407–22.

Wessendorf, S. (2014), *Commonplace Diversity: Social Relations in a Super-Diverse Context*. Basingstoke: Palgrave Macmillan.

Wicki, M., Haapio-Kirk, L. and Prokhorova, D. (2010), 'Little Georgia'. Film produced as part of the UCL Urban Documentary Film Workshop <http://www.youtube.com/watch?v=vqKSenB5XSc>

Wirth, L. (1928), *The Ghetto* (1988 edn), R.H. Bayer (ed.), with a new introduction by Hasia R. Diner. *Studies in Ethnicity*. New Brunswick and London: Transaction Publishers.

Wise, A. (2005), 'Hope and Belonging in a Multicultural Suburb', *Journal of Intercultural Studies*, 26(1): 171–86.

Wise, A. (2006), 'Multiculturalism From Below: Transversal Crossings and Working Class Cosmopolitans'. Paper presented at Everyday Multiculturalism Conference Proceedings, 28–29 September, 2006, at Macquarie University.

Chapter 4

Knowing our Communities: It Doesn't Have to be that Difficult

Michael Keating

A Forethought

Throughout the summer and early autumn of 2014 two high-profile events seemed to justify local government's critics. In Birmingham a so-called 'Trojan Horse' of Muslims was accused of creating an Islamist culture in a group of academies undermining 'British values'. The local authority stood condemned for its inability to challenge this or support the schools and their pupils. More shocking was the Jay report into children's services in Rotherham with its revelation that 1,400 young women had been victims of sexual abuse over several years. A central accusation was the failure of the local council and the police to provide proper care for vulnerable residents because a majority of the perpetrators were of Pakistani origin. In both cases the authorities seemed separate and distant from their communities. At the same time much of the commentary about the Scottish referendum vote and the success of the UK Independence Party in the Clacton by-election highlighted the inability of the British political system to respond creatively to changing views about identity and belonging (*Daily Telegraph*, 2014).

Reflecting on all this I wondered if I was deluding myself about the ability of local government to offer any meaningful lessons for these national debates. Would my arguments simply ring hollow, at best, or seem malign, at worst? It is easy to be intimidated by the headlines but once I began interviewing practitioners and exploring what was happening, I was reminded that it is in local places that the complexities are grappled with – we need to recognise this.

Introduction

Seemingly without end national debates about diversity, such as those above, demonise it with accounts of overburdened services, migrants exploiting the benefits system or providing cheap labour and 'British values' under siege. These claims build a picture of an insecure UK, fuelling anxiety. Meanwhile everyday life carries on, often messy but with communities working out ways of addressing their problems. Local government's role in this is rarely noticed. Undergoing huge reductions in resources, battered by negative media coverage, sidelined by successive governments and undermined by ongoing 'reforms' the best councils nevertheless continue to innovate and deliver services which meet the needs of their diverse communities.

Based on my experience of working with a range of local authorities, I am going to explore how councils who know and understand the communities they serve are better able to articulate challenges about difference and change – and in turn work out how to tackle them. On one level this understanding seems so obvious as 'local government' is anchored in 'local democracy'. Yet it continues to seem difficult, often needlessly when there is so much to learn from the experiences of others. Working out how local government can be more confident about its ability to know its communities could help shape a more optimistic reading of diversity in Britain as well as reasserting the key role of councils in shaping it.

In the following pages I explore the relationship between the national drivers for equality, the response of the local government sector and what happens on the ground in individual councils. Taking the Equality Act as my starting point I discuss how it offers an opportunity to think more creatively about the 'intersectionality' between understanding diversity, tackling inequality and the relationships required to do this. I describe how the Equality Framework for Local Government (EFLG)[1] provides a tool to refine practice anchored in 'knowing your community'. Looking at the work of Enfield, Hackney and Tower Hamlets, London boroughs assessed as 'excellent' by their peers in the last two years, I examine how they have managed the complexity of diversity in a context of austerity, welfare reform and growing inequality. They are a reminder of how local solutions provide lessons worth reflecting on more broadly.

Getting a National Lead

Included in the parliamentary wash-up just before the 2010 General Election, the Equality Act set out to strengthen protection, advance equality and simplify the law. It introduced nine 'protected characteristics' (age, disability, gender reassignment, marriage and civil partnership, pregnancy and maternity, race, religion or belief, sex and sexual orientation). The Public Sector Equality Duty (PSED) extended the existing public duties for race, gender and disability to these protected characteristics.[2] The Duty sets out that a public authority must, in the exercise of its functions, have due regard to the need to:

- Eliminate discrimination, harassment or victimisation;
- Advance equality of opportunity between persons who share a relevant protected characteristic and those who do not;

---

1 A glossary is provided at the end of the chapter.

2 Civil partnership and marriage is only covered by the eliminating discrimination duty of the PSED.

• Foster good relations between persons who share a relevant protected characteristic and those who do not.

Both the Act and the Duty gave the potential for a more sophisticated understanding of how individuals experience life, particularly the notion of the 'intersectionality' of the 'protected characteristics', for example the relationship between an individual's race, sex and religion. The main provisions of the Equality Act came into force in October 2010 and the PSED in April 2011.

Although the Act was passed with cross-support the Conservatives had made clear that they would not implement some elements of it, most strikingly the socio-economic duty. Following the election of the Coalition this proved to be the case and, while the Government does have an Equality Strategy, its implementation has been lukewarm although some issues, for example, gay marriage have been enthusiastically, and controversially, embraced. In early 2012 the Government also published its Integration Strategy outlining the approach to an integrated society and how to create the conditions for everyone to play a part in local and national life. Although it stated that communities are 'stronger when different people not only treat each other with respect, but contribute together', there was barely a mention of the Equality Act and the PSED or their connection to this work (DCLG, 2012).[3]

In May 2012 the Home Secretary announced a review of the PSED arising from the 'red tape challenge on equalities'. She restated the Government's commitment to equality of opportunity but also their 'strong desire to reduce unnecessary bureaucracy where it exists and consider alternatives to legislation'. The Review of the Public Sector Equality Duty: Report of the Independent Steering Group was published in September 2013 and concluded that it was too early to judge the impact of the Duty in relation to its costs and benefits. It had found broad support for the PSED but variable implementation, particularly an overly risk averse approach which created additional bureaucracy. In its response to the Review the Government stated that public bodies must be transparent about their objectives and performance on equalities and the Duty must support this. Implementation would be kept under scrutiny with the intention of a full-scale review in 2016.

The Act also introduced 'equality analysis' designed to improve the use of equality impact assessments (EqIAs), which had been in place since 2002 to help organisations tackle institutional racism following the Stephen Lawrence Inquiry. An EqIA provides an analysis of a proposed organisational policy and/or service, or a change to an existing one, assessing its disparate impact on persons with protected characteristics. They are often carried out by public authorities to assist compliance with equality duties and consequently they can be viewed as a 'tick-box' exercise. The Prime Minister confirmed this view when, in November 2012, he announced that government departments would no longer be required to carry out EqIAs, stating that while he cared 'about making sure that government policy

---

3   For contrasting analysis of cohesion policy, see Cantle (2014) and Jones (2013).

never marginalises or discriminates' this 'does not mean churning out reams of bureaucratic nonsense'. In fact there is no legal requirement to undertake an EqIA. Nonetheless for many local authorities they provide evidence of how decisions are taken – both to protect against judicial review and demonstrate that local needs have been considered. This is vital when the majority of decisions are about doing more with less resources – or cutting services (House of Commons, 2013).

Although I do not have the space to examine its role in any detail it is inescapable that media debates about diversity and equality are overwhelmingly critical focusing on 'political correctness' or the 'ideology of multiculturalism'. Discussion about the human rights of individuals and communities demonstrates this most clearly although ironically examples from Hackney and Tower Hamlets have inspired Europe-wide work to build the capacity of local and regional government officials (FRA, 2013). While this climate can stifle debate, nevertheless, during the PSED review, a group of 'excellent' local authorities submitted a joint statement.[4] They argued that high performing councils understand how people (both individually and collectively) experience age, disability, gender reassignment, pregnancy and maternity, race, religion and belief, sex and sexual orientation. Working collaboratively with communities and public, private and voluntary sector partners, these councils draw on this intelligence to make informed decisions about resource allocation, service design and delivery. Using the PSED, the Equality Framework for Local Government and related tools enabled them to be:

- Confident in their understanding of local communities and their ability to take a leadership role to advocate fairly in a period of scarce resources and community tensions;
- Collaborative in their approach to building and sharing this knowledge across different council services, with elected members and, in turn, with partners;
- Creative about how to use this understanding and these relationships to engage with communities in meeting their challenges;
- Committed to improvement in a way which motivates workforces and communities.

Improvements in equality have been supported by considerable public sector investment but in the context of unprecedented funding cuts, growing populations and increased demand it had become more important for local government to have the tools to continue to innovate and improve. Understanding the changing nature of local communities and ensuring that this informed decision-making had become more crucial because of a number of challenges including:

---

4   Brighton and Hove, Leeds, Newcastle and Nottingham City Councils, Essex and Leicestershire County Councils, and the London Borough of Tower Hamlets had all been assessed as operating at 'excellent', the highest level of the Local Government Association's Equality Framework for Local Government.

- A national funding gap in local authority funding of £16.5 billion a year by 2019–20, a 29 per cent shortfall between revenue and spending pressures;
- Growing populations particularly the increase in life expectancy with the accompanying higher demand for services for the elderly;
- Changing and growing responsibilities, for example councils are now responsible for public health and the move to integrating health and social care means a change in the relationship between the sectors, while there has been reductions in others, for example the decreased role in the local management of education;
- Rising need in some services, the so-called 'graph of doom' illustrates that, if nothing else changes, the cost of social care will rise so much that by 2028 this will account for all of a council's budget (*The Guardian*, 2012).

These sit alongside other challenges including increasing political fragmentation, the disconnection of many local residents from, and apathy towards, public institutions, and the ongoing risk of community tensions leading to social unrest.

This combination means that local government is required to make more difficult and unpopular decisions. If there is a failure to assess their impact the risk is poor and unfair decisions. While councils have been discouraged from undertaking exhaustive EqIAs, some local authorities have lost judicial reviews on the grounds that a sufficiently thorough information gathering exercise was not undertaken prior to a decision being made and had a negative impact upon a particular group or individual. Many high performing authorities therefore continue to use EqIAs discursively, both internally and with partners and communities, to collect and assess relevant evidence about inequality. This facilitates fair and proportionate decision-making and avoids costly and time consuming legal action.

These local practitioners believed the PSED is a driver to ensure equal treatment and outcomes remain at the heart of public sector bodies. They used the EFLG as a practical tool to help meet their duties in a way which drives service improvement rather than simply achieving legal compliance.

A Sector Response[5]

From 2002, after the report of the Stephen Lawrence Inquiry, councils became more mindful of their equality practice and had increasingly used the Equality Standard for Local Government (ESLG) to help them.[6] Following a growing awareness that it was too focused on processes rather than outcomes, in 2009 the Improvement and Development Agency, now subsumed within the Local Government Association (LGA), launched the Equality Framework for Local

---

5   This section draws heavily from Doran and Keating (2011).

6   The Equality Standard for Local Government assessed performance across five levels (with five as the highest).

Government designed to be simpler and strengthen the confidence of councils to understand how everyday service delivery is influenced by equality and how they can be seen to provide services fairly. It was also underpinned by a wider definition of equality that considered how the 'protected characteristics' influenced the experience of life chances, including physical security, health, education, families, participation and legal security (Equalities Review, 2007).

Developed in consultation with English councils, the EFLG has been refreshed twice, in 2011 and 2014, alongside two other LGA-owned frameworks for the fire and rescue service and social housing, to reflect the changing public sector context and the experience of practitioners. Based on three levels of achievement (developing, achieving and excellent) they focus on five performance areas: knowing your communities; leadership, partnership and organisational commitment; involving your communities; responsive services and customer care; and, a skilled and committed workforce. By analysing these, the Frameworks are designed to ensure decision-making is tailored to diverse needs and addresses gaps in services where it has been recognised that individuals or communities are experiencing disproportionately poorer outcomes. In addition they contribute to the evidence base underpinning changes to provision, help enhance reputation, support community engagement and empowerment, promote high standards of customer care and provide a standard approach to integrating equality into a council's work. They also demonstrate how organisations meet their statutory duties (LGA, 2014).

From the start self-assessment and peer challenge by councillors and officers was used to test effectiveness and exemplify a sector-led approach to support since it was agreed and owned by local government rather than dictated by central government or an inspectorate. This was designed to foster self-awareness by reflecting on existing practice and providing space for debate on the best approach to strengthening opportunity and outcomes. While every area must develop its own responses to community need, the EFLG was supported by a commitment to identify and share good practice.

Often equality has been situated outside or alongside the mainstream business of actual service delivery. 'Excellence' as conceptualised by the Framework depended on equality fundamentally informing how a council and its partners work, and the way they understand and relate to the local community. The importance of these structural and strategic factors – good and confident leadership and partnership and the ability to plan and respond effectively to change – are explored in the case studies later in this chapter. Councils and partnerships that manage to deliver real improved outcomes are those that have an overarching approach and a clear shared narrative, as well as individual examples of good practice.

The year after its launch, a survey of English authorities assessed how many were using the Framework and how useful it was. With a response rate of 65 per cent across all types of authorities and regions, 98 per cent of respondents were using the Framework or intended to do so. However, when asked about further areas for support and guidance, 'knowing your community' was the most common at 48 per cent, highlighting local anxiety about the nature of communities. This is often manifested in a search for accuracy that can sometimes act as a brake on actual policy and service development. Much of the discussion of equality therefore focused on measurement. For some councils this led to an attitude of 'doing the Framework' as though the achievement of a performance level was the main purpose. The peer assessment process could sometimes become a bureaucratic exercise rather than the opportunity to build a broader knowledge of what might be driving certain outcomes and how to address them.

The Framework therefore sought to advocate the vital and informed role of local councillors, staff and partners in delivering an overarching equality ethos. This can be challenging as public sector organisations are frequently the subject of local and national hostile media coverage, which is rarely interested in a sophisticated analysis of the complexities and controversies that can surround relationships within and between communities. This spotlight has often undermined the reputation of individual councils and the sector as a whole. The 'whole systems' approach to equality the Framework sought to foster was designed to build confidence and capacity.

The Framework was also shaped to respond to the lighter touch of the Coalition Government's approach to regulation across the public sector. This was where the view of peers was important but the external assessment has become less common not least because paying for it is seen as less of a priority when budgets are straitened. Nevertheless councils, fire and rescue services and social housing providers still believe in its importance (LGA, 2014). It is to three London councils that I now move to explore how work on equality runs through their corporate approaches and service delivery to:

- Manage the changing nature of suburban life in Enfield;
- Explore the challenges of gentrification in Hackney;
- Sustain excellent practice in Tower Hamlets.

A Changing Suburb

Enfield is a diverse outer London borough. The 2011 Census estimates a population of 322,426 with a quarter of its residents born outside the UK. The largest minority ethnic group is 'White Other' which includes communities from Turkey, Greece, Cyprus and Eastern Europe. Adopting the ESLG in 2003 Enfield was externally assessed at level three in 2008. The following year the Council set a target to achieve 'excellent' and, in 2011, an informal assessment concluded "the Council is broadly working at the excellent level of the Equality Framework across all the five themes". A successful assessment was eventually undertaken in 2013 (LB Enfield, 2013).

In early 2014 the borough was the subject of a series of articles, 'The Enfield Experiment: London's fortunes distilled into a single borough', describing 'the look of puzzlement that settles on the face of cosmopolitan journalists or government folk' when Enfield is mentioned or the comments of young people that 'nothing happens here' (*The Guardian*, 2014). Despite this, Enfield provides a perfect example of the changing patterns of work, family lives and home ownership that shows how suburbs are no longer places of 'archetypal Englishness', conformism and stagnation (Huq, 2013).[7] Recent work in Croydon, Kingston and Redbridge to develop a race scorecard to strengthen accountability of authorities to their communities is another demonstration of this transformation (The Runnymede Trust, 2013).

The Council used the EFLG to help navigate its way through the change in its communities and the implications for its role. As part of its assessment a programme of learning and development explored the organisation's confidence, collaboration, creativity and commitment to improvement. It identified that officers and members had a good understanding of Enfield, based on their (often) longstanding commitment to the borough, and recognised the change from a stable outer London suburb to a place with greater diversity and deprivation. This was matched by the expectation that the Council move from being a provider to a facilitator (via commissioning, partnerships and procurement) while retaining strong community leadership.

Although officers articulated a good understanding of local diversity there was a consensus that the Council did not capture information or share it effectively enough with councillors at a strategic level. Greater coordination was required to combine statistical information with softer data from day-to-day experiences to reinforce confidence and break down the silos between different services. In 2010 a more ethnically diverse and younger group of councillors was elected. This trend was confirmed in 2014 and has been seen as a strength particularly as, while bonding in Enfield's communities was strong, bridging between them was weaker. Elected members can therefore be facilitators of more positive relationships between different communities, as well as encouraging less vocal groups and individuals to have their say. The councillors are therefore community leaders, receptacles of community intelligence and knowledge and instigators of (potentially) strong partnership relationships. Nevertheless there remained potential for more problem-solving dialogue between members and officers.

With its large private sector inner city boroughs have for several years rehoused their poorer residents in Enfield. Following the welfare reforms this has increased and the borough now has the largest number of households affected by the benefit cap anywhere in the UK. Through the establishment of its Welfare Reform Taskforce the borough managed the day-to-day implications. At the same time members were concerned about how residential churn impacted on local cohesion and that moving people in and out of the borough would not be sustainable in the longer term.

---

7   Rupa Huq is a Labour councillor in the London Borough of Ealing, another suburb. See http://www.theguardian.com/commentisfree/2013/feb/21/flight-minorities-london-suburbs-white-flight for an example of other debates on this issue.

The ELFG assessment helped to strengthen local EqIAs, utilising stronger collective skills to ensure the process was not just a bureaucratic exercise. There was agreement to develop greater coordination and sharing of the organisation's knowledge about local communities, to ensure that equality analysis provided practical assistance in service planning, particularly in savings exercises, and communicated this broader understanding more robustly when explaining how Enfield responded to, and addressed, its key policy and service challenges.

By building on the professional expertise of officers and the diversity of members more grassroots interaction with local communities was built into annual work plans with working groups to support this and neighbourhood champions within each department. This type of interaction was promoted to test approaches with residents more proactively and establish credibility by tackling short-term issues as well as recognising longer-term ambitions. Using the banner of 'One Enfield – One Council' accentuated collective engagement to meet its challenges.

Achieving excellence was not the endgame and maintaining the qualities that the organisation had used to get to this point demanded ongoing work. The Council's equality objectives have been included in its Business Plan under the themes of fairness for all, growth and sustainability and strong communities (LB Enfield, 2014). These have been shaped by its learning from its experiences during the 2011 riots, via the National Riots Communities and Victims Panel, and as a pilot area for the implementation of welfare reforms. Regeneration schemes have been put in place to transform the more disadvantaged parts of the borough, such as Edmonton Leeside. The £2.1m Enfield Residents Priority Fund for communities has helped develop projects that improve their local areas and reduce deprivation.[8]

The third article in *The Guardian* series, 'Enfield tears up the rules in radical attempt to ease housing problem', countered those first impressions. Reducing dependence on private rentals by arranging a credit facility of £100m to bulk buy homes, a scheme to license private landlords, building council homes for the first time in 30 years and refusing to give tenants the 'right to buy' are some of the current initiatives. Based on its understanding of its local communities and building a partnership of officers and members that looks outside the Council, Enfield's work exceeds the expectations of what a suburb should be like (*The Guardian*, 2014).[9]

Grappling with Gentrification

Hackney has built a reputation as one of the most ambitious London local authorities and, particularly since Jules Pipe was first elected its Executive Mayor

---

8 For an example of an EqIA, see <http://www.enfield.gov.uk/search/results.php?q=meridian+water+master+plan+equalities+impact+assessment>

9 See, for example, <http://www.enfield.gov.uk/news/article/1298/handshake_secures_first_council_housing_scheme_in_30_years>

in 2002, has been on a journey of significant improvement. Under increasing focus for growth and development, the borough is on the edge of the City of London and the heart of East London. Around 40 per cent of the population come from black and minority ethnic backgrounds, 36 per cent are White British and 16 per cent 'Other White'. It has one of the largest communities of Charedi Jewish people in Western Europe, representing 7 per cent of the total population. Six per cent of residents were born in Turkey.

The population has grown by just under 20 per cent in ten years, particularly attracting young professionals and creative types in their 20s and 30s. This growth and increasing prosperity sits alongside the longstanding poverty of many residents, and with its neighbours, Tower Hamlets and Newham, it remains one of the three most deprived boroughs in the country. The changing demographics and rapid economic growth threaten cohesion by alienating the more deprived members of the community. This challenges the Council to harness the new opportunities to create ways into training, employment and prosperity. The nature of this challenge was demonstrated during the 2011 riots when Hackney was heavily affected.[10]

Harnessing the positive effects of change, while mitigating its negative ones, has been a consistent theme of the Council's work with its strategic partnerships, from its first Community Strategy in 2005, 'Mind the Gap', and an ambitious Sustainable Community Strategy running from 2008–18 (LB Hackney, 2009). Its role as an Olympic host borough featured highly in these debates, particularly its wider relationship with London and beyond, and how to re-define the Council's role as an 'active agent of social mobility'. Addressing inequality is at the core of this, exemplified by policies and programmes such as the Living Wage campaign, minimum wage enforcement, the Ways into Work service, promotion of apprenticeships, the 'Hackney 100' paid work experience scheme, the focus on provision of affordable housing, measures to address fuel poverty and raise educational standards and aspirations.

In 2008 the Council was peer assessed at level 3 of the ESLG and, two years later, was described as being on the 'cusp of excellence' against the EFLG. In 2013 it was judged as 'excellent' and the peer assessors reported,

> ... clear emphasis from the leadership on ensuring that the economic and social 'gap' is not widened as the borough changes and this is supported by a wide range of interventions in community safety, housing, employment, social care and education. The Council shows a high level of maturity in understanding and being prepared to have difficult discussions about issues such as the growing gentrification of the borough.

The report noted strong evidence of sharing data to benefit the community and using it to identify key issues such as the polarisation of 'Two Hackneys'. A vision

---

10 See Jones (2013) for a discussion of the longstanding nature of these local debates.

for equality was clearly articulated, recognising its greater importance in tough times. The evident commitment of the Mayor, his Cabinet and senior management was seen as inspiration to staff so that equality planning was integral to policy and service development. The assessors felt it was evident that tackling inequality was everyone's job, as the way in which 'we do things around here'. Satisfaction with the council and perceptions of cohesion had improved greatly in the last 10 years (LB Hackney, 2014).

While the organisation had a high level of maturity in understanding and being prepared to take difficult discussions about competing interests there was also an 'external perception that senior Council leaders are not confident telling their equality story to the wider public.' The Council has therefore begun to tackle this perception and reflected on using a Fairness Commission as an arena for local debate. However a criticism has been that, while the Commissions can identify local issues relatively easily, moving from recommendations to implementation and action is not so easy and therefore reduces impetus (Webb Memorial Trust, 2014).[11] Hackney has therefore decided to explore a more active engagement campaign fostering debate to allow the airing of anxieties about change, better communication about what the Council is already doing, and exploring with residents what else it may be possible to do – as part of a way of framing the next stages of its Corporate Plan. Among the issues to be explored would be jobs and access to training and employment for different groups, affordable housing, the provision of affordable childcare and addressing the fact that opportunities and outcomes for young black men are disproportionately worse than for the wider population.

Drawing on its work to date and its understanding of its community, Hackney is thus framing a debate to address the fundamental question of how the Council and its public sector partners talk about regeneration, rather than gentrification, and how its residents feel about the changing nature of the borough and the local authority's role in this.

Sustaining Excellence

Tower Hamlets is a borough of contrast and inequality. Home to Canary Wharf, at the same time 25,000 of its 60,000 families live on under £15,000 per year. There is a long history of migrant settlement. While its population is super-diverse, its predominantly Muslim Bangladeshi community comprises approximately one third of all residents. They have come under much (often critical) scrutiny in recent years particularly because of their active political engagement. The majority of Tower Hamlets councillors are of Bangladeshi origin. In 2010 the first Executive

---

11   In 2010 Islington held the first Fairness Commission. Since then there have been 15 more, including Croydon and Tower Hamlets as well as Camden's Equality Taskforce 'to explore our role in tackling inequality in the borough'.

Mayor from a black and minority ethnic background, Lutfur Rahman, was elected – and re-elected in 2014.

Since the 1990s the Council has placed equality at the heart of its work. It was the first local authority to be externally validated at Level 5 of the ESLG in 2007, the second to be assessed as 'excellent' against the EFLG in 2010 and the first to be successfully reassessed in early 2014. Among other achievements, between 2007 and 2013 it was the highest performing London local authority in the Stonewall Workplace Equality Index, thus championing sexual orientation equality as well as having the highest number of councillors from a Muslim background of any area in the country (LB Tower Hamlets, 2014).

Concluding their report, the peer assessors in 2010 noted that:

> … equality and diversity underpins everything the Council does with partners and stakeholders in the provision of services to its community. Looking across the Equality Framework we saw that LBTH has an in-depth and sophisticated knowledge of its community which informs service delivery; very strong political and managerial leadership on equality and diversity; good levels of equality and diversity resources and expertise and a national reputation for diversity and innovative community engagement.

At the same time they highlighted upcoming challenges and opportunities. Since 2010, 24 per cent of the Council's budget has been reduced with £91m of savings. Between the 2001 and 2011 census the population increased by almost 30 per cent, making it the fastest growing local authority area in the country. In 2011, 41 per cent of residents were born outside the UK and half had arrived in the last ten years. Just over 50 per cent of the population is from a black and minority ethnic community and around 40 per cent of all adults speak a language other than English at home with the highest proportion of pupils with English as an additional language in both London and England. It has the lowest proportion of residents aged 65 and older in London and nationally (6.1 per cent) and the working age population is the fastest growing in the country at 69 per cent. Housing costs are high so there is a significant reliance on benefits which means that welfare reform has had an adverse impact on many residents. In response to these changes the Council argues its focus on equality remains crucial.

In 2008, during discussions about refreshing the Community Plan, residents and partners expressed anxiety about how local progress could be undermined by the community tensions which have characterised local history. 'One Tower Hamlets' arose from this but there was a determination that it should be more than a unifying slogan, rather providing an overarching and embedded principle. 'One Tower Hamlets' was therefore defined in three mutually reinforcing ways as tackling inequality, strengthening cohesion and building community leadership. This was designed as a cycle of action whereby the successful development of services (to address local need) is dependent on strong working relationships (between different sectors, providers/users and citizens/politicians). Arising from this, dialogue with, and between, all sections of the community could drive new ways of thinking about changing need and other partnerships so that the cycle continues. At the same time the belief in how the diversity of community experience is fundamental to meeting the challenges caused by deprivation. Using the nine 'protected characteristics' then helps to understand how the interaction of all, or any of these, can define individuals (even when describing themselves as not being a particular characteristic) and, in turn, their place in wider society. In many ways therefore 'One Tower Hamlets' prefigured the general duties of the PSED and, at the same time, the EFLG provided a practical analysis of the action required.

In 2011 the Council developed its 'Single Equality Framework' (SEF), a high level strategic document designed to mainstream its equality work following significant restructuring to deliver savings and capitalise on the Executive Mayor as a single political figurehead to engage with and represent diverse local communities. In 2012 the SEF was embedded into the Strategic Plan to strengthen the delivery of key priorities where the primary intention was to reduce inequality between people. For example actions to tackle joblessness would need to address known differences in the employment rate of women and men, people from diverse ethnic backgrounds and those with disabilities. This was supported by performance measures, disaggregated to monitor outcomes by the different equality groups and track whether the Council and its partners were narrowing the gap in outcomes, in turn informing future business planning. In early 2013 the Council tried to strengthen this by developing a Borough Equality Assessment, which summarised its understanding of age, disability, gender, race, religion/belief and sexual orientation inequality locally.

The Council argued that these structures enabled it to adapt and innovate. This included a commitment to moral leadership so that, notwithstanding the challenging context, support for vulnerable people and tackling inequality, including poor housing, employment and community safety, continued to shape financial planning. Its local knowledge helped build an understanding of the impact not just of individual savings proposals, but also the cumulative effect of reductions in public spending. This was then used to minimise the impact on residents and ensure politicians had accurate assessments of the potential impact of different options when making difficult financial decisions.

In 2010 the peer assessors had also highlighted:

> It will be important to explore the tensions that can exist around the aspirations of ... communities and strengthen confidence locally about how to negotiate these sometimes complex differences ... Historically the Council has been generous in delivering services in a resource rich environment; this model is unlikely to be sustainable in the immediate future. Does the Council need to be engaging with its citizens differently to encourage and enable them to be less dependent and reliant on the Council in the future?

The approaches to this have varied. For instance, between 2011 and 2013, ten Neighbourhood Agreements were piloted identifying priorities for local areas with an assessment of how services and residents could work together, underpinned by two overarching aims to empower residents and encourage collaboration across communities. Fundamental to the programme was that the Council, its contractors and other public agencies relinquished control and adopted a more supporting role. Local residents had greater autonomy to work together with providers, identify local issues and design solutions. Seed funding and guidance were provided to unblock any issues, but residents were in charge of decision-making, delivery and assessing success.

Moving away from traditional performance measurement tools, the residents were supported to develop the 'Getting on Together toolkit' to measure the impact and strengthen good relations. Key was the recognition that the process of reaching the agreement, through meaningful interactions between different sections of the community, was as important as the actual agreement itself (Talk for a Change, 2012).

Building on this, as well as drawing on the positive atmosphere created by the Olympic Games, Local Community Ward Forums were set up to encourage and support further resident involvement. Recognising that to drive progress local areas would need committed community organisers, 86 Community Champion Coordinators were recruited to lead public forums representing each of the borough's seventeen wards. The process sought to ensure these champions reflected the local equality profile as evidence of 'how well people from different backgrounds get on'. The Council argued initiatives such as the Neighbourhood Agreements sit alongside work more directly targeted to address the kind of community tensions which have always brought attention to the borough.

Building on the local experiences following the 2005 London bombings and the national debates on cohesion, in 2008 the Community Cohesion Contingency Planning and Tension Monitoring Group (CCCPTMG) was established involving officers from the youth service, community safety, emergency planning and communications with the police, representatives of different faith communities, the lesbian, gay, bisexual and trans (LGBT) community forum, registered social landlords, youth organisations and the local further education college. The Group was formed to help develop a better understanding of the pressures which threaten community relations, create partnerships to prevent damage to these relations and put in place mechanisms for responding to cohesion related incidents and support emergency planning procedures. Between 2010 and 2014 the Group mobilised on six high-profile occasions.

In January 2011 stickers appeared across the borough with the words 'Gay Free Zone' and what appeared to be a verse from the Quran underneath. Following a high profile investigation two individuals were arrested. Although charged, they only received a fine which did not reflect the homophobic nature of their actions. This created significant anger and frustration and a group of national LGBT activists decided to run a gay pride event in the borough. Much of the commentary portrayed the borough as a place where LGBT people could not live safely and was also Islamophobic in nature. It subsequently turned out that there was far right involvement and the march was called off.

Between 2010 and 2014 the English Defence League (EDL) announced its intention to demonstrate in 'the heart of Britain's most militant Islamic area' on four occasions. Coming shortly after the summer riots, the demonstration planned for September 2011 was particularly high profile.[12] Although the Home Secretary banned a march the EDL was permitted to mount a static demonstration on the borough boundary. Widespread fear and anger was generated in the weeks preceding the event seeming to confirm once again that Tower Hamlets was a place of racial discord.

In January 2013 a group of young men began to harass members of the public in Whitechapel claiming to be 'Muslim patrols' and that certain behaviour (including drinking, wearing short skirts and being gay) was 'unIslamic' and not allowed near the East London Mosque. The 'patrols' filmed their activities and uploaded these on to YouTube.

These events generated significant media attention focusing on the 'otherness' of the borough, particularly its Muslim community, while the local partnership networks of the CCCPTMG went unnoticed. Each time the Group was able to manage the tension and potential disorder. This included working with local LGBT residents to organise a local gay pride event supported by the Mayor, with community and youth groups to recruit local volunteer stewards at the EDL demonstrations to help keep order and with the East London Mosque and others to promote messages of tolerance. Success was driven by the longstanding relationships that had been created and nurtured locally, based on an understanding of the complexity of the community and a willingness to explore and articulate this.

The strength of these strong local partnerships is most clearly demonstrated by the widely recognised and sustained journey of educational improvement despite Tower Hamlets having the highest proportion of children eligible for free school meals nationally (Collins and Keating, 2013). When the Council became an education authority in 1990 just eight per cent of its pupils achieved 5 + A-Cs at GCSE. There was little push for aspiration underpinned by the longstanding sense that working class children did not need to do that well at school and that local deprivation meant young people would always fail to match their counterparts in more comfortable areas. After the 1994 local elections a group of generally younger politicians, including a significant number from the Bangladeshi community, gained power. New community voices emerged including influential parent groups and notions of aspiration started to replace accepted views that local residents were simply victims of their class or ethnicity.

---

12 In contrast to both Enfield and Hackney, there was much less unrest in Tower Hamlets during the 2011 summer riots.

Political, officer and community leadership established a broad consensus to challenge low expectations and place education at the centre of the Council's agenda which also matched the longstanding commitment engrained in many of the local ethnic minority communities. From first becoming an education authority the Council had invested a lot of energy into building a relationship with its schools. Implicit was the belief that overcoming local challenges of child poverty and racial and faith tensions could not be done by one institution alone. Sustaining the partnership depended on understanding the dynamic between local politicians, their voters, the local authority, schools, teachers and parents but it also meant relationships had to be flexible, confident enough to articulate problems and open to finding mutual solutions.

Building these relationships had therefore to be based on the sophisticated understanding of what is happening locally. For instance, if the majority of school children are eligible for free school meals, their families will have low incomes (and likely to be in overcrowded housing with poor health), if they are overwhelmingly Muslim there is no point ignoring the role of mosques in local life or if there are strong links with Bangladesh it is likely that families may travel back and forth to visit relations. Ensuring that children achieve well at school cannot ignore these facts about their everyday lives. Tackling this inequality had to run hand in hand with specific commitments to improving exam results or reading scores.

The authority to drive through the changes came from this broad consensus forged through collaborative working alliances of active and accountable partners reflecting the different elements of local life. City firms were recruited to 'adopt' a school and every secondary school established a partnership with a major corporate partner. With Council funding the Improving School Attendance in Partnership was established at the East London Mosque working with identified families to support school attendance. In three years attendance at primary schools improved from the lowest in the country to the national average.

By 2013 achievement had risen to 61.9 per cent. Tower Hamlets and its schools were described as 'exceptional' with the major factors for this transformation including shared values and beliefs, highly effective and ambitious leadership, partnership working and community development. A report by academics from the Institute of Education outlined how Tower Hamlets demonstrated coherent and area-wide improvement which would not have been possible without strong political and professional leadership. The educational environment is however changing swiftly and the Council has to find new ways to exercise leadership and engage its schools. While the story is 'inspirational', worth celebrating and learning from, 'success was hard won ... It is not guaranteed in the future' (Woods, Husband and Brown, 2013).

In contrast to Hackney, Tower Hamlets began to grapple with this challenge by establishing a Fairness Commission to generate a fresh perspective on how to make the borough a fairer place to live in the current financial and political climate. The Commission's report was published in October 2013 with an ambitious set of recommendations for harnessing local financial and community resources to tackle inequality and unfairness in jobs, housing and income in the years ahead. The Mayor accepted all fourteen of the recommendations and work is underway to make them a reality (LB Tower Hamlets, 2014).

Lutfur Rahman was re-elected in May 2014 with a huge turnout and widespread support particularly from the Bangladeshi community. The result proved controversial with accusations of intimidation and an Election Petition was made to invalidate the election on grounds of electoral fraud. Earlier, in April, following accusations of corruption, the Secretary of State for Communities and Local Government, Eric Pickles, appointed Price Waterhouse Coopers as external auditors. Their report was published in November 2014 and provides evidence of cronyism and lack of proper procedures. Commissioners have been appointed to oversee grant giving, appointments, property deals and the administration of future elections until 2017. While making his statement to the House of Commons Pickles described the behaviour of the Mayor as 'to the detriment of integration and community cohesion in Tower Hamlets and in our capital.'

In April 2015 the Election Commissioner concluded that the Mayor had breached election rules and he was removed from office with immediate effect. A further poll will take place in June 2015 with, as much of the commentary noted, the potential for a campaign that polarises the community along ethnic and religious lines. Whether or not this controversy will derail the local authority's improvement journey is unclear but, undoubtedly, it will test the sustainability of 'excellence' (PWC 2014, *The Guardian* 2014, BBC 2015).

Lessons for Elsewhere?

Throughout this chapter it is clear that 'knowing your community' has an obvious benefit for delivering public services – and it does not have to be difficult if organisations are open to doing so. Yet it continues to feature as a recommendation in many studies about policy and services. A recent examination of migration in Derby and Newham, for instance, discussed the important lesson of 'understanding the particular life circumstances of individuals and households' (IPPR, 2014). An assessment of 'Local Welfare Assistance', a fund for councils to support people facing the greatest financial difficulty, highlighted how understanding local need is crucial to targeting scarce resources efficiently. An analysis of the Customer-led Transformation programme, to embed customer insight and social media tools and techniques in service delivery, emphasised engagement and understanding (LGA, 2014). These are valid conclusions but we need to reflect more on how it is done and what it can deliver – and that it is in local places where it has to happen. Recognising this could shape a more helpful approach to working out solutions rather than a succession of sweeping national statements about 'migrants', asylum seekers, Roma, East Europeans or whichever group is currently under the spotlight.

But does London have lessons on how to do this for elsewhere? During an online debate, the leader of Sevenoaks District Council, stated,

> I think there is a real danger of the debate focusing on the London bubble, most of local government is nothing like London and I think that is worth remembering.[13]

It is this kind of view that describes London's diversity as unlike any other part of the country.[14] There is of course truth in this uniqueness, as other chapters in this book evidence. Nevertheless the kinds of issues facing London communities are real and difficult – changing populations, welfare reform, lack of affordable housing, declining resources and uncertainty – and affect other places as well. They can be addressed by a robust assessment of how diversity and equality practice can drive the management of complexity and change, wherever the location. It was this that drove the publication of a collection of best practice case studies, 'Equality in London', explaining that,

> At a time when all local authorities are having to make decisions to withdraw or change services in order to balance budgets, having a proper understanding of how these decisions affect parts of the community can be the difference between better policy making and better decision making. (London Councils, 2013)

While the rural and urban contexts are clearly not the same, many of the basic dilemmas about difference are strikingly similar. Indeed it was the inspiration of London that led authorities in South West England to publish their own account, 'Achieving Equality and Efficiency in the rural South West', describing the work of Bournemouth Borough, Cornwall, Devon, Somerset and Wiltshire Councils. These areas are not as diverse as London and they have different political leadership. Nevertheless they are clear that 'consideration of service user needs through a robust impact analysis/assessment and consideration of equality duties can deliver savings'(South West Equality Network, 2015). A similar message emerges from a comparison of migration in Shropshire and Tower Hamlets, which argued that the 'exchange of experiences and lessons learnt ... would be mutually beneficial', a linkage that could extend beyond migration 'to cover issues that affect the populations in general' (Kershen, 2013).

What happens if local authorities do not engage with the reality of their communities? Running away from complexity will not make the challenges easier especially in the current context of austerity. On the contrary exploiting national

---

13   See: <http://www.theguardian.com/local-government-network/2013/may/07/equality-and-diversity-local-government-discussion?commentpage=1>

14   For an example, see <http://www.theguardian.com/politics/2014/sep/16/scottish-independence-catalogue-errors-union-uk>

drivers and drawing on lessons from across the local government sector help to assess policy and service delivery. Using these tools strengthens understanding of communities and builds the right kinds of relationships to explore what fairness means locally. Local government can give us inspiration that confidence, creativity, collaboration and commitment have helped find solutions in London in the past – and are principles worth remembering and emulating elsewhere.

Acknowledgements

For their ideas and support in writing in this chapter I would like to thank Deborah Carson, Rose Doran and Heather Wills (Local Government Association); Ilhan Basharan (LB Enfield), Joanna Sumner (LB Hackney), Frances Jones (formerly LB Tower Hamlets now Stoke City), Jane Graham and Samantha Jones (South West Equality Network).

Glossary

CCCPTMG	Community Cohesion Contingency Planning and Tension Monitoring Group
EDL	English Defence League
EFLG	Equality Framework for Local Government
EqIA	Equality Impact Assessment
ESLG	Equality Standard for Local Government
LGA	Local Government Association
LGBT	Lesbian, Gay, Bisexual and Trans(gender)
PSED	Public Sector Equality Duty
SEF	Single Equality Framework

References

BBC News (2015) 'Tower Hamlets election fraud mayor Lutfur Rahman removed from office', 23 April 2015 <http://www.bbc.co.uk/news/uk-england-london-32428648> accessed 27 April 2015.

Cantle, T. (2014), About Community Cohesion, <http://tedcantle.co.uk/resources-and-publications/about-community-cohesion/> accessed 27 April 2015.

Collins, K. and Keating, M. (2013), 'An East End Tale', in Marshall, P. (ed.), *The Tail: How England's Schools Fail One Child in Five – and What can be Done*, London: Profile Books.

Daily Telegraph (2014), Rotherham sex abuse: 'The utter brutality is what shocked me most', 30 August 2014. <http://www.telegraph.co.uk/news/uknews/

crime/11063874/Rotherham-sex-abuse-The-utter-brutality-is-what-shocked-me-most.html> accessed 7 July 2015.

Daily Telegraph (2014), 'Trojan Horse just the tip of the iceberg', 12 October 2014,<http://www.telegraph.co.uk/education/educationnews/11157116/Trojan-Horse-just-the-tip-of-the-iceberg.html> accessed 7 July 2015.

Department for Communities and Local Government (2012), *Creating the Conditions for a More Integrated Society*. London: DCLG.

Doran, R. and Keating, M. (2011), 'Social cohesion in the local delivery context: understanding equality and the importance of local knowledge', in Ratcliffe, P. and Newman, I. (eds), *Promoting Social Cohesion: Implications for Policy and Evaluation*. Bristol: Policy Press.

Equalities Review (2007), *Fairness and Freedom: The Final Report of the Equalities Review*. London: Cabinet Office.

Fundamental Rights Agency (FRA) (2013), *Joining up fundamental rights toolkit for local, regional and national public officials*. Vienna <http://fra.europa.eu/en/joinedup/home> accessed 7 July 2015.

House of Commons Library (2013), *The Public Sector Duty and Equality Impact Assessments*. London: Library Standard Note SN/BT/6591.

Huq, R. (2013), *On the Edge: The Contested Cultures of English Suburbia After 7/7*. London: Bloomsbury Academic.

Jones, H. (2013), *Negotiating Cohesion, Inequality and Change: Uncomfortable Positions in Local Government*. Bristol: Policy Press.

Kershen, A. (2013), *How does Middle England Compare with an Inner City London Borough? A Comparison of Local Government Responses to the Immigrant Presence in Shropshire and Tower Hamlets*. London: Centre for The Study of Migration.

Local Government Association (2014), *Equality frameworks*. London, <http://www.local.gov.uk/equality-frameworks> accessed 7 July 2015.

Local Government Association (2014), *Equality Peer Challenge Awards*, London, <http://www.local.gov.uk/web/guest/peer-challenges/-/journal_content/56/10180/3510141/ARTICLE> accessed 7 July 2015.

Local Government Association (2014), Customer-led Transformation Programme, London <http://www.local.gov.uk/web/guest/productivity/-/journal_content/56/10180/5681477/ARTICLE> accessed 7 July 2015.

Local Government Association (2014), *Local Welfare Assistance Delivering Local Welfare report and survey*, London, <http://www.local.gov.uk/finance/-/journal_content/56/10180/6031824/ARTICLE> accessed 7 July 2015.

London Borough of Enfield (2013), *Equality and Diversity*, <http://www.enfield.gov.uk/info/1000000152/equality_and_diversity> accessed 7 July 2015.

London Borough of Enfield (2014), *Borough Plan*, London, <http://www.london.gov.uk/priorities/planning/london-plan> accessed 7 July 2015.

London Borough of Hackney (2009), *Sustainable Communities Strategy 2008–18*, London, <http://www.hackney.gov.uk/Assets/Documents/scs.pdf> accessed 7 July 2015.

London Borough of Tower Hamlets (2014), *Equality and Diversity*, London, <http://www.towerhamlets.gov.uk/lgsl/851-900/861_diversity_and_equalities.aspx> 7 July 2015.

London Borough of Tower Hamlets (2014), *Fairness Commission*, London, <http://www.towerhamlets.gov.uk/lgnl/community_and_living/fairness_commission.aspx> accessed 7 July 2015.

London Councils (2013), *Equality in London: London local authorities delivering best practice* <http://www.rota.org.uk/webfm_send/227> accessed 7 July 2015.

PriceWaterhouseCoopers (2014), *Best Value Inspection of the London Borough of Tower Hamlets*, London <https://www.gov.uk/government/uploads/system/uploads/attachment_data/file/370277/140311_-_final_inspection_report.pdf> accessed 7 July 2015.

The Runnymede Trust (2013), *Croydon, Kingston and Redbridge Race Equality Scorecard Reports*, London, <http://www.runnymedetrust.org/projects-and-publications/community-cohesion/scorecard.html> accessed 7 July 2015.

South West Equality Network (2015), *Achieving Equality and Efficiency in the Rural South West* (forthcoming).

Talk for a Change (2012), *We need to talk about ... can discussing controversial issues strengthen community relations* <http://www.talkforachange.co.uk/wp-content/themes/haworth/publications/We%20Need%20To%20Talk%20About.pdf> accessed 7 July 2015.

The Guardian (2012), 'Graph of Doom: a bleak future for social services', 15 May 2012, <http://www.theguardian.com/society/2012/may/15/graph-doom-social-care-services-barnet> accessed 7 July 2015.

The Guardian (2014), 'The Enfield Experiment: London's fortunes distilled into a single borough', 3 February 2014, <http://www.theguardian.com/cities/2014/feb/03/enfield-experiment-london-cities-economy> accessed 7 July 2015.

The Guardian (2014), 'Enfield tears up the rules in radical attempt to ease housing problem', 1 September 2014, <http://www.theguardian.com/cities/2014/sep/01/enfield-experiment-housing-problem-radical-solution> accessed 7 July 2015.

The Guardian (2014), 'Eric Pickles takes over "rotten" Tower Hamlets', 4 November 2014, <http://www.theguardian.com/politics/2014/nov/04/eric-pickles-tower-hamlets-london-borough> accessed 7 July 2015.

Webb Memorial Trust (2014), *Approaches to Reducing Poverty and Inequality in the UK: A Study of Civil Society Initiatives and Fairness Commissions*, Edge Hill University.

Woods, D., Husbands, C. and Brown, C. (2013), *Transforming Education for All: The Tower Hamlets Story.* London: Tower Hamlets Council Communication Unit.

Chapter 5

London's 'Ghosts':
The Capital and the UK Policy of Destitution
of Refused Asylum-Seekers

Tendayi Bloom

> I do not want to be the Mayor of two categories of people in our great city,
> one group who live normally and another who live in the shadows unable to
> contribute fully to the rest of society.
>
> (Mayor of London, Boris Johnson, GLA 2009b)

This chapter introduces London's ghosts – those who, though refused asylum
in the UK, remain in the capital – and London's experience of policy leading
to their destitution. It presents a disenfranchised population taking what agency
they can, opting for invisibility and destitution in London rather than risk
deportation or dispersal. It also shows a city disenfranchised, receiving 'burden'
relief rather than acknowledgement of need and genuine assistance. London is
the UK city hosting the largest proportion of refused asylum-seekers and a city
hit by 'austerity cuts' in spending power. This chapter raises questions both for
the policy of destitution itself (which it argues is legally, logically and morally
unsustainable) and for the way cities and local authorities are forced to manage
its results. NGOs and activist groups have written extensively on the effects of
destitution on this group (e.g. Refugee Action 2006; Crawley et al. 2011) and
local and state-level government-commissioned reports have been very critical
(e.g. GLA 2009a; JCHR 2007). Yet surprisingly little academic work examines
this UK policy of refused asylum-seeker destitution (for example, Refugee
Action 2006, 31; Bloch 2013, 1507) and even less what it means for London and
London's local authorities.

**Introducing the Ghosts: Definitions and Contextualisation of the Policy
of Destitution**

The impossibility of the situation for refused asylum-seekers in the UK is
demonstrated in a 2009 judicial statement:

> Failed asylum-seekers ought not to be here. They should never have come here
> in the first place and after their claims have finally been dismissed they are only
> here until arrangements can be made to secure their return (Lord Justice Ward).[1]

This chapter adopts the terminology of 'ghosts' because it best reflects this group's physical presence coupled with political and legal invisibility. Refused asylum-seekers must navigate a system whose logic cannot accommodate them, in which meeting bare-life corporal needs for shelter and subsistence is made both illegal and practically extremely difficult. Like ghosts, they are forbidden from acting either humanly or politically. Refused asylum-seekers are not the only group at risk of this form of destitution in the UK (for example, Allsopp et al., 2014) but they are the asylum-seeking group most likely to be destitute (Crawley et al., 2011, 16). Their situation is the focus here because of its intractability and its legal and theoretical implications. This section explains how and why refused asylum-seekers become destitute in London, providing estimates of their numbers.

Definitions and Numbers

There is no internationally recognised definition of asylum-seeker (for example, Weissbrodt, 2009 111; Goodwin-Gill and McAdam, 2007) but in the UK context:

> 'Claim for asylum' means a claim made by a person [...] that it would be contrary
> to the United Kingdom's obligations under the [1951 Refugee] Convention for
> him to be removed from, or required to leave, the United Kingdom. (1993 Act (1))

An asylum-seeker is someone who has made such a claim. After examination by the Home Office, if the claim is considered unfounded, or insufficient for a humanitarian status, refugee or other, it is 'refused'.

There is no reliable data on numbers of refused asylum-seekers in the UK (for example, Allsopp et al., 2014, 10; Sigona and Hughes, 2012: 7), but the number *is* significant (though extremely low compared to other UK immigrants and tiny compared to asylum figures globally). In 2013, of over 17,000 final decisions on asylum applications 63 per cent were refusals (calculated from National Statistics 2014a). Of this number, almost 9,000 – 82 per cent – are recorded to have departed, either forced or 'voluntary' (calculated from National Statistics, 2014b). One must assume the rest, over 2,000 persons, remained, joining those from previous years. Public official data only exists from 2006, and post-2006 calculations imply there are over 48,000 such persons (see Figure 5.1). Official estimates for the period 1994–2005 are around 283,500 (NAO 2005, 13). Adding these very rough figures brings the estimated total to at least 332,288 persons. A 2009 LSE study puts the number much higher, at between 417,000 and 863,000 (Gordon et al., 2009).

---

1   *R (on the application of YA)* v *Secretary of State for Health* [2009] EWCA Civ 225.

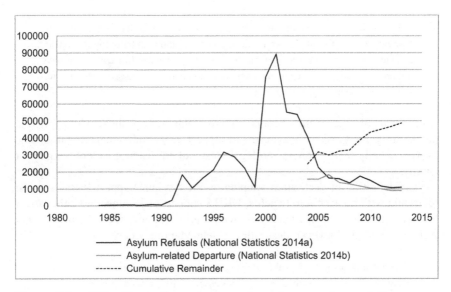

Figure 5.1   UK-wide asylum rejections, departures, and speculative cumulative remainder (based on available data) (National Statistics 2014a; b)

In 2000, the Audit Commission for Local Authorities estimated 85 per cent of asylum-seekers and refugees in the UK lived in London (Audit Commission, 2000) and the 2009 LSE study estimated that the proportion of the UK's refused asylum-seeker population living in London includes 80 per cent (+/-five per cent) of those from 2001 and gaining 60 per cent (+/-15 per cent) of that population's growth nationally from then on (Gordon et al., 2009, 49).

Once someone has been refused asylum in the UK he or she has 21 days to leave the country (1999 Act (94)(3)(B)), or ten days to lodge an appeal. After that period, the person, still forbidden from working, becomes ineligible for cash benefits, and in most cases also for most housing and welfare support and generally falls into the broad category of 'irregular migrants' (Bloch, 2013). A minority may apply for 'section 4 support', which, for a single person, is £35.39 weekly, upon demonstrating impossibility of return or that reasonable steps are being taken to leave and they would otherwise be destitute. However, few apply for such support, either lacking awareness of it or because application comes with requirements like regular in-person reporting to the Home Office (Crawley et al., 2011: 26). This is often seen as risky, associated with arrests leading to detention and/or deportation. This can make it preferable not to fulfil reporting requirements, cementing the situation of irregularity and removing any possibility of support (Crawley et al., 2011: 5; Bloch, 2013: 1512), rendering this population even more invisible. When applications are made, need for section 4 support is tricky to prove. For example, consider this extract from a Home Office letter:

> On your Section 4 application form you have mentioned that you were street
> homeless since this date [given earlier], you were hiding and moving from place
> to place, which is not a reasonable or credible statement. Moreover you have
> not provided any evidence to substantiate that you are destitute or with out (sic.)
> access to support. (ASAP, 2008: 15)

Other forms of support may be available to children, or to those who applied at
port of entry. For those without access to support, as the individual remains unable
to work legally there becomes no legal means of subsistence except begging or
charity.

The definition of destitution adopted by the Asylum Support Partnership is:
'currently with no access to benefits, UKBA support or income, and either street
homeless or staying with friends only temporarily' (Smart, 2009: 4). In the 1999
Act Section 95(3), however, destitution is defined more widely:

> …a person is destitute if – (a) he does not have adequate accommodation or any
> means of obtaining it (whether or not his essential living needs are met);
> or (b) he has adequate accommodation or the means of obtaining it, but cannot
> meet his other essential living needs.

The apparent contradiction that leads to destitution, no legal work and no benefits,
is not a legal oversight. In 2007, a Home Office document explained the thinking
behind the policy:

> [refused asylum-seekers] should be denied the benefits and privileges of life in
> the UK and experience an increasingly uncomfortable environment so that they
> elect to leave (Home Office, 2007: 17).

As well as being unable either to work or to claim benefits, since 2004, refused
asylum-seekers are also ineligible for NHS hospital healthcare beyond emergency
treatment and screening for infectious diseases (see Amnesty International, 2006).
Despite these conditions, many remain in the country. Reasons for this are the
subject of the next section.

So Why Do They Stay? Becoming a Ghost as an Active (Albeit Tragic) Choice

> No failed asylum-seeker need face destitution if they comply with the law and
> the decisions of our courts and go home when required and able to do so. (Home
> Office Statement, for example, in Nye, 2013)

> [29-year-old Esrafil] had no money and no home because his asylum application
> had been refused and his support cut off. He was ill and could not find a doctor
> who would treat him. Although terrified of return to Iran, and convinced he had
> not had a fair hearing, he could not find a lawyer to take on his case. He set fire

to himself in the office, and died six days later in hospital. (Refugee Action, 2006: 10)

Having been refused asylum in the UK, there are three primary reasons people do not leave (Crawley et al., 2011: 17):

- Removal is not possible;
- Fearing return, persons abscond; and/or
- Desire to ensure claim is given proper consideration.

Regarding the first, central government acknowledges that many destitute refused asylum-seekers come from countries with 'ongoing conflict or political instability' (HAC, 2014: s3). Return may be impossible because of this instability, lack of cooperation from home country authorities, or a lack of safe routes (Finch and Cherti, 2011: 107) as well as medical reasons making the person unable to travel (1999 Act (4)(5), 2005 Regulations 3(2) note wording: *may* provide support). In such cases persons may apply for section 4 support but, as mentioned above, application rates are low (e.g. Crawley et al., 2011: 26). As such, not only are persons denied the right to work or claim benefits, they may also be officially unable to leave (indeed, persons unable to leave will not be considered for section 4 support unless they are otherwise demonstrably destitute).

Second, though refused humanitarian status, persons may still fear return to their home countries. A 2012 report of the UK's Refugee Council found a quarter of clients accessing their destitution services were from five countries (DRC, Eritrea, Somalia, Sudan and Zimbabwe). Table 5.1 shows the high rates of asylum refusal for persons from these countries (from Refugee Council, 2012: 26).

Table 5.1   Proportion refused asylum in the UK 2002–2012 from five origin countries

Country of origin	Proportion refused asylum 2002–2012
Democratic Republic of Congo	80%
Sudan	76%
Zimbabwe	74%
Somalia	54%
Eritrea	52%

Alongside fearing return, persons, particularly from these countries, mention feeling injustice at the belief that their claim has not yet been properly considered. Indeed, this may be well-founded. In 2011, 26 per cent of appeals on negative asylum decisions decided were allowed (Refugee Council, 2012: 27), nearly 28 per cent in 2012 (Ghelani, 2014). This represents large numbers that could otherwise have been returned to persecution (Weissbrodt, 2009: 147) and motivates people to seek review even though difficult and, like initial decisions, slow.[2]

Choosing destitution renders potentially productive London inhabitants 'useless' (e.g. Dorling et al., 2012: 14). This is mentioned in almost every report on this situation, highlighting wasted human resources, deskilling, psychological effects and dehumanisation. The absurdity is shown most clearly through the case of an obstetrics and gynaecology consultant who lived comfortably in Senegal, training UN staff and occasionally flying to London for conferences at the London School of Hygiene and Tropical Medicine. He was a campaigner for minority rights and for independence for South Senegal. These latter activities led him to be detained twice and tortured by his government. He explains: '… my life was saved by one of the guards who recognised me as the doctor who had helped his wife to give birth' (quoted in NNLS, 2014). He fled to the UK, claimed asylum, and at the time of writing sleeps on buses and on a mattress in a shared room in a night shelter, reading medical journals in the library to follow current research (NNLS, 2014). The difference in his status in London now compared to that of his past is striking. It is also striking that he chooses this lifestyle over return to Senegal.

If the aim of the destitution policy is to make people leave, it is not proving generally successful. Studies show the policy has driven people neither to leave nor to stop claiming asylum though it has driven them to become more invisible (see for example, Blitz and Otero-Iglesias, 2011; SHSH, 2007; OECD, 2011). Destitution is not short-term. In a 2009 UK-wide study of visits by destitute persons to Red Cross support centres, 62 per cent of refused asylum-seekers had been destitute for over six months (calculated from Smart 2009 6). Indeed, the length of destitution is often longer, with 31 per cent of visits by persons who had been destitute for over two years, (calculated from Smart, 2009: 16). Other studies suggest destitution may be for considerably longer. Alongside analysing this as policy-implication, the length of destitution demonstrates a form of agency, showing the level of hardship London's ghosts will suffer in order to remain in the capital.

London and Two Decades of UK Asylum Policy

This section charts how national policy around the protection of refused asylum-seekers over the past two and a half decades has affected London disproportionately. Reasons for this include the significantly higher density of asylum-seekers and refused asylum-seekers per head in the capital, high levels of poverty, and the

2 Endemic inefficiencies in the British asylum system have frequently been highlighted and in 2012, the Independent Chief Inspector of Borders and Immigration report into this led to the break-up of the UK Borders Agency (UKBA, created in 2008), relocating systems to the Home Office and answerable to ministers (HAC 2012). Recent 2014 suggest this has not had the desired effect.

'austerity'-induced reductions in financial and housing capacity in these local authorities. Rather than supporting local authorities sufficiently to provide for asylum-seekers in their jurisdiction, central government (under all three recent administrations: Conservative, Labour and Coalition) has developed two main policy strategies: dispersal and destitution. These reinforce that, while immigration and asylum decisions are the protected purview of central government, resourcing the resulting social situations is the domain of local authorities.

Dispersal

In the 1990s, London was already the main destination for asylum-seekers in the UK (Allsopp et al., 2014: 13), giving this region disproportionate responsibility for asylum-seekers' welfare. Indeed, pressure in the capital may have influenced the development of the dispersal scheme (e.g. Audit Commission, 2000: 5). Dispersal was introduced at the end of the 1990s, a decade in which new asylum legislation introduced every three years gradually reduced welfare obligations towards asylum-seekers. It was also a decade of increasing popular and political suspicion of 'bogus asylum-seekers' and indeed of economic migrants *per se* in the middle of this period, and towards the end of John Major's Conservative administration, Peter Lilley MP explained the rationale of the latest, 1996, Act, as to:

> [E]nsure that the UK remains a safe haven for those genuinely fleeing persecution; to deal more speedily with their claims; and to discourage unfounded claims from people who are actually economic migrants. (Lilley, 1996)

In 1997, the new Labour government of Tony Blair did not noticeably alter the evolution in asylum policy. Terms like 'illegal' and 'bogus' asylum-seeker peaked in the national press in 1998 and in 2002–3 (Gabrielatos and Baker, 2008: 30), along with a conflation of the phrases 'asylum seeker' and 'illegal immigrant' (IPPR, 2006: 7; Goodwin-Gill and McAdam, 2007: 385) and a culture of disbelief of asylum claims developed (e.g. Weissbrodt, 2009: 146). It is particularly interesting that low points in the use of these terms in the press occurred in 1996 and 1999, when key Acts were passed, each time followed by a sudden rise in their usage (see chart, Gabrielatos and Baker, 2008: 32). The rhetoric from all sides has continued to appeal to moral and national values, whether regarding suspicion-worthy welfare-scroungers or British values of public welfare. Once the 1996 Act was passed, asylum advocates turned to the postwar anti-Poor Law National Assistance Act 1948 to circumvent the worst privations.

In September 1999, the Audit Commission recorded just over 9,000 asylum-seeking households covered by homelessness legislation living in temporary accommodation in London, almost a quarter of the city's homeless households. In some boroughs it was more like 60 per cent (Audit Commission, 2000: 8). Local authorities were already spending significantly more on asylum-seekers than was recoverable from central government (Audit Commission, 2000: 12). In five cases, this represented a shortfall of ≥25 per cent of total gross expenditure on housing benefit (Audit Commission, 2000: 13), something particularly difficult for some of the UK's already poorest and most densely populated local authorities.

It was in this context that the 1999 Act removed significant welfare rights and introduced the dispersal policy, by which asylum-seekers were sent to social housing initially in 12 parts of the UK (Birmingham, Bradford, Coventry, Hull, Leeds, Glasgow, Greater Manchester, Liverpool, Newcastle, Nottingham, Plymouth, Sunderland). The dispersal policy was controversial, not least because it relocated these vulnerable populations to some of the UK's other poorest areas. The notions of burden and the suspicion of asylum-seekers continued. Rather than removing the pressure on local services, dispersal moved it to local services in other poor areas (e.g. Sigona and Hughes, 2012: 48) leading to further resentment and even violence (Burnett, 2010). It had been hoped the 1999 Act's creation of NASS (National Asylum Support Service) might relieve those most stretched councils, as central government would take up the monetary costs alongside NASS coordination of dispersal to areas with less demand on housing stock (Bloch and Schuster, 2005: 506). But it did not work out that way.

Among migrants, too, the policy was unpopular. In practical terms, dispersal locates people far from co-linguistic, co-cultural communities and can involve frequent moves, with most asylum-seekers moved two or three times and others significantly more. One case study describes a mother and small child moving eleven times in half as many years (Children's Society, 2013: 21). Yet it seems, to a limited extent, that dispersal had an intended effect. Asylum-seekers, attracted to areas with established co-linguistic, co-ethnic communities, are now more likely than before to settle outside London, leading to some natural dispersal also of refused asylum-seekers.

However, London continued to attract large numbers of asylum-seekers, particularly those making their own accommodation provisions, moving pressure from public housing to migrant communities or leaving people street-homeless. Various studies have found asylum-seekers returning to London from dispersal areas, demonstrating with their feet the policy's limitations, giving reasons like: 'feelings of isolation from community and/or harassment in the dispersal regions' (Allsopp et al., 2014: 28). Consequently, in 2005, 71 per cent of the UK's asylum-seeking population was still found in London (Allsopp et al., 2014: 14). London and London's local authorities were therefore still disproportionately responsible for meeting asylum-seekers' welfare needs, even including the now reduced claim to public services.

Removing Support

Alongside reducing asylum support generally, the 1999 Act introduced a new unique benefit for refused asylum-seekers, a reduced 'Section 4 support' (HAC, 2013: s3). And, moving into the 2000s, while dispersal remained, the emphasis on withdrawing from obligations developed. Despite the measures of the 1990s, there were descriptions of a 'housing chaos' arising from pressures on social services in London and the South East, with social services in London alone supporting 57,000 asylum-seekers (Allsopp et al., 2014: 15). The policies of the 2000s aimed to respond to this, by adding more wide-ranging removal of benefits from asylum-seekers in a new way. As a result:

> [l]ocal authority housing departments, traditionally the first port of access for refugees and asylum-seekers, were barred from providing accommodation for asylum seekers, with a few exceptions. (Allsopp et al., 2014: 15)

Research commissioned by the Labour Mayor of London Ken Livingstone predicted that an estimated 10,000 asylum-seekers, including those refused and those with claims ongoing, would be made destitute annually by these measures (MoL, 2004). And a 2009 study found that the highest percentage of visits by destitute persons to Red Cross and other voluntary services in the UK were by failed asylum-seekers (Smart, 2009). In London and the South East, this proportion is lowest, with 45 per cent of recorded visits to destitution service-providers made by refused asylum-seekers, compared with 81 per cent in Wales and the South West (Smart, 2009: 31). However, rather than indicating that fewer refused asylum-seekers are destitute in London, these figures reflect the much higher proportion of Convention Refugees and asylum-seekers also destitute. This is corroborated by London support agency data. For example, almost 30 per cent of Centre Point's homeless young clients are asylum-seekers, including refused asylum-seekers and refugees (quoted in Allsopp et al., 2014: 28).

Meanwhile, other changes were going to make conditions increasingly difficult. Towards the end of the 2000s, the existing budgetary shortfalls in London's local authorities increased and at the decade's end, the central government's *2010 Spending Review*, commissioned by the new Conservative-Liberal Democrat Coalition Government, led to wide-ranging cuts to central government financial contributions to local governments and to benefits and services more generally. The review indicated support of 'increasing delivery through the voluntary and community sector' (HM Treasury, 2010), something already characteristic of asylum provision. While the *2010 Spending Review* mentioned asylum directly only once (in terms of the logistics of asylum processing within the context of border control, HM Treasury, 2010: 55), refused asylum-seekers were heavily affected by the wider cuts to public services, legal aid and local budgets impacting upon all those vulnerable to local authority support.

The 1999 Act had introduced the cashless voucher system for 'Section 4 support'. Removed in 2002, this had been reintroduced in 2004, primarily as the 'azure card', only valid in specified shops. Receipt of Section 4 support (which, for a single person, is £35.39 weekly) does not prevent poverty. In 2014, the British Red Cross surveyed 74 organisations assisting people receiving this support. Many organisations were supplying food, clothing, baby items and toiletries, indicating that those using their services were otherwise unable to obtain these items (Carnet et al., 2014: 27). Basic needs became hard to meet, reinforcing the status of 'ghosts'.

Refused asylum-seekers were now commonly street-homeless, or else staying with friends or family, reliant on the charity of persons, themselves on either Section 95 or Section 4 support. Destitution policy does not, then, alleviate their needs but shifts the responsibility to meet them onto society's poorest. This concern is voiced in the London Mayor's Refugee Integration Strategy:

> Evidence suggests high rates of homelessness and destitution among asylum seekers and refused asylum seekers. This can place a burden on refugee communities and inhibit integration. (GLA, 2009a: 14)

The first decade of the millennium ended, then, with an explicit UK policy of enforced destitution of refused asylum-seekers. Rather than reducing pressure on the London local authorities with the highest refused asylum-seeker populations, it has entrenched refused asylum-seeker poverty in these areas and has made responding to needs even more difficult.

Local Authority Response to Destitution

Unpacking the implications of the policy of destitution in London is tricky. On the one hand, it freed local authorities from providing services to refused asylum-seekers, relieving pressures on service-providers. On the other hand, and as decried by a growing number of local authorities, it forbade assisting this vulnerable population, with knock-on effects on public health, criminality, disorder, as well as moral obligation (e.g. Refugee Action, 2006: 13). A London borough interviewee for a 2002 study noted: 'what is beginning to emerge as an issue is if someone is vulnerable do you, or do you not, as a local authority, have a responsibility towards them?' (Morris, 2002: 419). The response of the UK's cities and local authorities to the policy of destitution has been mixed.

At the time of writing, (November 2014), ten local authorities outside London have passed motions condemning destitution among asylum-seekers (Glasgow, Bristol, Sheffield, Oxford, Bradford, Leeds, Liverpool, Kirklees, Swansea and Manchester) and eight have joined the Still Human Still Here coalition (Bradford, Bristol, Kirklees, Leicester, Liverpool, Manchester, Oxford and Swansea – two of which have been key dispersal destinations), while London Assembly Members have pushed the Mayor to join the campaign on their behalf. Meanwhile, landmark cases have been brought against local authorities, predominantly in London, following each Act. Nineteen cities have joined a coalition working with Central Government Interventions and Sanctions Directorate staff to ensure better immigration laws enforcement.

The UK's first directly elected mayor, the Mayor of London was instituted in 2000. As leader of the Greater London Authority, the London Mayor has no jurisdiction over local authority services (indeed four London Boroughs have their own directly elected mayors for this purpose) and also has no jurisdiction over asylum decisions, which are the reserve of the Home Office. Indeed, when it was contacted for interview or further information for this research project, the Office of the London Mayor responded:

> Unfortunately the Mayor does not have power over asylum processes including refused asylum applications. It is the responsibility of the Home Office. You may wish to contact the Home Office. (email received by author)

The London Mayor's role in the debate is, therefore, complicated. Two key initiatives, the LSMP (London Strategic Migration Partnership) and MRAP (Migrant and Refugee Advisory Panel) have been created and both incumbents, Labour Ken Livingstone and Conservative Boris Johnson have commissioned reports into homelessness among irregular migrants and asylum-seekers in London (MoL, 2004; GLA, 2009a).

It was in response to the 2009 report that Boris Johnson made the comment at the head of this chapter. His call is not humanitarian and is not like Walzer's disagreement with 'live in servants', supplying labour without the protections of membership (Walzer, 1963: 56). Instead he argues that persons who cannot be removed should be able to work and pay tax. In a 2009 BBC Panorama television documentary programme he stated 'let me be clear I am in favour of sending them back but we must be realistic'. He has elsewhere elaborated:

> If an immigrant has been here for a long time and there is no realistic prospect of returning them, then I do think that person's condition should be regularised so that they can pay taxes and join the rest of society.[3]

Johnson criticises the illogicality of preventing irregular migrants from working and so paying taxes whilst using services, and the resulting creation of two classes of Londoners. However he does not address the fundamental intractability of refused asylum-seekers, denied both the right to work and access to benefits. This was an opportunity missed and the following year, London Assembly Members called upon Mayor Johnson to lobby central government on behalf of London local authorities and the destitute asylum-seekers they host (GLA, 2010). In particular, they wanted him to demand refused asylum-seekers receive the right to work. Amnesties for irregular immigrants is something that Boris Johnson has supported and which has been unpopular within his party.

It is crucial not to miss the role of NGOs in London and elsewhere filling gaps in service-provision (e.g. see Allsopp et al., 2014: 35), lobbying and campaigning. There is an interesting character to London's contribution to the Still Human Still Here coalition, the main body working in this area. Of the 68 coalition member

---

3   In a speech at the London Citizens Mayoral Assembly 2008 <www.youtube.com/watch?v=OMQGLVhzB2Y> accessed 10 November 2014.

organisations, 56 per cent are London-based, though only three are London-focused.[4] London remains the focus for the UK's refused asylum-seekers and for UK asylum policies. It must, therefore, also be the focus of any solution to their destitution.

Destitution in London: International Obligations and Local Responsibilities

The destitution of refused asylum-seekers comes into conflict with two different sorts of international commitments: Refugee and Human Rights Conventions; and global commitments to reduce poverty (MDGs/SDGs). It also conflicts with local commitments to equity in wealth-distribution and poverty-prevention.

Legal Worries: Refugees, Stateless Persons and Inhuman and Degrading Treatment

This subsection presents three legal worries about the destitution of refused asylum-seekers: the right to seek asylum; protecting stateless persons; and prohibition on inhuman and degrading treatment. These relate to international commitments made by the UK central government.

A Right to Seek Asylum

While there is no formalised international definition of asylum-seeker, nor category of rights associated with them, the Universal Declaration of Human Rights (UDHR) recognises a right to seek and to enjoy asylum (Art.14(1)) and the Refugee Convention requires that a person seeking asylum not be penalised on the basis of irregular border-crossing (Art.31). The policies described in this chapter contravene these rights. It is useful to see this in context. While the original proposed text of UDHR included a right to be granted asylum, this was amended to the UK-promoted version with what Goodwin-Gill and McAdam refer to as 'the vaguer and far more innocuous "and to enjoy"' (2007: 359). This wording has remained through subsequent instruments and makes granting asylum dependent on the goodwill of states.

Despite this, the UNHCR maintains that a person 'does not become a refugee because of recognition, but is recognised because he is a refugee'. As such he or she should be eligible for Convention protections even without recognition (UNHCR, 1992: 28). In the case of refused asylum-seekers, it may appear that their failure to meet the definition criteria has been demonstrated. However their continuing decision to remain in the country, the high rates of successful appeal and the explanations given for remaining suggest otherwise. Furthermore, as a

---

4   These figures derive from a study of the membership listed on the 'still human still here' website.

2001 UNHCR document regarding the treatment of asylum-seekers argued, the 1951 Convention provisions not linked to lawful stay or residence should apply 'in so far as they relate to humane treatment and respect for basic rights' (UNHCR, 2001, quoted in Goodwin-Gill and McAdam, 2007: 412), demonstrating the need to emphasise human rights obligations throughout the asylum process, even without a refugee determination. Presumably, even if refused, if unable to leave, persons must also be accorded the same protections. Finally, explicitly trying to make life so unbearable that someone leaves conflicts with the provision against refoulement and forcing 'voluntary return' in exchange for access to basic food and shelter is a cause for worry.

Some Refused Asylum-Seekers may be Stateless Persons

According to the 1954 Statelessness Convention, a person is 'stateless' if he or she is 'not considered as a national by any State under the operation of its law' (Art.1). Arguably, then, refused asylum-seekers unable to return should be included under the Statelessness Conventions as they 'lack an effective nationality or cannot legally be returned to their country of origin' (e.g. Blitz and Otero-Iglesias, 2011: 658). Indeed, the majority of those considered to be stateless in the UK in a 2011 UNHCR report were refused asylum-seekers. That report also suggested that the lack of a statelessness determination procedure at that time meant that the only status such persons could apply for was asylum (UNHCR, 2011: 45; 100). In 2013, the UK became one of the slowly growing number of states to have a statelessness determination procedure. Recognition of a Statelessness status would give a person a right to work, and to benefit from some social security benefits. But it would not remove the underlying problem of a series of Acts intentionally rendering a substantial population destitute.

A Prohibition on Inhuman and Degrading Treatment

The provision against inhuman or degrading treatment is found in the European Convention on Human Rights (ECHR Art.3) as well as in a number of international agreements (e.g. UDHR 1948 Art.5; ICCPR 1966 Art.3,16; Convention Against Torture 1984) and was already used against the policy of destitution in 1996 for reasons described in this chapter. A 2007 government report made the following statement (JCHR, 2007: 41):

> We have seen instances in all cases where the Government's treatment of asylum-seekers and refused asylum-seekers falls below the requirements of the common law of humanity and of international human rights law.

This emphasises that it is not because such persons might be eligible for refugee or statelessness status that there is a problem with their destitution. It is that this policy falls below the accepted standards of treatment for them as humans. The report explains (JCHR, 2007: 5):

> ... the Committee concludes that by refusing permission for asylum-seekers to work and operating a system of support which results in widespread destitution, the Government's treatment of asylum-seekers in a number of cases breaches the Article 3 ECHR threshold of inhuman and degrading treatment.

One 2011 study found that interviewees who had been denied refugee status cited the lack of access to five key rights as having the biggest effects on their lives: to work, to have a bank account, to hold a drivers' licence, to lease a mobile phone and to enter education, while the cancellation of financial benefits gave rise to significant financial difficulties and the overall situation led to a lack of control over 'major live decisions' (Blitz and Otero-Iglesias, 2011: 684, based on interviews in Oxford and London). Interviewees in another study, carried out in London, the Midlands and the North West of England, referred to being 'trapped', 'locked up', 'in prison' (Bloch, 2013: 1520) despite being apparently physically free. As such, the destitution illegally forces people to live as ghosts, trapped in a limbo between physical being and legal non-being.

Broader Commitments: Development Goals and Destitution as a Policy of Extreme Poverty

The Millennium Development Goals (MDGs) sought to eradicate extreme poverty by 2015. People in a situation of extreme poverty are defined as those 'whose income is less than $1.25 a day', without access to productive employment and decent work, and 'people who suffer from hunger' (Targets 1A, 1B and 1C). This description fits those described in this chapter, especially where $1.25 is off-set for Purchasing Power Parity (PPP) in one of the world's most expensive cities. According to World Bank indicators,[5] this would convert, in the UK, to £1.38. However, London is ranked 15th in the Economist Intelligence Unit Cost of Living Report 2014 and the way in which public salaries in London are adjusted in comparison to salaries elsewhere in the UK, referred to as 'London Weighting', can help to indicate perceived difference in purchasing power. For example, state-school teacher starting salaries in London are 20 per cent higher than in the rest of the country. Increasing the poverty threshold in this way moves it to at least £1.65 per day.

Those who obtain section 4 support receive £5.06 per day (the national minimum wage for over 21s is, at the time of writing, £6.50 per hour) and an Oxfam study found that destitute asylum-seekers working illegally were receiving between £1 and £3 per hour (Crawley et al., 2011: 6). However many record a lack of any income, or any reliable income, and other UK-wide studies record unpaid

---

5   See <data.worldbank.org/indicator/PA.NUS.PPPC.RF> accessed 10 November 2014.

work in exchange for accommodation, for example, including child care and sex work, or committing minor criminal offences (Bloch, 2013; Refugee Action, 2006: 13; from 77).

Much of the discourse about the MDGs, particularly the first Goal, has focused on developing countries, including developing countries as recipients of aid. This is a discourse that has continued in the formulation of the post-2015 Sustainable Development Goals (SDGs). However, while it is vital to reduce the unacceptable scale of extreme poverty globally and a considerable reallocation of resources, as well as an altering of global systems is needed, the extreme poverty described in this chapter suggests the absence of a genuine global culture of collaborative poverty eradication per se. Destitution of refused asylum-seekers in London is an example of invisible avoidable extreme poverty. Ending it requires only will, since the jurisdiction within which the law changes, funds and infrastructure would be needed are one and the same and the capacity exists. This illustrates the practical and symbolic importance of explicitly including the needs of migrants in the SDGs.

The peculiarity of this level of poverty in a country of such wealth (the UK is ranked 14th in the 2013 Human Development Index) is not lost on those caught up in it. One informant in a 2011 study mentioned:

> It never came into my mind that one day I'd be destitute myself, especially in this country, which is ruled by civilised people. On paper they seem to be feeling sorry for people like me, but in the back of their minds I think they are happy. (Crawley et al., 2011: 18)

This arises from a prior perception of the UK as a land of promise and of London as a city where a person can pursue his or her ends. The human implication is that those persons not receiving even section 4 support are forced into extreme poverty. This is not something that local authorities can manage on their own, but simple policy changes and central/local government cooperation could still eradicate this poverty within the MDG timeframe and lead the way for other developed countries and cities especially in designing the SDGs. It would also add credibility to commitments to a global effort to end extreme poverty.

London Local Authorities: Between a Rock and a Hard Place

Jeremy Waldron's critique of homelessness (1993) is particularly useful in showing the absurdity of the destitution policy and this helps to identify the difficulty for local authorities. Waldron criticises as ludicrous policies that make unavoidable human activities illegal. For example, if people are homeless and 'urinating is prohibited in public places (and if there are no public lavatories) then the homeless are simply unfree to urinate' (Waldron, 1993: 329). This is the situation into which London's ghosts are placed. Unable to leave, forbidden from working, from receiving benefit, indeed, often homeless, they are forbidden from carrying out unavoidable human activities. Consequently, London's ghosts will necessarily carry out these activities within local authorities irrespective of what central government policy allows.

London local authorities have continued to suffer from cuts. From 2010 (when the *2010 Spending Review* was published) until 2014, spending power in London local authorities has fallen by well over 20 per cent while for other UK local authorities it fell by less (see chart Hastings et al., 2013: 9). That said, the figures for services look different (Hastings et al., 2013: 12) and some argue that London experiences a privileged place among local authorities in terms of investment (e.g. Massie, 2013). However, the effects of cuts to London's local authorities' budgets are exacerbated by high and still rising costs of housing in the capital (e.g Pickford, 2013) and the higher density of persons in this refused asylum-seeking population to support.

Nationally, the numbers of refused asylum-seekers are small, particularly when compared to the 7.5 million foreign-born persons found in the 2011 Census to be living in England and Wales. It is also tiny compared to global asylum figures. However, when the responsibility for supporting this population falls primarily to a capital city and to its poorest local authorities in particular, then it is harder to manage. This chapter has presented how the UK policy of refused asylum-seeker destitution has arisen as a result of a failure of central and local government collaboration. Moreover, the implications of the policy are to create situations of extreme poverty in London and other cities with secondary consequences of financial, housing, and other pressures put on the city's poorest, also resulting in difficulties in terms of non-reporting of illness and crime, making it more difficult for cities to manage other policy areas.

Members of the London Assembly see a role for London, as a city, to defend those seeking asylum in the capital. This can be seen in the calls to stand against the policy of destitution in cases like that of Nigerian refused asylum-seeker Isa Muazu who, in December 2013, undertook a 90 day hunger strike giving as his reason fear of attack from Boko Haram on return to Nigeria. The London Assembly voted unanimously for London Mayor Boris Johnson to intervene with central government on their behalf (though this is based on only 13 members voting). He did not, not publicly, at least.

London will need financial support to meet refused asylum-seeker needs in a time of austerity, though this will be politically difficult initially. Without directly addressing the situation, and doing it with cooperation between central and local government, change is unlikely.

Conclusions and Recommendations

> They kill me already. I feel like the walking dead.
> (refused asylum-seeker quoted in Dorling, et al., 2012: 14)

This chapter has argued that policies both of dispersal and of destitution seem aimed at apparently pushing obligation away from the state. The first redistributed persons within the country, including to already poor constituencies, putting the economic burden on those political entities already most stretched. The second policy moved obligation away from political entities and onto civil society and migrant communities, often the poorest persons within the country's poorest jurisdictions. These policies, pursued by Conservative, Labour and Coalition governments alike, were coincident with a rhetorical move against asylum-seekers and refused asylum-seekers in particular, characterising them as 'bogus', 'illegal' and as 'scroungers'. As such, UK asylum policy, and in particular, the policy towards refused asylum-seekers, needs to be seen within a wider context of inequality and a rhetoric of deservingness in a period of austerity. London and London's local authorities have been significantly affected by these policies. It is clear that the International Conventions relating to refugees, statelessness and human rights cannot be met without partnership between central and local governments. The Millennium Development Goals are not only to be achieved somewhere far away. If the goal of ending extreme poverty is genuine, it should include an end to intentional policies of destitution in wealthy states like the UK. The current fine-tuning of the post-2015 Sustainable Development Agenda could be used to help focus efforts, for example, in this area, explicitly including migrants within the goals and the consequent indicators.

This is part of a much larger question. Economic shortfalls are being felt in many countries and similar discrepancies between the rates of asylum rejection and rates of departure exist in many Western European countries (e.g. Weissbrodt 2009, 141), and a failure to meet their needs is not uncommon. There has been a growing awareness of the importance of cooperation between central and local and city governments in meeting international obligations. This is seen, for example, in the cities' meeting at the High-level Dialogue on International Migration and Development (HLD) in New York in October 2013 and the subsequent development of the Mayoral Forum on Mobility, Migration and Development, first held in Barcelona in July 2014. This was not attended by London or any other UK city, though this may reflect the short timeline between the HLD decision to hold the event and the event itself as well as the fact that there were other (not specifically migration related) cities' events taking place at the time. The nature of these obligations and the role of cities still needs to be established.

This chapter advocates the development of a strategy for collaboration as part of a global move towards city empowerment and partnerships between cities and between cities and central government. Further, it advocates that governments support the explicit inclusion of migrants into the SDGs, either within a stand-alone Goal or singled out within other goals, particularly those relating to poverty-reduction and access to labour and health systems. Finally, this chapter calls for a greater visibility for London's ghosts and a greater debate

in London and elsewhere about the ethical limits of immigration control within
state borders.

Acknowledgements

The author thanks the visitors and volunteers of NNLS Asylum Seekers' Drop In
and Hackney Migrant Centre for generously helping deepen her understanding,
and Jenny Altschuler, Deborah Koder and others for in-depth conversations. She
also thanks Katherine Tonkiss and Anne Kershen for their kind reading and wise
comments.

References

Amnesty International (2006), *Down and Out in London*. London: Amnesty
    International UK.
ASAP (2008), *Not Destitute Enough*, London: Asylum Support Appeals Project.
Audit Commission (2000), 'A New City', briefing July 2000, The Audit
    Commission for Local Authorities and the National Health Service in England
    and Wales, London.
Allsop, J., Sigona, N. and Phillimore, J. (2014), *Poverty among refugees and
    asylum-seekers in the UK*. IRiS Working Paper Series, No. 1/2014, University
    of Birmingham.
Blitz, B. and Otero-Iglesias, M. (2011), 'Stateless by Any Other Name: Refused
    Asylum-Seekers in the United Kingdom' *Journal of Ethnic and Migration
    Studies*, 37(4): 657–73.
Bloch, A. (2013), 'Living in Fear', *Journal of Ethnic and Migration Studies*
    40(10): 1507–25.
Bloch, A. and Schuster, L. (2005), 'At the extremes of exclusion', *Ethnic and
    Racial Studies* 28(3): 491–512.
Burnett, J. (2011), 'Public Spending Cuts Savage Dispersal System', Institute of
    Race Relations.
Carnet, P., Blanchard, C. and Ellis, J. (2014), *The Azure Payment Card: The
    Humanitarian Cost of a Cashless System*. British Red Cross Report, London.
Children's Society, The (2013), *Report of the Parliamentary Inquiry into Asylum
    Support for Children and Young People* <http://www.childrenssociety.org.uk/
    sites/default/files/tcs/asylum_support_inquiry_report_final.pdf> accessed 23
    October 2014.
Cholewinski, R. (1998), 'Enforced Destitution of Asylum-seekers in the United
    Kingdom', *International Journal of Refugee Law*, 10(3): 462–98.
CIPFA (2014), *Austerity and beyond: a local government discussion paper*,
    London: The Chartered Institute of Public Finance and Accounting.

Crawley, H., Hemmings, J. and Price, N. (2011), *Coping with Destitution*. Oxfam Research Report, February.

Dorling, K., Girma, M. and Walter, N. (2012), *Refused*. London: Women for Refugee Women.

Finch, T. and Cherti, M. (2011), *No Easy Options*. London: Institute for Public Policy Research (IPPR).

Gabrielatos, C. and Baker, P. (2008), 'Fleeing, Sneaking, Flooding', *Journal of English Linguistics*, 36(5): 5–38.

Ghelani, S. (2014), 'Government in the dock', article on open democracy website, <www.opendemocracy.net/5050/sonal-ghelani/government-in-dock-destitution-and-asylum-in-uk> accessed 16 June 2014.

Gibney, M. (2009), 'Precarious Residents', *Human Development Research Paper 2009/10*, UNDP.

GLA (2010), 'Assembly calls for change in employment rules for asylum seekers', <www.london.gov.uk/media/assembly-press-releases/2010/10/assembly-calls-for-change-in-employment-rules-for-asylum-seekers> accessed 29 October 2014.

GLA (2009a), *London enriched*. London: Greater London Authority.

GLA (2009b), 'Mayor condemns Government immigration failure', <http://www.london.gov.uk/media/mayor-press-releases/2009/03/mayor-condemns-government-immigration-failure> accessed 20 June 2014.

Goodwin-Gill, G.S. and J. McAdam (2007), 'The Concept of Asylum', pp. 354–417 in Goodwin-Gill, G.S. and J. McAdam (2007), *The Refugee in International Law* Third Edition, Oxford: Oxford University Press.

Gordon, I., Scanlon, K. Travers, T. and Whitehead, C. (2009), 'Economic impact on the London and UK economy of an earned regularisation of irregular migrants to the UK', LSE report for the Greater London Authority, London.

HAC (2013), *Asylum*. Home Affairs Committee. London: The Stationery Office.

HAC (2012), *The Work of the UK Border Agency (July–September 2012)*. Home Affairs Committee. London: The Stationery Office.

HM Treasury (2010), *Spending Review 2010*. London: The Stationery Office.

Home Office (2007), *Enforcing the Rules*. London: The Stationery Office.

Home Office (2005), *Controlling our borders*. London: The Stationery Office.

IPPR (2006), *Irregular Migration in the UK*. London: IPPR.

JCHR (2007), *The Treatment of Asylum-seekers*, the House of Commons and the House of Lords Joint Committee on Human Rights, London: The Stationery Office.

Hastings, A., Bailey, N., Besner, K., Bramley, G., Gannon, M. and Watkins, D. (2013), *Coping with the Cuts?*, Joseph Rowntree Foundation Programme Paper, University of Glasgow, Glasgow.

Lilley, P. (1996), Presentation to the House of Commons, *Hansard*, HC Deb 11 January, vol. 269 cc331–45.

Massie, A. (2013), 'London is different', *The Spectator* blog 4 December 2013.

MoL (2004), *Destitution by design*. London: Greater London Authority.

Morris, L. (2002), 'Britain's Asylum and Immigration Regime: the Shifting Contours of Rights' *Journal of Ethnic and Migration Studies*, 28: 409–25.

NAO (2005), *Returning failed asylum applicants*. National Audit Office. London: The Stationery Office.

National Statistics (2014a), 'Table as_01', *Asylum data tables immigration statistics April to June 2014 volume 1*, Home Office.

National Statistics (2014b), 'Table rv_01', *Removals and Voluntary Departures data tables immigration and statistics April to June 2014 volume 1*, Home Office.

NNLS (2014), Asylum Drop-In Report, February, New North London Synagogue.

Nye, C. (2013), 'Glasgow's destitute asylum-seekers', BBC News Scotland website: <http://www.bbc.com/news/uk-scotland-21835432> accessed 16 June 2014.

Refugee Action (2013), *London Migrant Homelessness Conference*. Conference Report, London.

Refugee Action (2006), *The Destitution Trap*. London: Refugee Action.

Refugee Council (2012), *Between a Rock and a Hard Place*. Refugee Council, December.

SHSH [Still Human, Still Here] (2007), *Briefing paper on destitute refused asylum-seekers*. The campaign to end destitution of refused asylum-seekers. Amnesty International.

Sigona, N. and Hughes, V. (2012), *No Way Out, No Way In.* Research Report May 2012, ESRC Centre on Migration, Policy and Security. Oxford: Oxford University Press.

Smart, K. (2009), *The Second Destitution Tally*, Asylum Support Partnership Policy Report.

Stevens, D. (1998), 'The Asylum and Immigration Act 1996', *Modern Law Review* 61(2): 207–22.

UNHCR (2011), *Mapping Statelessness in the United Kingdom*. United Nations High Commissioner for Refugees / Asylum Aid, London.

UNHCR (2001), 'Reception of Asylum-Seekers, including Standards of Treatment, in the Context of Individual Asylum Systems', *Global Consultations on International Protection*. United Nations Document EC/GC/01/17.

UNHCR (1992), *Handbook on Procedures and Criteria for Determining Refugee Status*. United Nations High Commissioner for Refugees.

Waldron, J. (1993), *Liberal Rights: Collected Papers 1981–1991*. Cambridge: Cambridge University Press.

Walzer, M. (1983), *Spheres of Justice*. New York: Basic Books.

Webber, F. (2012), *Borderline Justice*. New York: Basic Books.

Weissbrodt, D. (2008), *The Human Rights of Non-citizens*. Oxford: Oxford University Press.

Chapter 6

Undocumented and Unseen: The Making of the Everyday in the Global Metropolis of London 2015

Parvati Nair

> In a classic tale of rags to riches, Dick Whittington dreamt as a boy that the streets of London were paved with gold. Having made his way to the capital, this young immigrant found himself labouring as a scullion, underpaid, exploited and almost enslaved. The church bells, however, tolled and promised him that he would, one day, be Lord Mayor of the city, which, indeed, he went on to be. This is a tale of inequality and dreams of material empowerment. This is a tale of London – of urban promise, of immigration and of the dream of a better life.[1]

A decade and a half into the new millennium … and London towers as a mega metropolis, a financial, cultural and political hub from where global trends emanate in finance, politics, trade, culture, fashion, popular music and so much more. This capital has long been a gateway to power, as evidenced by its imperial history and the dynamic of its famed square mile, the City, home to one of the most important stock markets in the world, as well as to a plethora of major, globally connected financial houses. Geo-culturally, the expanses of London encompass an extremely wide array of diversity of social class, ethnicity, religion, language and levels of education. From the council estates of East London, to the terraced houses of Hackney, to the Georgian homes of St John's Wood and to the mansions of The Bishop's Avenue, the city houses a very wide spectrum of social classes and ethnicities. In the many layers of urban expansion, transformation and gentrification that have altered the cityscape over centuries, London's pulse is one of hybridity, cross-pollination and mutation. To quote Peter Ackroyd, 'London is so large and so wild that it contains no less than everything.' (2001: 7). Ackroyd compares London to a living body, its dynamic of growth multi-faceted and multi-dimensional, defiant of any single mapping. It merits, he states, not a history as such, but a biography – or, perhaps, many, competing biographies.

Within the myriad narratives that attempt to encompass this mutating city are the traces and shadows of many more that remain untold. Today, despite the financial crisis of 2008, London continues to grow, drawing daily to its urban maze people from poorer, more unstable, or less empowered parts of the world, all seeking a better life. London is a major arrival point for immigrants, both internal and international, and has been so for the past century and more. The city throbs

---

1 For the story of Dick Whittington, see *Troll Books*, 1989.

with the dreams of a million Dick Whittingtons. The metropolitan area of London is today home to more than 13 million people. Over 300 languages are spoken daily in Greater London alone. A unique and intense experience of diversity is on offer here, and hence also one of concomitant hybridity and difference. London is a contradictory city of major class differences and of startling contrasts and combinations of cultural diversity. In the 21st century, the stratification of long existing and increasing divisions between rich and poor, citizens and non-citizens, the secure and the insecure, combines with an effervescent and seemingly unstoppable mixing in the everyday that evolves continuously across the uneven and shifting urban landscape. Driving the hybridity of London's cultural scenario, and commercialising it in terms of food, demographic patterns, neighbourhood identities, high street shops, restaurants, artistic ventures and other ways is a powerful financial engine that propagates itself on the back of London's growing diversity and difference.

Since the turn of the millennium, and especially in the wake of the wars in Afghanistan and Iraq, as well as more recent conflicts elsewhere, the inextricability of economic migrants from refugees and asylum seekers is hard to contest. Subsumed within this context is the larger need for these groups to survive displacement in the face of stringent immigration laws and policies in much of the Western world, as is the case especially with the United Kingdom. A brief glance at Calais and other ports connected to Britain will offer a sense of the numbers and flows of migrants who seek entry, many fleeing conflict zones and endemic poverty. For these global refugees, migrants and displaced people, London, as a capital city of global stature, easily the most powerful of European capitals today, is a focal point for relocation. Legal residence in the United Kingdom, however, is increasingly difficult to obtain and, for those who do enter the country by whatever means, can involve a long and arduous struggle for citizenship. In the course of this struggle, these arrivals must find ways of eking out a living. Alongside London's might as a global financial centre, and linked to this in a million unseen ways, is a thriving informal economy, one where irregularities of wages, fiscal declarations and employment occur in the everyday. Many immigrants survive in ways that defy legislation and accountability. Such work is all too often underpaid and such workers do not access the norms set in place by law. It is in part through their labour, their energy and their exploitation within the urban maze that the city thrives and grows. The undocumented contribute in a myriad of small, unseen, but important ways to the urban weave from below, from the thickly matted underbelly of the city, where rights, recognition and representation often remain at bay.

The focus of this chapter will be on the reliance and centrality of undocumented labour through the informal economy in supporting and enhancing the globalised drive of urban expansion. There is little doubt that irregular migrants play their part in the maintenance and development of London as a global capital. It is important to note two key facets to this issue: firstly, hidden in the crevices of the urban everyday are the often-unrecognised ways in which central aspects of the mainstream urban dynamic are sustained and fuelled by the contributions and presence of irregular migrants; secondly, and although leading marginal existences, the availability of the undocumented for unregulated labour impacts up the labour chain, affecting thus the more vulnerable layers of society, who, in turn, are also forced into compromised labour situations. Thus, a key determiner of global urban expansion in cities such as London is one where irregular employment is engaged in by undocumented immigrants, who thereby contribute in unacknowledged ways to the daily making and remaking of the city. Two factors work together in this context: undocumented migrant labour receives no formal recognition, but is fuelled by the dream – or, all too often, the illusion – of recognition in the future. By framing such dreams and using them in the name of growth, the city expands and thrives, forging new borderlands as it grows. My claim here is that irregular migration plays a certain role in sustaining London life and in sustaining London's status as a global capital through largely underpaid and unrecognised contributions that aid and abet the flow of capital through the city. Of particular relevance here are the fundamentally *unseen* ways in which such migrants contribute to the city, because it is precisely through this invisibility and the mantle of irregularity that is forced upon them by immigration laws and border controls that the city as a whole, and hence the more affluent citizens of London together with their economic, political and ideological interests, are able to benefit from their efforts. Undocumented immigrants find themselves forced into arenas of non-recognition in a bid for survival. Indeed, urban expansion is itself symptomatic of urban immigration, and, in the cases of globally attractive cities, such as London, undocumented immigration must be understood as a key element in the dynamic of urban growth. As such, this chapter will argue that a close connection exists between the erection of borders that constrain the undocumented to non-recognition and the expansion of London as a global capital, both in geopolitical and economic terms.

The theoretical framework for this analysis brings together firstly a reflection on the vital links between the market economy of globalisation, of which London forms a vital part, and labour exploitation, an extreme form of the latter being the unregulated labour market. This idea of the city as dependent upon its 'arrivals' for growth will then invite a reflection on David Harvey's reworking of Henri Lefebvre's notion of the 'right to the city' (2008). While Harvey notes that this right, in an increasingly urbanised world, forms an important aspect of human rights, in a global context where human rights are all too often sidelined by 'market rights', this chapter will also seek to situate the discourse of human rights, and hence the right to the city, within the larger, and more overriding, framework of borders that demarcate, regulate and shape the socio-economic pathways open to migrants. In considering London as a prime example of a mega-city that flourishes within the framework of the globally dominant and profit-oriented market economy – its hypermodernity drawn from the sheer pulse of capital that comes to it, is produced by it and flows through it – this chapter will situate it as exemplary of modernity's intrinsic reliance, stronger than ever before in the 21st century, on the systems and structures of the market economy. This is one that is reliant on the continuous production of borders, both as points of obstruction and as points of contact or privileged crossings. In such a scheme, human rights, and thus the right to the city for the undocumented and irregular, remain marginalised, sidelined by the overriding forces of the market. While the advocates of globalisation propose numerous discourses on freedoms and rights, often professed in tandem with a commitment to democracy, what gets lost from view or mention is, indeed, the right to the city for those barred from papers. As such, freedoms and rights in the city, and to it, become exclusionary practices, enforcing borders that emerge across the city's many topographies. Such exclusionary practices are those that delimit an individual's ability to integrate or claim citizenship (i.e. enter into the community of the documented, the mainstream and the recognised), whilst simultaneously inscribing their contribution as necessary for their future non-integration. These turn London into a dynamic conglomerate of border-scapes through which the city evolves. Inevitably, these borders are not static or dormant. In keeping with Ackroyd's notion of the city as an organism, there is a border dynamic at work here that both manages and produces exclusions. As a result, borders demarcate and produce irregularity through their exclusionary force. On occasion, they also function as contact points and entry points, at times confounding the demarcations between the documented and undocumented, the regularised and the irregular. Borders also shift and relocate in accordance with larger economic and political contexts, displaying a surprising agility and responsiveness that belie their presumed intransigence. In such a landscape, irregularity has many facets: it is an imposition on those it marks, a strategy of survival for the disempowered, as much as it is a method through which capital grows and expands, securing London's pre-eminence on the global financial and urban stage. In this contradictory scenario, the globalised urban setting connects irregular migrants to the city and its citizens, but also constantly restricts them to the margins.

Irregular migration forms an important but often unseen aspect of the social fabric, with many such migrants entering irregularity by overstaying tourist visas or student visas. The authorities acknowledge that there is, in fact, a lack of governmental control on exits from the United Kingdom, a gap in the system of migration control that enables immigrants to overstay or 'disappear.'[2] Many who are in the United Kingdom on student visas enter irregularity by working longer hours than their visas allow them to. These are the moonlighting students, who service restaurants, gas stations, bars and pubs in plenty in order to pay off student fees and living expenses. Others manage to pass through immigration on false passports, pretending to be citizens of the European Union, with rights to live and work in the UK. According to an article published in the *Economist*, 'Nobody knows quite how many people live in Britain illegally. A plausible estimate by the London School of Economics in 2009 put the number at 618,000,

---

2   See Alan Travis's article in the *Guardian*, 'Britain's immigration system in intensive care, says MPs': <http://www.theguardian.com/uk-news/2014/dec/20/britain-immigration-system-in-intensive-care-mps> accessed 20 December 2014.

around 70 per cent of whom live in London. That study relied on census data from 2001, and had a margin of error of 200,000.' (26 October 2013).³ More recent estimates vary between one million and eight hundred thousand. With London and the south east of England established as the wealthiest parts of the country, the majority of undocumented migrants on British territory seek to live and work here. Undocumented migrants, engaged in irregular employment, inevitably nourish the hope that the irregularity of their situation is temporary and that, in due course, they will regularise their situation.

In this context, it is important to note that irregular migrants may have many motivations for enduring the conditions they find themselves in. Firstly, there may often be the short-term aspirations of somehow making enough money not merely to survive, but also to send remittances home. A key factor here is the purchasing power of sterling in comparison to the currencies of many less economically developed nations. In the longer term, however, when immigration laws bar access to the city and when economic and legal borders block their path, irregularity becomes a strategy through which the right to the city is claimed by these unrecognised (non-)citizens. Yet, such claims, when made through irregular means, emanate from boundaries that contain and channel the path of migrants, fencing them within zones of non-recognition and rendering them part and parcel of the larger structures that position them often permanently in illicit border zones whose function remain pivotal to the dynamic of capital. As such, the very phenomenon of irregular or undocumented migration must be seen as integrated within the structures of a larger global economy, one that creates, and is also propelled by, the interstitial forces of the undocumented. In short, London supports and opens up pathways for the undocumented as part and parcel of the networked global routes of capital that rely on labour exploitation and political non-recognition as fuel for economic, political and cultural growth. In this sense, undocumented migrants both resist the system and are formed within it. It thereby becomes clear that globalisation produces, invites, sustains and is sustained, in part, by such irregularities.

A Day in the Life of London

The film 'A Day Without a Mexican' (dir. Sergio Arau, 2004) satirizes the fate of California should the state be deprived for a day of its immigrants. What would happen to London if its irregular population were to disappear for a day? Before dawn, the fresh produce arriving at London's markets would remain unloaded. Market stalls would be unmanned. Produce would not be distributed across the city to supermarkets or grocers. The fruit and vegetables might last a day, but not

---

3 'Over the Top', *Economist*, 26 October 2013, online article <http://www.economist.com/news/britain/21588362-perhaps-half-million-people-live-illegally-britain-governments-draconian-new> accessed 14 August 2014.

the fish. But there would be no one to throw the fish away, so it would sit in the crates. At 6am, the cleaners, especially those habitually relegated to deal with the more unattractive jobs, would fail to turn up. In offices, waste-paper baskets would remain full all day and toilets would not be cleaned. Across the city, cafés would be short-staffed, unable to manage the queues of customers wanting to quickly buy a coffee and a croissant on their way in to work. In restaurants, the pot washers would be absent and the dirty pots would pile up in sinks; vegetables would be left without prepping as kitchen assistants fail to turn up. The middle class would find that the domestic helper who arrives at 8am every morning to get their children ready for school has not turned up. They would have to ring work to say they will be late – the meeting set for 9am would have to be rescheduled. Joan Smith, aged 84 and only just mobile, would wait patiently, and then impatiently, for the woman who comes to her house at mid-day every day to help her get ready and make her a hot cup of tea.[4] In small shops in every locality, the owners would work overtime to step in for the underpaid and irregular immigrants who regularly lighten their load. Ali Mustafa, the Somali-born owner of a mini cab company, would find that the calls from customers are coming in as usual, but he is without drivers.[5] João Santos, born in Brazil and British for over thirty years now, runs an electrical repair business.[6] The clients would call him angrily. Non-stop. No one would have turned up to repair their faulty lines. Near the Barbican, the city broker would return to his flat to find his washing up still in the sink and his shirts for the next few days un-ironed.

Worst of all, yes … worst of all, building works across London would come to a halt. From small repairs, to roof replacements, to loft extensions, to reconversions and renovations, to the erection of architectural wonders that are intended to become landmarks of London, nothing, absolutely nothing, would progress. And if building works fail to progress in London, then London itself fails to progress.

Indeed, central to the prosperity of London is the asset value of its properties, many of which are burgeoning redevelopments. Since before the turn of the millennium, and despite the financial crisis of 2008, urban regeneration has been a major preoccupation of those governing London. To quote Ben Campkin, 'In millennial London … there has been a massive drive led by the state, and by the Urban Task Force established by the New Labour government in 1998, 'to … achieve an urban renaissance.' (2013: 2). Campkin notes 'a feverish new appetite for the regeneration of cities.' (2013: 2). Urban regeneration in London has been critiqued

---

4   Joan Smith, resident of the borough of Barnet, interviewed on 24 August 2014 in Barnet.

5   Ali Mustafa, owner of a minicab company in Finsbury Park, Borough of Haringey, interviewed on 20 August 2014 in Finsbury Park.

6   João Santos, self-employed as an electrician who sub-contracts as needed, Bethnal Green, interviewed in Bethnal Green on 18 August 2014.

by many as urban gentrification, the appropriation and transformation of localities by powerful property developers at the cost of displacing older inhabitants. More than any other commodity, properties in London confirm and secure London's place in the steep financial ladder of the market economy. In her book *Ground Control* (2012), Anna Minton challenges the notion of regeneration by arguing that this has devolved into the building of, in this millennium, mega shopping malls, such as the two Westfield malls in west and east London respectively, into gated properties for the financially privileged, and into extremely profitable ventures for developers at the cost of ordinary citizens who can no longer afford such homes. Instead, these properties are sold to another type of immigrant, a global elite of the super rich, who come and go freely through the UK's borders by dint of generous bank accounts in the country. Minton writes of a culture of fear, one controlled by the overwhelming presence of CCTV and the iron grip of financial powerhouses that has emanated through such 'regeneration'. Within this scheme of fear, at its base and upholding it, often quite literally on their shoulders, are the undocumented masons, bricklayers, cement mixers and carpenters of London, who have come from elsewhere in search of work. They, too, live and work in fear – that of being discovered and deported.

Indeed, if the undocumented seek to be in London, it is because work is more on offer here than elsewhere. Notable in this new millennium in London has been the building of one impressive architectural landscape after another. The construction of the Olympic village alone led to a chain of employment from contractors to subcontractors that slid at times down the pole of legality into illegality, creating informal labour opportunities for many. Indeed, many of these workers were from accession countries of the European Union without full rights as yet to work in the UK or, in some instances, from countries with no rights in the UK at all. Take the case of Constantin,[7] a 42-year-old Macedonian worker, who arrived in London in 2008 and worked until 2009 on the Olympic village as one of a large team of East Europeans employed by a company hired to work on the site. The reason for his presence in London stemmed from the fact that, for some years, he had worked as a construction worker in Spain, but the financial crisis of 2008 had then pushed him and his wife to look further and come to London. While the celebration of the Olympic Games has generally been heralded as a British success, what is less known or mentioned is the role played in the preparations for these games by irregular migrants. When such mention has surfaced, it has inevitably led to expressions of anxiety at the lingering presence of irregular workers in the UK.[8]

Constantin and his wife, like so many new arrivals in London, are part of the many waves of immigrants who seek the better life in London, due largely to the

---

7   Interviewed in London on 24 August 2014.

8   <http://www.independent.co.uk/news/uk/home-news/uk-inspectors-quietly-sack-200-romanian-olympic-site-workers-1522970.html> accessed on 10 September 2014) and <http://www.telegraph.co.uk/sport/olympics/news/9369389/London-2012-Olympic-torches-made-by-illegal-immigrants.html> accessed 10 September 2014.

plethora of economic opportunities that appear in contrast to many other parts of the world. They live in East London, in a house shared with ten others, all irregular workers like themselves, sub-let to them by a Romanian with rights to live and work in the UK. When Constantin lost his job at the Olympic village, he did not panic. His wife, a cleaning lady, was earning over £500.00 per week by working informally in four houses a day, six days a week, always earning money in cash. It was enough to support them for a while. Soon, however, Constantin found another work opportunity. A property maintenance company on his own high street took him on, sending him to do small repairs in homes across the East London area. Constantin was not skilled in all the jobs he was faced with, but he learnt to do them anyway as best as he could, as he too was being paid in cash. Constantin and his wife have one principle aim: to work in London and save enough to go back home and start a business. They also share one fear, that of running up against the authorities and being locked up in a deportation centre. Constantin's life offers a living example of globalisation in practice, seen in the everyday and negotiating, as it does, the limited opportunities and channels for upward mobility that the larger, overriding system of the free market and of globalisation, opens up for them.

Economic Expansion and Urban Borders

To understand the inter-reliance between borders, exclusion, exploitation and the marketplace, it is perhaps useful first to go back somewhat in time, and to reflect on the early phase of globalisation, when Empire was at its height, and the fundaments were laid to ensure London's growing stature as a city of international reference. The hyper-reflexivity of latter day modernity (Delanty, 2000) may have done away with some of the stark and shocking practices of those days, but the fundamental structures of inequality that were cemented then and that reinforced imperial structures continue, albeit in somewhat veiled forms, to ensure ongoing growth of hegemonic heartlands, London being securely located within the latter. It was precisely in the sixteenth, seventeenth and eighteenth centuries, when globalisation as we know it today took on its incipient form as the intercontinental colonial trade of highly marketable and profitable material resources, that our modern era began to emerge as inextricably wedded to the ideology and practices of capitalism. Supporting its growth and development was the practice of slavery, one that relied on colonial and racial supremacy and that was central to the propelling of natural resources across the globe. In his book, *Capitalism and Slavery* (1944), Eric Williams states that 'slavery was an economic institution of the first importance. It had been the basis of the Greek economy and had built up the Roman Empire. In modern times it provided the sugar for the tea and the coffee cups of the Western World' (1944: 5). Williams explores the early phase of globalisation, the result of colonial trade ventures, reliant as it was on the slavery and labour exploitation of slaves. His work, controversial in the postwar years when it emerged against a backdrop of the Cold War and of political commitment in the West to capitalism as synonymous with freedom, focuses upon the inextricability of exploitation from expansion. Slavery was central to laying down the systemic structures of capitalism as we know it today and of the acceleration of processes of globalisation.

While slavery involved the forced migration and dislocation of Africans to the Americas and elsewhere and has been officially abolished, slavery persists in our contemporary world in myriad forms and contexts – as child labour, trafficking, prostitution and labour exploitation (Bales and Sealy, 2008). As Kevin Bales and Mark Sealy (2008), show through a focus on documentary photography, there is, in the contemporary age, a growing link between slavery in diverse forms and the rise of a global economy. Global economic heartlands, such as London, both benefit from such rises and remain at the helm of global economic power through the exploitation of such forms of slavery. Enmeshed into the very fabric of this city, therefore, are the exploited, amongst whom the undocumented and the immigrant remain all too often the most vulnerable and the most entrapped.

Labour exploitation is thus both an economic issue and one of human rights. When Henri Lefebvre issued a call for the 'right to the city', he invited reflection on existing structures of urban (dis)enfranchisement. Amongst the most disenfranchised in the city are undocumented immigrants. Lefebvre states that the right to the city:

> ... should modify, concretise and make more practical the rights of the citizen as an urban dweller (citadin) and user of multiple services. It would affirm, on the one hand, the right of users to make known their ideas on the space and time of their activities in the urban area; it would also cover the right to the use of the center, a privileged place, instead of being dispersed and stuck into ghettos (for workers, immigrants, the 'marginal' and even for the 'privileged'). (Lefebvre, 1996: 34)

For Lefebvre, the right to the city was twofold: for the inhabitants of a city, regardless of their legal status at national level, to be able to determine the uses of the city and its spaces, and hence to participate in the expansion and making of the city; and for them also to have rights of access to the city, and hence to be able to claim their place in the city. This two-fold right is one that would lift the entire existing range of urban borders and so open up citizenship to the undocumented. Lefebvre's work, through its focus on cities as icons of modern economic expansion, is a critique of capitalism, as a system that establishes processes and practices of exclusion. In this critique of capitalism, it is precisely the undoing of these borders that he calls for in his chapter entitled 'The Right to the City' (Lefèbvre, 1996: 147–59). In short, the political and spatial boundaries of the city would dissolve through this right, removing both ghettoes and the privileged zones of the elite, thus empowering denizens to become citizens in the true sense of the word.

While Lefebvre issued this call for the right to the city, and hence for an urban revolution, he did not lay out the ways in which this right may be implemented. As such, there is no map for ways forward to altering the status quo. In his critique of Lefebvre's call for the right to the city, David Harvey explores the increasing distance in the context of globalisation between Lefebvre's utopian vision of urban justice and urban realities. He states, making reference to Mike Davis's book *Planet of Slums* (2006), that 'urbanisation, we may conclude, has played a crucial role in the absorption of capital surpluses, at ever increasing geographical scales, but at the price of burgeoning processes of creative destruction that have dispossessed the masses of any right to the city whatsoever. The planet as building site collides with the "planet of slums"'.[9] The building site, locus of immigrant labour, on occasion undocumented if transnational, is the epitome of economic success, raised on the shoulders of those who endure economic and political marginalisation. Harvey points out the irony that while human rights are today more centre-stage in political discourse than ever before in human history, they simply do not challenge the supremacy of market demands and the overriding priority of profit over people. On the contrary – the repeated discourses of human rights, and, as Harvey points out in his essay, within this frame that of the right to the city, have become blanket references for processes and practices of economic acceleration. 'Urbanisation', Harvey states, 'has always been ... a class phenomenon, since surpluses are extracted from somewhere and from somebody, while the control over their disbursement typically lies in a few hands'.[10]

This is also a point made by Doug Saunders in his *Arrival City* (2010). The phenomenon of mass global urbanisation in the 21st century is brilliantly explored in this book through a sustained focus on the everyday lives and experiences of precisely those who form the mass of global urban expansions. Saunders makes the point that metropolitan influx forms the most important mass migration of this century. For transnational migrants without high levels of skills or income, irregular migration is often the sole way in which they can become part of this great global heave and flow towards the great city. Worth noting here is the fact that urbanisation is itself one of the great hallmarks of the global market economy, a symptom of the thriving marketplace and economic priorities of the modernity that we all know and are part of. Without doubt, London, together with a handful of other global capitals, is one such city. This is so especially in the 21st century, when border controls sieve the skilled and the well-to-do from those without. Equally, and as Saunders points out, it is precisely through the unstoppable flow of immigration that such cities grow, develop, expand and gain importance. Within this scheme, irregular migrants live as denizens, on the ambiguous margins of the city, but inhabiting it nonetheless and contributing to its dynamic. Saunders considers London's East End, with its many layers of immigration, as the crucible of urban growth, its vast council estates excluded from the privileges of the City

---

9   <http://newleftreview.org/II/53/david-harvey-the-right-to-the-city>
10   Ibid.

and, yet, intrinsic to the upholding of the latter. Saunders hones in on the grind and the grit of immigrants, a rising global population of the hopeful, who relocate to urban margins from across the globe in order to stake their claim in the promise of the city. On the one hand, theirs is the struggle for the right to the city. On the other hand, their efforts are also the force with which the city builds its forts and barriers that work to exclude, marginalise and alienate, but also attract, the disempowered and the displaced.

A reading of Saunders' work alongside Harvey's essay shows clearly how urbanisation and urban growth are processes and pronouncements of class, tied intrinsically to the idea of difference, and thus borders. Modernity, as practised in the twentieth and twenty-first centuries, comes into view as a spiralling system of exclusion, especially in light of the centrality of urbanisation. In such a light, London in 2015 is at once a crucible for cultural hybridity and city of sharp differentiations of social class and power. The irony here is that the excluded are intrinsic to the functioning of this system and yet barred from its gains, exploited as they are to build the very borders that produce their exclusion. Harvey states in no uncertain terms that in this day and age of increasing urbanisation and mass migrations to cities, the potential for revolution necessarily emerges from urban hubs. If Lefebvre's proposal of the right to the city is to have any pragmatic validity, this can only happen from within the city. Global cities, of which London is a prime example, offer the most fecund ground from which this struggle for urban citizenship can take place precisely because they combine powerful channels of capital with the desires, dreams and labour of the undocumented. Indeed, as Saunders shows, this 'revolution' has long been underway in London, not in the sense of a mass revolt, but in and through the strategies of survival of the newly arrived, their occupations of city space, their contributions to the city's life and their indelible mark on the weave of the urban fabric. Citizenship, most often forged through the making of home and work in the city, is a process of social – and class – mobility that may take a generation or two or more to make the transition from the margins to the mainstream. Contemporary London, in its great diversity, exemplifies the borders that must be negotiated in this slow and arduous process that awaits the undocumented when they arrive in this city.

Indeed, in their book, *Border As Method* (2013), Sandro Mezzadra and Brett Neilson argue that globalisation is a system of border proliferation – a far cry from the supposedly open and free space of the global marketplace that it is often associated with. Economic life and, alongside it, political life become privileges of a global elite in a world that is increasingly divided. Mezzadra and Neilson make the important point that, in fact, the very epistemology that shapes and conceives practices, methods and modes of globalisation are shaped by the idea of the border, so that the latter becomes a central trope of the contemporary world. Undocumented migrants and the contexts they face play a crucial role in revealing the prerogative of the borders that run through the social, political and economic life. To quote:

... [M]igration is increasingly marked by the emergence of various zones and experiences of waiting, holding, and interruption that assume many institutional forms ... The figure of the "illegal" migrant emerges on the world stage in the wake of tumultuous transformations of capitalism that begin to unfold in the early 1970s ... Central to the emergence of this figure was a marked shift in public and policy discourses, a new international institutional environment for the generation of knowledge about and the forging of strategies to manage migration, a reorganization of labour markets to accommodate processes of informalization and flexibilization, and a disruption and multiplication of migratory routes and patterns across diverse geographical scales. (2013: 143)

Mezzadra and Neilson cite Walter Mignolo's concept of *border thinking*, the epistemological pathway of modernity that is solidly symptomatic of the historical legacies of colonialism in latter-day guises (2013: 18). Borders, they state, are 'sites of struggle' (2013: 18), exclusionary in their role and inherently violent therefore. At the extreme, and once again as revealed by the experiences of undocumented migrants, borders can involve questions of life and death. Global capitals, such as contemporary London, act as laboratories of both heterogeneity and differentiation, where, as they state, '"third world" conditions often apply.' (2013: 64). In such a scenario, the undocumented migrant is not only defined by the borders that surround her or him, but also a key agent in the production and maintenance of such borders. In other words, undocumented migrants play a central role in reshaping, challenging and defining citizenship. An important way in which they do so within the larger scheme of the marketplace is through their labour, work being a key bridge between the marginal and the mainstream.

Borderline London

London offers a superb example of the global city, where urban development rides on transnational flows. What we witness in terms of urban growth is not merely the migration from rural to urban areas within nation-states, but, symptomatic of globalisation's cross-border and transcontinental relations, the great international magnetic force of global mega-cities, with their lure of wealth and power. For example, migrants from rural Punjab, from rural Somalia, from rural Turkey and from rural Eastern Europe rub shoulders in London, as do their more urban compatriots. The city, by definition, mutates and changes, evolving through the patterns of settlement and resettlement that define its borderlands. And when cities change, economies do too. In a city such as London, where approximately one out of every twenty people is undocumented, irregular immigration is fundamentally linked to economies of labour. This is so because irregular migrants must work to survive, having recourse to no, or limited, benefits and rights from the state. As such, what emerges is a portrait of a city at work, where it is not merely human presence and labour that remains undocumented, but also the production and exchange of capital from such sources that remains so. The informal economy evolves, thus, in tandem with the formal one. More importantly, and given the fundamentally fluid and migrant nature of capital itself, there are numerous junctures where the informal economy merges with the formal one, or blends into the latter, so that the economy itself must be viewed as a hybrid process of irregular mixing. This is by no means a smooth crossing. Take, for example, the case of Felipe, a cleaner from Colombia, who has obtained a false National Insurance number and pays taxes on his earnings.[11] He presents a case of an undocumented worker who seeks illicit means to find work and is thereby simultaneously contributing to the economy by engaging illicitly in labour and yet paying taxes to the state. He remains barred from citizenship in the full sense of the word, but also contributes financially as a citizen would, but with the aim of remitting hard-earned funds back to his family in Colombia. This is just one example of numerous ways in which the undocumented survive in the city. The links between the licit and the illicit that run through London are broken, jagged and uneven, hard, often, to align, a process where borders both block and bleed.

Global arrival cities, such as London, may thrive off the flow of capital, but this same process requires routes and channels – in other words, the erection of borders and valves, or gate points, to ensure that the flow of capital is primarily directed towards the centres of wealth and away from its peripheries. This demarcation of centre and periphery is not a spatial one. Rather than being distinct zones, these are, in fact, distinct classes, kept so by the many borders that proliferate in the processes of capitalism, but also connected to one another and in close contact precisely through these same borders. Thus, it is important to note that borders are both sites of contact and separation. They mark difference, but also simultaneously support proximity to alterity. A key feature of the globalised city, as iconic product of the capitalist system, is the interweave of alterity in the here and now, contributing in essential ways to the flow and weave of the urban process. Despite this dynamic, and despite a certain cultural hybridity that inevitably ensues from the presence of irregular migrants from across the world in London, what is also important to note is that irregular migrants, devoid of legal recognition, make their ways through the city behind the borders imposed upon them by their condition of irregularity. They are denizens of the city, without rights to the latter, but also inherently a part of this and thus connected, though invisibly so, to the larger economy of the city and its dynamic.

The border functions at many levels and in many spaces. The undocumented migrant labourers of London may occupy the sites of greatest exclusion. Nevertheless, and as exemplified by the border's paradoxical ability to both confine and connect, the availability of unregulated and informal labour impacts vertically upward in the labour chain. This has been especially so in this new millennium, most importantly in the wake of an economic crisis that has imposed

---

11   See the article by Jon Manel entitled 'The tax-paying illegal workers living in London' at <http://www.bbc.co.uk/news/10515357> accessed 5 January 2015.

displacement and dispossession on many members of the working class. The legalisation and introduction of zero hour contracts imposes financial uncertainty on workers, who often already belong to the more vulnerable sectors of society. According to Andrew Sayer, in his book *Why We Can't Afford the Rich* (2014: 371), in 2014, there were 1.4 million workers in the United Kingdom on zero hour contracts. Such workers often rub shoulders with the undocumented, from whom they may be separated by legal regularity, but with whom they share economic uncertainties, labour vulnerabilities and questions of dignity in the everyday. As London's stature as a global capital commands the global financial landscape, what remains less in view are these cracks that run deep through the city, where urban anxieties proliferate in the everyday. This, though, is part and parcel of the life force that energises the flow of capital in the direction of hegemonic and elite groups, institutions and systems.

While the urban contributions made by undocumented migrants are rarely noted by the mainstream in London, there is, nevertheless, a sustained discourse both in the press and amongst politicians on the undesirability of undocumented migrants. Indeed, many would not hesitate to align the lack of legal documentation with criminality. The recent rise of the far right-wing party UKIP in Britain only serves to exacerbate the discourse, policies and practices that confine irregular migrants in London to invisibility. In response to the rising popularity of UKIP, the more established parties in the political spectrum have also vocalised their commitment to border controls and to the deportation of irregular migrants. What is curious here, though, is the fact that a paradox is at play: on the one hand, border controls and the visibility of the United Kingdom Border Agency in the mainstream have increased dramatically in recent years, but, on the other, borders remain porous filters, both deterring irregular entries and yet never fully preventing them. In turn, this ensures the continued and streamlined contribution of an irregular labour force to the economy. There is, at play, a dynamic that should be duly noted, whereby, on the one hand, London's eminence as a global capital attracts immigrants who seek whatever means available to them to be here and whereby, on the other hand, the city itself expands in part through irregularity as a *modus vivendi*. Indeed, this is so to the extent that it becomes difficult, if not impossible, to extricate the irregular from the regular, although the former remains in the shadows and interstices of the seen, known and recognised aspects of the city.

Wave upon wave of immigration has brought to London, over the decades, a cultural vitality that places it in a league apart from its European counterparts. The postcolonial immigration that occurred in the postwar period has long been layered over by the arrival of a global populace in search of economic and political stability. This dynamic urban weave depends on a network of connectivity across differences, across strata, one that links the financial with the ethnic, the cultural, the political and the documented – or undocumented – in surprisingly subtle and invisible ways. The social topography of this mega-city is variegated, interwoven and complex. The margins of London, be these geographical or economic, are vital to the bolstering of its centres, and the stability and the development of London as a major financial and cultural powerhouse on the global map are inextricable from its ability to daily reinvent its margins, making it a city of a million, mutating borderlands.

References

Ackroyd, P. (2001), *London: The Biography.* London: Vintage Books.

Arau, S. (dir.), (2004), *A Day Without A Mexican* (film).

Bales, K. and Sealy, M. (2008), *Documenting Disposable People: Contemporary Global Slavery.* London: Hayward Gallery Publishing.

Campkin, B. (2013), *Remaking London: Decline and Regeneration in Urban Culture.* London: I.B. Tauris.

Davis, M. (2006), *Planet of Slums.* London: Verso.

Delanty, G. (2000), *Modernity and Postmodernity.* London: Sage Publications.

Harvey, D. (2008), 'The Right to the City', *New Left Review* 53, September–October <http://newleftreview.org/II/53/david-harvey-the-right-to-the-city> accessed 14 August 2014.

Lefebvre, H. (1996), *Writings on Cities,* Eleonore Kofman and Elizabeth Lebas (Trans). Oxford: Blackwell Publishing.

Mezzadra, S. and Neilson, B. (2013), *Border As Method, or, The Multiplication of Labour.* Durham, NC and London: Duke University Press.

Minton, A. (2012), *Ground Control: Fear and Happiness in the Twenty-first Century City.* London: Penguin Books.

Saunders, D. (2010), *Arrival City.* Portsmouth, NH: Heinemann Press.

Sayer, A. (2014), *Why We Can't Afford the Rich.* Bristol: Policy Press.

Troll Books (1989), *Dick Whittington.* London: Troll Communications.

Williams, E. (1944), *Capitalism and Slavery.* Richmond, Virginia: University of North Carolina Press.

Chapter 7

Who Speaks for the Subaltern in a Postcolonial Metropolis? Representing the Lives of Migrants in London through Novels, Films and Oral History[1]

John Eade

This chapter explores the ways in which cultural difference has been constructed through artistic modes of representation in Britain during both the colonial period and postcolonialism. This relationship between past and present is explored by an analysis of novels and films produced during the inter-war period and recent contestations involving artists and community activists who seek to represent the social and cultural identity of minority ethnic groups in contemporary multicultural Britain. Attention is paid to London in particular, given its key role as the centre of national and colonial government and its development as a global city, whose increasing cultural diversity has been shaped by postcolonial migration.

Introduction

The debate, encouraged by Gyatri Spivak in 1988 about the relationship between the role of Indian intellectuals in establishing a space through 'subaltern studies' where the voice of marginalised groups could be heard, raised crucial questions about the nature of representation in the context of the colonial traces across a supposedly decolonised world. These questions are also relevant in the former colonial metropoles such as London where the settlement of people from ex-colonial territories reveals the continuing influence of colonial discourses and practices. Recent discussions concerning London's reinvention as a 'global city' frequently underestimate these continuities with the former 'imperial capital'. Furthermore, the complexity of who seeks to speak for or about another is highlighted by the sometimes fraught relationship between artists, who draw on their family ties with former colonies, and London's 'black and Asian communities'.

This chapter will focus on artistic representations of issues involving minorities and how ethnic community activists in particular reacted to these. The aim is to

---

1   This chapter first appeared in *Przestrzeń Społeczna* [Social Space] 1(5), 2013: 29–46.

explore questions concerning the relationship between the representer and the represented and the boundaries between insiders and outsiders. The practice of artistic representation forces artists to distance themselves from what they seek to represent. Their reflexivity inevitably moves them away from the centre to the periphery of their 'community'. They become cultural mediators and, thereby, are no longer pure insiders. Indeed, this process of social and cultural distancing may result in their being criticised as outsiders by local community representatives. Communities become sites of contestation which highlight the complications involved in attempting to speak for others. Texts produced by themselves and others were written from a particular position. Although minorities were usually presented in multicultural discourse as coherent entities grounded in certain cultural traditions, this was a convenient myth. There was no integrated community whose voice could be articulated through its representatives but, rather, a range of voices expressing different and sometimes conflicting views in fields of power and knowledge shaped by the traces of empire.

Multicultural Representations of London across Time: Developments before the Second World War

The celebration of London's cultural diversity has usually focused on the effects of immigration since the Second World War. However, a number of studies have revealed the extensive lineage of this diversity (see, for example, Fryer, 1984; Visram, 1986, 2002; Chatterji and Washbrook, 2013). Yet this diversity largely escaped the attention of artists, novelists and ethnographers before the Second World War. Those arriving from Britain's expanding empire sometimes appear as servants in 18th century portraits of aristocrats, for example, or are mentioned in such pioneering urban ethnographies as Henry Mayhew's *London Labour and the London Poor* (1861) and the contribution by Beatrice Webb (nee Potter) on the 'East End' in *Inquiry into the Life and Labour of the People in London*, Charles Booth's magisterial series published between 1886 and 1903. Migrants were primarily associated with poor, working class areas despite the arrival of some professional people, university students and Indian princes from the late 19th century onwards (see Visram, 1986). If they were noticed the usual assumption was that their presence was temporary: they would return to the colonies where they 'belonged'. They were viewed with a mixture of suspicion and patronising interest – exemplars of exoticism and orientalism (see Said, 1978) – but those who exposed the cleavages of race and class in British society before the Second World War were not intimately associated with empire. The largest number of migrants were Irish Catholics and therefore British subjects before 1922. They were the targets of religious prejudice, while the arrival of Jews from Poland and Russia during the 1880s excited anti-semitic feeling. The other substantial influx of migrants – German Protestants – created far less interest until the rise of anti-German feeling before the First World War.

Representations of outsiders were shaped, therefore, not just by the class cleavages of an increasingly industrialised and highly urbanised society but by discourses and practices, which revolved around race, religion, gender, sexuality and language. During the period between 1800 and 1950 the ambiguities and uncertainties of the relationship between the British nation and its empire were concealed to some extent by a process of boundary maintenance. The boundary distinguished between an Anglo-Saxon Protestant majority and others – Catholic and Jewish immigrants, temporary migrants from the colonies and those who decided to stay on rather than return to the far-flung empire. These outsiders were largely confined to the inner recesses of Britain's cities – if they moved out into the expanding suburbs they had to assimilate as much as possible to narrow the distance between themselves and the national majority.

How did these 'outsiders' represent themselves artistically to a national audience before the Second World War? Although individual writers, musicians and other creative spirits operated during the 19th century, the most significant development was the emergence of Jewish novelists from London's East End between the two world wars. They were brought up in Jewish working class communities, which were heavily dependent on certain industries, especially the manufacture and trading of textile goods. They engaged with the political struggles of the day – trade union organisation, political mobilisation by Labour, Communist and Zionist groups over unemployment, housing conditions and rising fascism. They also took a keen interest in international developments such as the development of the Communist state in Russia, the rise of anti-colonial movements, Jewish migration to Palestine and conflicts in Spain leading to the civil war. Their ethnic and class background differed strikingly from writers associated with what came to be broadly known as the 'Bloomsbury group' and they sought to contribute to what became known as the 'working class novel' with its emphasis on social realism and political engagement (see Worpole 1983). Their Left-wing sympathies led them to criticise the social and economic inequalities of British industrial capitalism and to identity with anti-colonial movements across the British Empire. London was, in their view, the centre of an exploitative political and economic system and, for some at least, the imperial capital represented the antithesis of the new social relations being forged in the USSR.

The impact of Jewish writers during the inter-war period was confined largely to left-wing circles and the East End. A wider awareness of the social and cultural issues they explored was encouraged by individual artists, particularly with the arrival of the multi-talented black American artist, Paul Robeson, during the late 1920s. He articulated many of the political and social issues with which the Jewish writers were grappling – racism, the divisions of industrial capitalism, colonialism and fascism. Although he appeared in the British experimental silent movie, *Borderline* (1930) which explored racial and sexual tensions, his involvement with local communities was limited. Within Britain his closest contact with working class communities was forged through his focus on the plight of unemployed Welsh miners. During 1928, while he was performing in the musical *Showboat* in

London, he met a group of unemployed miners, who had come to the capital on a 'hunger march' from the South Wales coalfield. He visited the coalfield during the 1930s to perform and in 1934 he sang in the North Welsh town of Caernarfon to raise money for families devastated by a major disaster at a colliery where 264 miners had died. Robeson's commitment to the cause of the Welsh miners was also expressed through the 1940 film, *Proud Valley*, which was set in a South Wales mining locality and where he plays a 'kind and generous and good natured' worker'.[2]

Artistic Representations after the Second World War and the Growth of Identity Politics

Despite the continual flow of people from the empire before the Second World War, the students, sailors, servants and aristocrats did not intend to stay long. Those who settled were too few in number to create a significant local presence, even if some were able to facilitate the later growth of urban communities through their social networks. The arrival of workers from the empire from the late 1940s onwards led to a radical change in the ethnic and racial composition of many British cities, particularly London. The changes taking place within Britain were intimately linked to global developments as the empire began to unravel and artistic representations sought to express these transformations by drawing on the everyday lives of the emerging communities.

During the 1950s and 1960s those representations focused primarily on the political and cultural life of migrants from the Caribbean. The issue of 'inner city' racial tensions had been highlighted by the so-called 'Notting Hill riots' of 1958, increasing anti-immigrant political agitation and legislation designed to restrict immigration from the 'New' Commonwealth. These political tensions formed the backdrop to a growing body of artistic representations, which sought to reflect the interests and aspirations of both the first and the emerging second generation of 'black British' citizens. They drew on cultural traditions from the countries of origin as well as resources provided by the British cultural industry (music, poetry, novels, film, television and radio). In cinema Robeson and other African-American actors were followed by those from the Caribbean and Africa such as Robert Adams, who appeared in films from the 1920s and took the lead role in the 1946 film, *Men of Two Worlds*, where after a period as a musician in London he returns to his African village to teach music.[3] Films begin to move from black characters as itinerants to placing them within black communities from the late 1950s. *Sapphire* (1959), *Flame in the Streets* (1961), *A Taste of Honey* (1962), *The L-Shaped Room* (1962) and *To Sir With Love* (1967) explored racial and sexual tensions in London locales. This development went in parallel with the contribution

---

2   <http://www.screenline.org/film/id/500677/index.html>
3   <http://www.imdb.com/title/t0038736/>

by gifted 'black and Asian' writers such as Naipaul, Selvon, Chaudhuri, Collis, and Lamming. Yet these artists had little contact with the emerging migrant locales – their focus was on the white-dominated literary elite, the mainstream publishing industry and employment opportunities within the BBC (see Sandhu, 2003). It was in the area of music that a closer relationship was forged between artists and local black and Asian neighbourhoods, leading to the explorations by an increasing number of 'black and Asian' academics from the 1980s such as Stuart Hall, Paul Gilroy, Sanjay Sharma and Claire Alexander.

These artistic and academic representations have also been accompanied by the growth of local 'black and Asian' community and political activism. Community organisations, trade unions and political parties provided the platforms on which activists were able to build their following, emerging as borough councillors during the 1970s and 1980s mainly in 'black and Asian' concentrations across London. In the 1987 general election a break-through was made at parliamentary level with the election of three 'black' Labour Party MPs. During the 1990s and 2000s the growing strength of 'black and Asian' representatives from working class ethnic enclaves has been accompanied by a similar development in the spheres of artistic production and the professions.

Artistic Freedom, Religion, Gender and Community Representation

The Satanic Verses saga of 1989 dramatically signalled that the artistic treatment of certain topics could deeply offend religious and political representatives at both local and global levels. The burning of the book in Bradford at a public meeting held by the Council of Mosques in 1989 was one of the most well-known demonstrations of anger by local community representatives and their supporters. The threat to Salman Rushdie's life after the fatwa pronounced by the Iranian leader, Ayatollah Khomeini, and his subsequent going into hiding powerfully challenged western liberal notions of artistic freedom and demonstrated the ability of local leaders to mobilise local minority support and attract mainstream public attention.

As identity politics among British minorities during the 1990s and 2000s became more focused around religious issues so other minority writers could be subjected to the wrath of local activists. In 2004, for example, the play *Behhzti* (*Dishonour*) written by a second generation British Sikh woman, Gurpreet Kaur Bhatti, attracted considerable hostility when it was performed in a central Birmingham theatre. She had worked, like many other 'black and Asian' writers for the BBC in London and contributed to two major television 'soaps' – *Crossroads* and *EastEnders*. On the topic of writing Asian storylines for such programmes she had declared, perhaps naively, that 'if your heart is in the right place, if you ask the right questions, if you make the right choices, anybody can write about anything. ... It is just about doing it with sensitivity and care and passion'.[4] However, her

---

4   <http://news.bbc.co.uk/1/hi/uk/4109017.stm>

play, which involved a Sikh 'priest' raping a woman and murder in a *gurudwara* (Sikh temple), led to protests and some violence, as well as death threats made against the author. The president of a local gurudwara in Birmingham claimed that the main problem was:

> ... having these things take place in a temple. Any religion would not take such a slur ... We are concerned that people out there who don't know anything about Sikhs will see this and what sort of a picture will they have in their mind? ... They will paint all Sikhs with the same brush.[5]

Although the theatre argued that 'the play is a work of fiction and no comment is being made about Sikhism as a faith', the Roman Catholic Archbishop of Birmingham spoke up for religious institutions in general – '[s]uch a deliberate, even if fictional, violation of the sacred place of the Sikh religion demeans the sacred places of every religion'.[6] The play was quickly called off and in the subsequent discussion it was alleged that the protest had been highjacked by 'extremists' linked to terrorist groups in India and 'outsiders'.[7] Given London's economic, cultural and political importance within Britain and its large concentrations of 'black and Asian' residents a range of artists have sought to reflect on the issues of race, religion, gender and class through representations of everyday life. Over the last 30 years Hanif Kureishi has produced the most sustained and well-known body of work beginning with his screenplay for the film *My Beautiful Laundrette* (1985), to his novels *The Buddha of Suburbia* (1990), and *Intimacy* (1998) (adapted for a film in 2001), the film *London Kills Me* (1991), *The Mother* (2003) and the screenplay *Venus* (2006). While he tackles highly controversial issues such as sexual attraction between a young British Pakistani man and a white National Front sympathiser in *My Beautiful Laundrette* and a mixed race adolescent's escape from London's suburbia to a bohemian life in west London in *The Buddha of Suburbia*, he has not attracted the kind of local community agitation sparked by the publication of the novel, *Brick Lane* (2003), by another 'mixed race' writer, Monica Ali (her father came from Bangladesh and her mother from northern England). A close inspection of this agitation enables us to explore more deeply the relationship between artistic representations of London's cultural diversity and the local community settings for those representations.

The Brick Lane Dispute, 2003–2006

The title of the book refers to a street which runs through the heart of East London's Bangladeshi settlement. The story revolves around a young woman, Nazneen,

---

5   <http://news.bbc.co.uk/1/hi/england/west_midlands/4109255.stm>

6   <http://news.bbc.co.uk/1/hi/england/west_midlands/4107437.stm>

7   <http://www.thetimes.co.uk/tto/news/uk/article1920632.ece>

who has come from a Bangladeshi village with her two daughters to live with her husband on a run-down public housing estate near Brick Lane. By joining a group of fellow Bangladeshi women to work on garments for the local textile industry, she gradually frees herself from the traditional role of a Bangladeshi housewife. Her 'emancipation' leads to tensions with her bombastic and unsuccessful husband, who eventually returns to Bangladesh to look for better prospects. Nazneen is drawn towards a young local Bangladeshi community activist, who campaigns for a return to a pure Islam but she finds freedom not in an adulterous relationship but through close relationships with her daughters and her group of garment workers. This story of female emancipation contrasts with her sister's elopement from the village with her lover and subsequent hard times in Dhaka, Bangladesh's capital – a story told through the letters in faulty English to her sister in London.

The book was very well received by London's media elite. In 2003 it was shortlisted for the prestigious Booker Prize and won the British Book Awards 'Newcomer of the Year'. Its commercial success led to the release in 2007 of the film, based on the novel. However, this enthusiasm was not shared by some local community activists and their objections were outlined in an 18-page letter to the publisher by the Greater Sylhet Development and Welfare Council. Since the vast majority of British Bangladeshis were linked to the district of Sylhet in north-eastern Bangladesh, this organisation sought to defend the honour of not only those in Britain but also their district of origin. The community representatives claimed that the book portrayed Sylhetis as ignorant economic migrants and a BBC report on the protest highlighted a passage from the novel where Nazneen's husband refers to local Bangladeshis as 'uneducated. Illiterate. Close-minded. Without ambition'.[8] The publisher responded in familiar fashion by asserting that the book was a fictional account and that it found 'both the accusations against it and any demand for censorship ludicrous' (idem.).

The reference to censorship clearly reflected concern among the media elite that the controversy might result in the book and its author suffering a similar fate to *The Satanic Verses*. Although the dispute died down in 2003, it revived when permission was given to use Brick Lane for filming during 2006. This time the protest was led by Bangladeshi entrepreneurs from the Brick Lane Business Association, which claimed to be speaking on behalf of the Bangladeshi community as a whole:

> People are disgusted about the film, and while the authorities have given permission for it to be filmed here, it does not mean they have permission from the community. ... We will do what the community wants us to do. We are not going to leave it as it is.[9]

---

8   <http://news.bbc.co.uk/1/hi/entertainment/arts/3287413.stm>
9   <http://news.bbc.co.uk/1/hi/entertainment/5190990.stm>

Given the substantial number of Bangladeshis in the borough council this was a serious threat. What rankled with this group was that Monica Ali was assumed to know about the lives of British Bangladeshis as an insider. In other words, it was not just a work of fiction:

> She is not one of us, she has not lived with us, she knows nothing about us, but she has insulted us. ... This is all lies. She wanted to be famous at the cost of a community (idem.)

The dispute did not just entail a local minority group pitting itself against the media industry. A leading writer, Germaine Greer (2006), also criticised the book in an article in the *Guardian* during July 2006:

> Ali did not concern herself with the possibility that her plot might seem outlandish to the people who created the particular culture of Brick Lane. As British people know little and care less about the Bangladeshi people in their midst, their first appearance as characters in an English novel had the force of a defining caricature. The fact that Ali's father is Bangladeshi was enough to give her authority in the eyes of the non-Asian British, but not in the eyes of British Bangladeshis.

Greer then raises the issue of the relationship between fact and fiction and the use of stereotypes:

> Brick Lane is a real place; there was no need for Monica Ali to invent it. In giving her novel such a familiar and specific name, Ali was able to build a marvellously creative elaboration on a pre-existing stereotype. English readers were charmed by her Bengali characters, but some of the Sylhetis of Brick Lane did not recognise themselves. Bengali Muslims smart under an Islamic prejudice that they are irreligious and disorderly, the impure among the pure, and here was a proto-Bengali writer with a Muslim name, portraying them as all of that and more. For people who don't have much else, self-esteem is crucial. (idem.)

Germaine Greer's intervention quickly drew a rebuke from another major writer, Salman Rushdie, who had been offended by her criticism of *The Satanic Verses* back in 1999. In a letter to *The Guardian* he accused her of being ignorant, racist, pro-censorship and treacherous. Her article was:

> ... a strange mixture of ignorance (she actually believes that this is the first novel to portray London's Bangladeshi community, and doesn't know that many Brick Lane Asians are in favour of the filming); pro-censorship twaddle ... and ad-feminam sneers about Monica Ali ... . At the height of the assault against my novel *The Satanic Verses*, Germaine Greer ... [described] me as "a megalomaniac, an Englishman with dark skin". Now it's Monica Ali's turn to be

deracinated: "She writes in English and her point of view is, whether she allows herself to impersonate a village Bangladeshi woman or not, British." There is a kind of double racism in this argument. To suit Greer, the British-Bangladeshi Ali is denied her heritage and belittled for her Britishness, while her British-Bangladeshi critics are denied that same Britishness, which most of them would certainly insist was theirs by right.[10]

Given the history of protest against Salman Rushdie's book, it was not surprising that Bangladeshi protesters threatened to burn Monica Ali's book at a public rally in spite of the film company announcing that it would abandon its plans to film on Brick Lane. The lead 'convener of the Campaign Against Monica Ali's Film *Brick Lane*' declared that 'the rally would be peaceful and potentially violent "fringe elements" would be deterred from attending but added that if the author had 'the right to freedom of speech, we have the right to burn books. We will do it to show our anger. We don't like Monica Ali. We are protecting our community's dignity and respect' (Lewis, 2006).

The book-burning threat was quickly withdrawn but in an article describing the rally the journalist raised another issue at the heart of the dispute – the role of women in British Bangladeshi society. When asked about the striking lack of women at the rally, protesters referred to the influence of religious conservatism – 'Muslim women are very conservative and they don't feel comfortable coming here' while another claimed that the protest had been 'organised at short notice and obviously our families have children. So who looks after them? ... My wife wanted to come and face this, but at the moment I have guests' (Cacciottolo, 2006). Ironically, this relationship between Bangladeshi women's domestic roles and their public activities was central to Monica Ali's novel.

Oral History – An Authentic Representation of Minority Communities

If artistic explorations of minority issues in multicultural London could be criticised for conflating fact and fiction by people who did not really belong to the communities portrayed in their novels, were oral histories a more authentic guide? This question has particular resonance because of the many oral histories undertaken by ethnic community organisations and supported by the Heritage Lottery Fund (HLF). The oral histories were hailed by the HLF as giving 'a voice to ordinary people' and helping to 'shape the heritage of the future'.[11] Yet they did not escape the constraints of representing others which dogged other texts – they were written from a particular position and were shaped by the questions asked and by the people selected for interview. While groups involved in oral history

---

10   <http://www.guardian.co.uk/books/2006/jul/29/comment.letters>

11   <http://www.hlf.org.uk/ourproject/projectsbysector/cultureandmemories/Pages/index.aspx>

projects were encouraged by the HLF to represent 'their' community as insiders, their attempts were always partial and highly selective.

In the light of the controversy swirling around Monica Ali's novel, an oral history project led by Swadhinata Trust, a British Bangladeshi heritage group based near Brick Lane, provides a useful illustration of this relationship between the myth of community and the reality of selective representation. The group was founded in 2000 with the aim of promoting 'Bengali history and culture to ensure its representation as an essential part of the history of Britain and by extension, our contemporary world'.[12] It also sought to empower young Bangladeshis and help them engage with 'mainstream culture':

> The need for such a Trust has arisen from a sense that, an absence of documentation and social data representing Bengalis' heritage, historical presence and achievements, can contribute towards a sense of marginalisation, low self-esteem and alienation of young people in particular, as part of a minority ethnic community within wider society. This in turn, can limit their participation and contributions to mainstream culture. (idem)

The project 'looked at three generations of being Bengali in multicultural Britain' by interviewing over 50 people and focusing on three themes – (a) the 'dialogue between first and third generation on the history of Bangladesh and the 1971 war of independence', (b) the 'dialogue between second and third generation on welfare and community involvement in the UK, from the 1970s–80s' and (c) the development of popular culture 'focusing on traditional and more recent British Bengali musical heritage' (Eade et al., 2006: 70).

Swadhinata's leaders described it as 'a London based secular Bengali heritage group that works to promote Bengali history and heritage amongst young people'.[13] As a result, even though religious issues had become increasingly important for Bangladeshis in both Britain and Bangladesh, and the leaders of the East London Mosque in particular had gained considerable influence, no religious representatives were interviewed. The sidelining of religion was pursued in Swadhinata's other projects such as the heritage trail which guided visitors around Brick Lane and its environs ('Banglatown and the Bengali East End') and another Heritage Lottery Fund project, this time in collaboration with London Metropolitan University. This project explored the history of the Bengali seamen (*lascars*), who 'served on British naval and merchant ships from the 17th century onwards' through a heritage trail across the borough of Tower Hamlets to 'key landmarks such as the docks and buildings' associated with them' (idem.).

Although the vast majority of British Bangladeshis were Muslims, the only mosque included in both these guides was the London *Jamme Masjid* (Great

---

12   <http://www.swadhinata.org.uk>

13   <http://www.swadhinata.org.uk>

Mosque) on Brick Lane. The building had become a well known symbol of the area's multicultural and migration history since it began as a French Protestant chapel during the 1740s and later became a synagogue before starting a new career as a mosque in 1976. However, the largest and only purpose-built mosque in the borough was the East London Mosque, whose origins can be traced to 1910 even though it did not occupy local premises until 1940–1941.[14] The mosque provided a much wider range of resources than the Great Mosque and supported local welfare and interfaith activities. This openness to outsiders was affirmed in language which neatly fitted government discourse:

> Our vision is to provide a range of holistic, culturally sensitive services for the communities of London, drawing on our Islamic values and heritage, with a view to improving quality of life and enhancing community cohesion.[15]

Colonial Traces in a Postcolonial City

So far this chapter has examined the contested and positional character of textual representations among those who drew on their origins in the former empire. Yet in what ways are those representations influenced by colonial traces? The answer can be found in the relationship between colonial policies and secular nationalism after colonies gained their independence. By the time the British left India in 1946, for example, local communities had come to be officially differentiated through cultural traditions whose 'natural' guardians were religious leaders and other members of literate elites. The colonial state, on the other hand, sought to confine itself to such secular issues as maintaining law and order and economic affairs. This separation between cultural communities and a supposedly legal-rational state informed Indian nationalists' understanding of secularism after the British left in 1947.

Although the secular nationalist rhetoric of the Bangladesh government after independence in 1971 has been muted by a turn towards Islam, Bangladeshi activists in Britain have operated within an official environment where the colonial tradition of separating the legal-rational state from 'native institutions' still predominates. The growth of minority organisations, including a plethora of religious centres and representatives, has only encouraged government at central and local levels to encourage uniformity and hierarchical organisation. This centrifugal pressure 'simplifies the task of representing such rich cultural diversity and conforms to the mode of regulating difference with its colonial resonances'. (Thomas Blom Hansen, personal communication).

---

14   <http://www.eastlondonmosque.org.uk/history>
15   <http://www.eastlondonmosque.org.uk/vision>

Conclusion

This chapter has explored the issue of artistic representation in the context of Britain's national capital, London. Its prime focus has been the ways in which artists have sought to represent the capital's racial and ethnic diversity not just since the Second World War but before 1939. This approach contributes to the growing realisation that the city's multicultural diversity has roots which developed well before the much-celebrated arrival of the M.S. *Empire Windrush* from the Caribbean in 1948. In other words, the problems involved in representing marginalised people across contemporary London and Britain, more generally, are shaped by traditions which emerged during colonialism. London's status as a global city can conceal a much longer history as a colonial metropolis. The policies and practices, which emerged during the expansion of colonial territories, were not just applied by the British government 'overseas' – they also informed modes of power and resistance within Britain's rapidly expanding towns and cities during the 19th and early 20th centuries. Indeed, migration brought these two worlds of governance together during this period since the largest number of overseas immigrants came from Britain's nearest colony – Ireland.

Before the Second World War the novel and film constituted the two prime vehicles for representing London's social differences shaped by class, ethnicity and race. Although the cinema hosted films which explored class and race through the controversial black American singer and actor, Paul Robeson, the novel was the main arena where the city's working class artists sought to represent 'their world' to outsiders. In London's 'East End' class, ethnicity and race were brought together in the writings of the Jewish second generation. Given their immigrant origins these novelists showed a keen awareness of life beyond Britain – not the British Empire but the heir to another empire – Russia – and the international struggle between communism and capitalism and against the rising tide of fascism. Indeed, their engagement with these two inter-war conflicts provided a link with Paul Robeson, since he visited Russia in 1934 and supported, during the Spanish civil war, the Republican side against an opposition aided by Italian and German armed forces.

Before the Second World War the divisions of class, ethnicity and race were explored, therefore, by both professional artists and London's working class residents through a lens which gazed at both national and international conflicts and exposed their interconnections. Migration from the unravelling British Empire after 1945 widened the lens through which local, national and global processes could be represented. Multicultural policies and practices, which included substantial funding, provided a bridge between artistic representations of London's growing diversity and local minority community consciousness, on the one hand, and government on the other. These policies and practices encouraged the growth of local activists who increasingly challenged the authority of artists to represent 'their community'. This contestation raised important issues about artistic freedom which were shaped by global conflicts and were most dramatically reflected in the controversy sparked by the publication of Salman Rushdie's book, *The Satanic Verses*, in 1988. The question of who represented whom was posed in a potentially lethal form but it also highlighted the competing claims of local activists to represent 'their community'. Despite attempts by government and local activists to portray communities as homogeneous entities – a practice forged during colonialism – London's inhabitants have shaped a complex web of diverse identities which is reflected in the competing representations and voices described in this chapter.

Acknowledgements

This chapter draws on my involvement in two projects. The first one is the Writing the British Asian City project which was funded by the UK Arts and Humanities Research Council Diasporas, Migrations and Identities programme, 2006–2009. A related chapter 'Representing British Bangladeshis in the Global City: Authenticity, Text and Performance' appears in *Writing the City in British Asian Diasporas* (Routledge, 2014), edited by Sean McLoughlin, William Gould, Ananya Jahanara Kabir and Emma Tomalin. The second one is the study of transnational religion in London, Kuala Lumpur, Johannesberg and Durban funded by the Ford Foundation, 2006–2008.

References

Cacciottolo, M. (2006), 'Brick Lane protesters hurt over "lies"', BBC News 31 July <http://news.bbc.co.uk/1/hi/uk/5229872> accessed 19 December 2010.

Chatterji, J. and Washbrook, D. (eds), (2013), *Routledge Handbook of the South Asian Diaspora*. London and New York: Routledge.

Eade, J. et al. (2006), *Tales of Three Generations of Bengalis in Britain*. London: Roehampton University.

Fryer, P. (1984), *Staying Power: The History of Black People in Britain*. London UK and Sterling VA: Pluto Press.

Greer, G. (2006), 'Reality bites: People in Brick Lane are in uproar about a plan to film Monica Ali's novel. Do they have a point?', *Guardian*, 24 July <http://www.guardian.co.uk/film/2006/jul/24/culture.books> accessed 19 December 2010.

Lewis, P. (2006), 'Brick Lane protests force film company to beat retreat'. The Guardian, 27 July. <http://www.guardian.co.uk/uk/2006/jul/27/film.books> accessed 19 December 2010.

Said, E. (1978), *Orientalism: Western Representations of the Orient*. London: Routledge and Kegan Paul.

Sandhu, S. (2003), *London Calling: How Black and Asian Writers Imagined a City*. London: HarperCollins.

Spivak, G. (1988), 'Can the Subaltern Speak?', in C. Nelson and L. Grossberg (eds), *Marxism and the Interpretation of Culture*. London: Macmillan.

Visram, R. (1986), *Ayahs, Lascars and Princes: Indians in Britain, 1700–1947*. London: Pluto Press.

Visram, R. (2002), *Asians in Britain: 400 Years of History.* London UK and Sterling VA: Pluto Press.

Worpole, K. (1983), 'Out of the ghetto: The literature of London's East End', in K. Worpole, *Dockers and Detectives*. London: Verso Books.

<http://news.bbc.co.uk/1/hi/entertainment/5190990.stm> accessed 5 May 2009

<http://news.bbc.co.uk/1/hi/entertainment/arts/3287413.stm> accessed 19 December 2010.

<http://www.guardian.co.uk/books/2006/jul/29/comment.letters> accessed 19 December 2010.

<http://www.hlf.org.uk/ourproject/projectsbysector/cultureandmemories/Pages/index.aspx> accessed 21 December 2010.

<http://www.swadhinata.org.uk/> accessed 21 December 2010.

<http://www.eastlondonmosque.org.uk/history>, accessed 21 December 2010.

<http://www.eastlondonmosque.org.uk/vision>, accessed 21 December 2010.

Chapter 8

Migrants and Descendants: Multi-Generations of the Irish in London in the 21st Century

Bronwen Walter

Introduction

The Irish were the largest birthplace group in London from outside Britain until 2001. However the position changed rapidly between 2001 and 2011 when the ranking of the Irish fell sharply to fourth overall by birthplace amongst the incomers, after Indians, Poles and Pakistanis, and ninth by ethnic group. In 2012–13 Irish were placed only eleventh for new migrants seeking National insurance numbers in Britain, many fewer than Poles, Lithuanians, Hungarians, Italians or Portuguese, though of course some young Irish people will have worked in London previously (Kennedy et al., 2014: 26–7). But Irish migration to London has a much longer history and Irish experiences offer an unusual opportunity also to explore multi-generational ethnic identities as they persist, hybridise and lose visibility over time.

Tony Murray describes ways in which 'The Irish have been deeply woven into the fabric of London life for centuries' (2012: 21). Irish settlement in London was recorded in the Middle Ages, becoming more permanent in the Elizabethan period (MacRaild, 1999: 1). Numbers increased in the 18th century, especially in the area of St Giles, part of Holborn, with outer settlements in the east of the city, Whitechapel and Southwark. From the early 19th century numbers in the centre continued to expand. Although London is now the prime destination of the emigrants from Ireland, with nearly half the total by 2010–11, before the mid-20th century other parts of Britain had larger shares especially North West England and the West of Scotland. In 1841 only 18.0 per cent of the total share was located in London, falling to 11.8 per cent in 1871 (MacRaild, 1999: 55).

Far from being a long-settled group with a fading historic background the Irish population is therefore constantly replenished by succeeding 'waves', often precipitated by cycles in the Irish economy which have had emigration as a 'safety valve' for large numbers of unemployed people (Mac Laughlin, 1997). The latest inflow followed the collapse of the Celtic Tiger economy after 2006. This wave shares many of the characteristics of previous flows, but with a much greater concentration of the highly-educated whose careers in Ireland were abruptly stalled in the middle of the 2000s (Irial et al., 2013).

As a consequence of the longevity of links with London and the changing social and economic character of migrants, the Irish 'community' is very diverse. It includes a great variety of degrees of settledness amongst both migrants and generations of English-born descendants. The Irish have interacted and intersected with many other migrant groups over time, in the process becoming an important part of the 'mainstream' as well as the wider multi-cultural mix.

Present-Day Settlement: A 2011 Census Portrait

The 2011 Census allows us to identify key demographic and socio-economic features of the present-day Irish population in London, map its changing locations and identify related policy issues. An additional source of diversity is the inclusion of migrants from two jurisdictions, the Republic and Northern Ireland. This analysis includes both parts of the island where possible, drawing attention to differences which arise from migrants' social, economic and political backgrounds, including political and religious affiliations. Importantly statistics are collected in different ways in the Republic of Ireland and the UK so that findings from the two parts of the island cannot necessarily be aggregated or compared to provide a full picture (Walter, 2008: 184–5).

The Census data show that the total Irish-born population in London in 2011 was 162,581, of whom 80.1 per cent were born in the Irish Republic and 19.9 per cent in Northern Ireland. A much higher proportion of the total Republic Irish-born population in England is located in London, 34.2 per cent compared with 17.5 per cent of those from Northern Ireland. Larger proportions born in Northern Ireland have settled in the North West, the Outer South East, East and South West of England.

Year of arrival in the UK is one of the statistics provided for Republic-born migrants only. This confirms that in the period 2001–2011 numbers rose sharply to 25,914 after a comparative lull in the 1990s when only 11,891 arrived. The Republic-born population in London consists of three main 'waves' in the post-Second World War period so that of the present-day population, almost half arrived before 1970, a smaller 'bulge' of 15 per cent in the large Irish recession of the 1980s and a further 20 per cent in the most recent decade. This pattern has very strong implications for the character and experiences of the population as a whole, suggesting that age and period of arrival are another important source of internal diversity.

Data are also available on age at arrival in the UK of Republic-born people resident in London. Of those living in the city in 2011, 72.5 per cent were aged 24 years or younger when they arrived, with a smaller proportion (20.5 per cent) aged between 25 and 34. This tells us that the large number of older Irish-born people have been resident for almost all their adult lives and are therefore very long-settled members of London's population. It also confirms that the latest 'wave' of arrivals between 2001 and 2011 are young people in their 20s and 30s. There are thus at least two important categories of the Republic Irish-born – the long-settled born before 1945, many of whom will be parents and grandparents to London-born second- and third- generations – and the young, much newer arrivals who may or may not be settled in London or established in families.

Yet although there was a sharp increase in new arrivals between 2001 and 2011, overall the number of the Irish Republic-born in London fell by 17.5 per cent, a higher rate of decline than for the Northern Irish-born (-12.8 per cent). This reflects two processes which are specific to the Republic-born and partly explain the changing location of the Irish in the numerical hierarchy of migrants in London. One is high levels of mortality in the ageing 1950s generation. At the same time new arrivals have not increased as fast as in other groups, especially those from Poland. However a second factor is return movement to Ireland, which is not captured by the UK Census (Irial et al., 2013: 76). The Celtic Tiger economic boom was still attracting young and middle-aged returners from London in the early years of the 21st century, though this rapidly declined after 2006.

Within London the Irish-born are scattered throughout the city, but also strongly clustered by borough. The six with the largest Republic-born populations are contiguous west of the centre, in three Inner London boroughs Islington (2.8 per cent Irish-born), Hammersmith and Fulham (2.7 per cent), Camden (2.4 per cent), and the adjacent Outer London boroughs of Brent (2.9 per cent), Ealing (2.3 per cent) and Harrow (2.1 per cent). These have been 'Irish' areas of London throughout the post-1945 period, with a gradual outward shift reflecting rising owner-occupation and movement away from inner city renting. The Northern Irish-born share a higher concentration in the Inner London boroughs but have not participated in the outward movement to the same extent (see Chapter 2, p. 14, Figure 2.1).

Birthplace data helps to paint a demographic portrait of the Irish groups, but a much fuller range of socio-economic statistics is available for the White Irish ethnic group. This category was first included in 2001 after a sustained campaign by Irish welfare and community groups who argued that the Irish had been disadvantaged by exclusion from the new ethnic category introduced in 1991 (Walter, 1998). This precluded recognition of specific Irish need, for example in ethnic monitoring exercises aimed to identify discrimination and disadvantage, as well as for funding in areas such as housing and health (Hickman and Walter, 1997).

However the composition of the White Irish category is complex to interpret, especially in 2011 when the ethnic categories were changed so that 'Northern Irish' became part of the 'White British' category. Many Northern Irish-born people who ticked 'White Irish' in 2001 may have changed to this category in 2011 hindering accurate analyses of trends over time. Over 80 per cent of those born in the Republic ticked White Irish in both censuses, whereas only 22.7 per cent of those born in Northern Ireland did so in 2011 compared with 36.8 per cent in 2001. This must be borne in mind when the findings are considered. As will be discussed later, one per cent of people born in England also identified as

White Irish, presumed to be second- or third-generation Irish people who chose this identification.

Bearing in mind these inclusions and exclusions from the White Irish category, levels of qualification by ethnic group point up some important characteristics of the group. As expected from their periods of arrival, the White Irish are recorded at both ends of the socio-economic scale. They have the largest proportion of any ethnic group with no qualifications, if the very small 'White: Gypsy or Irish Traveller' category, which also of course includes Irish people, is removed. Amongst those aged 16 and over in the main ethnic groups, 26.1 per cent of the White Irish have no qualifications, substantially more than 20.9 per cent of the White British and well above those identifying in Asian (1.2 per cent) and Black (14.3 per cent) categories. In part this reflects the much older age structure of the Irish-born, many of whom arrived in London with very basic schooling. It also relates to the types of 'unskilled' work for which the Irish were recruited, men in heavy manual labour and women in domestic work.

At the other extreme, in 2011 the White Irish had close to the highest levels of tertiary level qualifications. In total 37.3 per cent had degrees or equivalent, almost identical to the White British and exceeded only by White Others with 42.5 per cent and Asians with 39.7 per cent. If age was taken into account the higher levels of education amongst the White Irish would be much more apparent. The young age profile of White Others for example is signalled by their low levels of retirement, 6.2 per cent compared with 26 per cent of the White Irish, the highest all groups.

These two broad categories of migrants, the older group employed in, or retired from, manual work, and the young, well-educated 'high flyers' have very different profiles and make contrasting contributions to, and demands on, life in London. But it must not be forgotten that new arrivals still include young people with few qualifications who continue a very long tradition of 'escaping' from unemployment or low-paid, insecure jobs in Ireland (Mac Laughlin, 1997; Walls, 2005; Tilki et al., 2009). Unemployment in the Republic grew from around five per cent in the mid-2000s to over 15 per cent in 2011. There are also other welfare needs which may be available in London, such as women needing access to abortions, legally even more restricted from 2014 in the Irish Republic (Rossiter, 2009; *Guardian*, 2014). Thus there are clear threads of continuity over time as well as sharp alterations in direction matching fast-changing economic contexts.

Young professional people from Ireland see their stay in London very differently from earlier generations. For many this is part of a wider global pattern of mobility rather than a permanent move. Moreover some are 'Eurocommuters' who return to permanent homes in Ireland on a regular, perhaps even weekly basis, either by lifestyle choice or the necessity of remaining in a negatively-mortgaged house in Ireland (Ralph, 2014). A recent report has examined the recruitment of Irish teachers to British schools, many of those interviewed being based in London (Ryan et al., 2014). Using qualitative methods including interviews and a discussion group, the research found that 68 per cent gave 'no jobs in Ireland' as their main reason for leaving. Most had arrived after 2010 and their average age was 28. They were part of the extensive Irish diaspora, about 60 per cent having links of family and friends in Britain and one-sixth had previously worked in another country, mainly the US, Australia and New Zealand. A number anticipated further moves in future. On average they returned to Ireland four times a year and only about 30 per cent expected to stay at least five years or even permanently.

This occupational group illustrates many of the characteristics of other post-Celtic Tiger young professional migrants in London. In contrast to the older, long-established Irish migrants, recent arrivals did not have links with Irish community groups and welfare organisations. But they continued to live in 'Irish worlds' to some extent, frequently socialising with Irish friends and taking part in Gaelic Athletic Association activities. Although it is widely assumed that anti-Irish racism is no longer expressed in Britain, 34 per cent of the teachers said that they had encountered anti-Irish sentiment, although this was considerably stronger outside London which was seen as much more accepting of ethnic diversity.

However, by far the largest section of the migrant population is aged over 55. Relatively few of the 1950s and 1960s cohort returned to Ireland in the 1970s when economic conditions improved. By then many had started to raise families, were buying their own homes and had become established in their jobs. Unlike recent migrants there was much less fluidity in their movements, both because of travel costs and greater rigidity in employment patterns. Over a quarter of the White Irish are now retired, and another important section are in the pre-retirement age group (50–59 for women and 50–64 for men), a very different pattern from other ethnic groups in London. Although there is considerable variation in the lives of this population, overall those from the Republic are more likely to take part in Irish community and cultural events and to have specific socio-economic characteristics and cultural needs. Qualitative research in the Borough of Brent showed this has led to the development of a 'community saved', with a strong internal cohesion based on shared cultural values (Malone, 2001). By contrast migrants from Northern Ireland were less likely to engage with 'Irish diaspora culture', perceiving this to be 'Catholic, Southern Irish or working class' (Devlin Trew, 2013: 117).

Although many long-established Irish-born people in London made adequate livings, ensuring that their children were well-educated and could be upwardly mobile, not all succeeded in this way. A report entitled *The Forgotten Irish* was completed in 2009 and identified key areas of ongoing need for support (Tilki et al., 2009). The major differences from the British population as a whole included: larger proportions single and living alone, long-term health problems or disabilities, a history of working in occupations with health risks, poor housing conditions and living in areas of multiple deprivation. In particular men who had worked 'on the buildings' experienced isolation and poverty, often building lives around the pub, with attendant dangers of alcohol misuse (Leavey et al., 2004: 775). Mainstream care providers frequently showed cultural insensitivity, related to the long history of anti-Irish racism. In many ways, therefore, the Irish have specific needs as long-term migrants, which continues to set them apart from more recent arrivals in London.

The invisibility of this section of the population both in London and in Ireland was highlighted by a very influential documentary entitled *Lost Generation* broadcast by RTÉ in the respected *Primetime* slot just before Christmas 2003 (Rouse, 2003; Department of Foreign Affairs, 2014). The filming showed extreme poverty amongst older Irish men in London, Coventry and Manchester causing a public outcry in Ireland. It demonstrated the failure of the Irish Government to honour the promise of greater financial support to emigrants in need, made in 2002 following the Report of the Task Force on Policy Regarding Emigrants (Department of Foreign Affairs, 2002). The showing forced the announcement of a change in policy and led to the establishment of the Irish Abroad Unit in the Department of Foreign Affairs. In 2005 the amount allocated to the Irish voluntary sector in Britain, was doubled to nearly £6 million pounds, resulting in substantial increases in funding to community and welfare groups in London (*Irish Post*, 2004b).

A section of the Irish population which is particularly invisible is Travellers. Although they were included as an ethnic group in the 2011 Census for the first time, there was undoubtedly serious undercounting. Those whose presence was recorded as 'White: Gypsy or Irish Traveller' numbered 8,196 in London and had very distinctive features (Ryan et al., 2014: 16–17, 22–7). They included large numbers of children, over one third of the population being aged 0–15. Conversely less than four per cent were aged 65 or over, indicating very high rates of early mortality. Just over half (54.3 per cent) had no qualifications, compared with 17.6 per cent average for all ethnic groups. In total 35.9 per cent were recorded as 'never worked and long-term unemployed' compared with 5.6 per cent of the White Irish. This population had the highest rates of limiting long-term illness and those aged 50+ who rated their general health as 'bad' or 'very bad', and by far the largest proportions in prisons.

The Irish-born population in London is very diverse, but there are distinctive features which have persisted over time. Until the recent arrival of large numbers of East Europeans there has been a tendency to overlook 'white' migrants in surveys of London's incomers. But the Irish share many aspects of the positionings and experiences of those acknowledged as minority ethnic groups as well as intermixing with them in later generations.

Second-Generation Irish Identities in London

Recognition of the Irish as an ethnic group is relatively recent. The Greater London Council made the historic step of including the Irish in minority ethnic community funding initiatives in 1984 (Greater London Council, 1984). But by 1994 only 14 local authorities in London included the Irish as a category in monitoring procedures. Awareness of the issue was boosted by the publication in 1997 of the Commission for Racial Equality report *Discrimination and the Irish Community in Britain* which used London as one of its major case studies (Hickman and Walter, 1997). An important outcome was the inclusion of White Irish as a separate ethnic group in the 2001 Census.

Whereas birthplace references only those born in Ireland, ethnicity potentially captures their English-born children, grandchildren and even more distant descendants who choose this identity. However, despite great efforts on the part of Irish organisations in the lead-in to the 2001 and especially the 2011 Census, only a small proportion is captured in the White Irish category. Most people of Irish descent do not tick this box, either because the wording confusingly points them towards White British as their national affiliation or because recognition of a 'second-generation Irish' identity is not encouraged in Britain (Hickman et al., 2005; Walter, 2005/6; Hickman, 2011). Some of course may prefer to identify as English, perhaps having lost strong family connections with Ireland.

Only 49,000 people born in England and living in London in 2011 ticked White Irish, compared with 162,581 Irish migrants who did so, so that they constituted just under a quarter of the total (Ryan et al., 2014: 12). Yet estimates show that children of at least one Irish parent outnumber the Irish-born at least twice and so the number could potentially have been closer to 330,000 (Hickman et al., 2001). The most accurate enumeration of parents' birthplaces in the UK was in a single Census, 1971. This showed that 241,220 people living in London at that time were born in the Irish Republic and 515,310 residents had an Irish parent giving a ratio of slightly over 2:1. An even greater proportion was recorded in 2004 when a Greater London Authority representative and weighted sample survey of London residents found that 11 per cent had at least one parent born in either part of Ireland and 19 per cent had a grandparent born there (*Irish Post*, 2004a). Including both first and second generations, as is commonly the case for other minority ethnic groups, would place the Irish higher up the list numerically, close to the Black/African/Caribbean/Black British: Caribbean group which numbered 344,597.

The absence of census data and the complexity of identities in the second generation means that qualitative material is most useful in exploring British-born Irish generations. The most extensive was the ESRC-funded research study entitled *The second-generation Irish: a hidden population in multi-ethnic Britain* (2000–2), known as the *Irish 2 Project*. This explored senses of identity of people with Irish parents, selecting five locations of which London was one. Qualitative methods were used, including focus groups with target populations (professional women, professional men, mothers and people of mixed ethnic parentage) and 25 individual interviews based on demographic, socio-economic and cultural quotas. Most participants were in their 30s and 40s, the children of the 'bulge' of postwar migrants in the 1950s. The findings go some way to explain the apparent low rate of claiming Irish identities in the 2001 and 2011 Censuses.

Discussing the issue of identity, focus group members strongly asserted their ongoing senses of Irishness, but explained the difficulties in expressing this in the face of English people's denials and accusations of inauthenticity from people in Ireland. The key 'proof' laid down by both challenging groups was the lack of an Irish accent. Many *Irish 2* participants had decided that the best description of their ethnic identity was 'London Irish', a diasporic term which hybridised their family origins and their personal background. In the professional men's group there was broad agreement about this.

> Finbarr: I was born here, been brought up in London and I feel, I feel more of a relationship to London, rather than the United Kingdom. But I am Irish, I can't help it. I can't deny that. It's the blood that's been passed down.

Seamus agreed:

> Seamus: I'm not Irish Irish but I'm very, well I'm London Irish and I'm proud of my London roots as well, but as your man here says, it's just a London thing.

> Moderator: Yeah.

> Seamus: 'Cause I was, went to school here, you know, I went, I was confirmed here, I went to church here but it was always going back home to Ireland for every holiday. We were sent back for six weeks. So that was, I think that's, that was a good thing as well because I've got friends similar background to my own, but their mother and father didn't, they probably lost their religion or something. But religion was important to me growing up because, you know, it was all part of being Irish. And seeing friends and that so, you know, but yeah certainly not British that's, that's what I'm like. Not that I'm anti-British, it's just that it's not me.

> Moderator: Yeah.

> Seamus: That's, that's how I feel comfortable describing my own self.

Seamus's elaboration brings out many aspects of the London childhoods of Irish migrants' children. It has already been shown that there was distinctive geographical clustering in the inner west London boroughs so that local Catholic church attendance and schooling brought together children of a similar background. Moreover frequent visits to Ireland, especially in the school holidays also reinforced connections with families in Ireland (Walter, 2013).

However self-description as 'London Irish' may not be without problems for the second generation. Malone and Dooley (2006), drew on focus group discussions with eight women in Brent to argue that the second generation feel much less anchored in their neighbourhoods than their migrant parents.

The London Irish women, in marked contrast, are self-perceived outsiders from both mainstream British society and, in particular, from the current urban life given their stated preoccupation with the desired or imagined environment of a rural Ireland of their own memories of summer holidays, their 'inherited memories and recollections of their parents or – rather more likely – a bit of both'. (p. 23)

In particular the second-generation participants lacked the practical and emotional support of belonging to a migrant network, leading to a greater sense of anonymity in the city.

But the second generation is also placed within a larger picture of multiple ethnic settlement in London, especially as their inner city neighbourhoods are homes both to other migrant groups as well as the settled English or British populations. Their substantial numbers and long-established family connections as well as their joint inside/outside status have provided a distinctive location within the ethnic mix. In certain situations, one consequence of long settlement can be the establishment of strategic alliances between different minority ethnic groups. As Hickman et al. (2013) report:

In Kilburn, the shared experiences of discrimination and migration of African Caribbean long-term residents and their Irish counterparts were cited by interviewees from both groups as the source of the ease with which these two groups were able to live together.

An illustration of this 'identity alliance' was given by a young long-term settled Irish man:

It's Irish and Caribbean youngsters, and they do round here, which is quite confusing, not like anywhere else they plot together. And here in Stonebridge they plot together. They hang round together. Whereas in Hackney or somewhere like that, or New Cross in Lewisham, or whatever, there is big Irish communities and Caribbeans that live next to each other but they don't mix. But here for some reason they mix … I sort of know why, it's, you know, back ages and ages ago when everyone came over, some Irish people would buy up and then let Caribbeans stay. And then some Caribbeans would buy up and let Irish stay. So it's a sort of mutual respect thing. From Ladbroke Grove it started up and just moved up towards here like. (2013: 154)

As the participant suggests, Kilburn presents an unusual case of cooperation and respect between the Irish and Caribbean populations. Areas with fewer Irish people, or a different social status, had less positive relationships between groups. John Walsh, in his memoir *The Falling Angels* (2000) describes his Irish mother's sharp exchange with the driver of an old car who was about to place it unhelpfully on her doctor husband's parking space in Battersea, south of the Thames.

She strode over to the Austin, where the driver was yanking on the brake and rapped sharply on the window. A black face looked out. 'Would you mind offaly' said Mother in her most piercingly polite voice, 'not parkin' here ...' [explaining the doctor's need for quick access to his car].

'Lady', said the man in the car, equably. 'Why don't you go back where ya came from?'

She flinched as if she had been hit in the face. 'Lookit', she said. 'I was living in London a long time before *you* fellas came near the place'. (p. 53)

This anecdote illustrates the second-generation son's awareness of his Irish mother's class and ethnic pretensions, signified by accent and demeanour, which could easily be punctured to reveal her insecurities. It references continuing negotiation between insiders and outsiders which has both spatial and temporal dimensions.

It is not surprising therefore that mixed race partnerships are more common amongst the Irish than the British (Walter, 1988: 22). The *Irish 2 Project* interview sample included two young people each of whom had one Asian and one Irish parent. Tariq had an Irish mother who converted to Islam when she married his Pakistani father. He explained his experience of living in London.

Interviewer: What kind of neighbourhood do you recall growing up in as a child, what was the ethnic mix?

Tariq: I grew up in Balham, South West London where my parents still live. It was very mixed, there were families from Caribbean, South Asia, Irish families as well, I remember it being very mixed, comfortable in the sense it was at ease. I also went to a school in South London that attracted people from a number of different backgrounds. My whole upbringing as far as where I grew up and went to school, where I spent most of my time, was what we call today multicultural I guess, that is what I got used to. If I don't have that around me that is what I look for.

Interviewer: So that is what you are comfortable with, a cosmopolitan multicultural area.

Tariq: Yes, it reflects what I am, who I am, mixed background myself, a religion that is different to most people that I grew up with, living in London. I am not sure whether London, just being in London had as much influence over what I wanted from life, and what I found comfortable in life, whether that had as much influence over me as my parents' background. I think it is a very special place in that sense, London.

Tariq realised that he had taken London's diversity for granted and not understood the significance of location when he applied to university.

> Tariq: After all that I said about needing that diversity around me, I just picked Exeter because of the course. I had no idea where I was going to, or what I was letting myself in for. You could count the number of non-white people on both hands walking through campus each day.

> Interviewer: Which is quite a tough thing.

> Tariq: It was very difficult, I didn't realise it at the time how much that place was not for me. I was eighteen.

Tariq was far more connected with his father's generous and inclusive Pakistani family than his mother's less welcoming Irish one, and therefore identified more with second category in his self-description as 'Irish Pakistani'. But the other mixed race participant, Yasmeen, experienced great difficulty in locating her identity between the two backgrounds. In contrast to Tariq's safe, middle-class upbringing her working-class childhood had been very unhappy with a violent Pakistani father and abusive Irish uncles. In her 30s she had decided that she was simply 'Irish and Pakistani, mixed race'. Both Tariq and Yasmeen fitted the typical pattern of Irish mothers and Asian or Caribbean fathers which are echoed in other case studies mixed race children in London (Twine, 2004; Ifegwunigwe 1999; Harman 2010).

The distinctive experience of being second-generation Irish in London drew heavily on, and contributed to, notions of multi-cultural identities in the city. As the Kilburn case study showed, the Irish were well-placed to offer a more inclusive attitude to later arrivals than people who simply saw themselves as the ethnic majority whose entitlements were under threat. But as the Census debate about ethnic inclusion exemplified, this also placed them in a 'double bind'. Whilst they were often able and willing to 'make their cultures inclusive and accessible in order to contribute towards a liberal-pluralist celebration of 'cosmopolitan' diversity and cross-cultural citizenship', they needed to establish significant differences in order to claim much-needed resources (Nagle, 2009: 5).

An event which epitomises the place of the wider Irish community in London is the St Patrick's Day Festival, one of eight cultural events organised and funded by the Greater London Authority. The others were the Feast of St George, Vaisakhi Festival, Eid, Diwali Festival, African Festival, Liberty Festival and New Year's Eve Fireworks. The revival of the Irish Festival and parade in 2002 after thirty years of the Northern Ireland 'Troubles' signified the recognition of a newly-acceptable population. Initially confined to a site on the south bank of the Thames, after 2005 it moved to Trafalgar Square, described as a symbolic arrival in 'the heart and hegemonic centre of Britain that from which the marginalised Irish had previously been proscribed' (Nagle, 2008: 191).

St Patrick's Day both proclaims the specificity of Irish culture and includes many 'honorary Irish' who are invited to join in. In 2006 President Mary McAleese linked these groups into the notion of a 'global family'

> I wish to send warm greetings on this St Patrick's Day to Irish people at home and abroad, and to Ireland's friends around the globe.
>
> Today is a day of celebration in Ireland and for all our global family throughout the world.

Rather than seeing it as part of the 'double bind', Mary Hickman offers a more positive interpretation. She suggests that 'a policy that aims at achieving cohesion by celebrating unity and difference, rather than dissolving difference, is one for our hybridised times' (Hickman, 2014: 126).

Multi-Generational Identities of Irish Descent: East End of London

There is no doubt that the long history of Irish settlement in London is deeply embedded in the ancestry of the population as a whole. The present-day second-generation Irish population is scattered throughout London but the largest numbers identifying as White Irish in the census are now located in the inner west boroughs close to where their migrant parents live. However, this spatial concentration dates only from the 1950s (Weindling and Colloms, 2002: 128). Between the mid-19th century and the Second World War, the largest Irish settlement was in the East End. This is therefore a particularly interesting area in which to explore more distant Irish backgrounds. Although many will have moved away, especially in the 'slum clearance' programmes of the early postwar period, the spread of Irish grandparents and great-grandparents through mixed marriages over several generations makes it likely that a significant proportion of the 'white working class' in the East End has Irish antecedents. Indeed Dench et al.'s controversial monograph *The New East End* (2007: 15) noted that 'to this day a large proportion of the white people in Bethnal Green have Irish surnames'.

For several centuries the East End has been a 'reception area' for immigrants seeking manual labouring jobs and cheap rented housing in the capital. In the 19th century Irish men dominated dock work, for example, and lived close to the river in areas like Wapping and Shadwell. Many Irish women were employed as domestic servants and thus had a wider distribution within London, working for poorer families, including Jewish households, in the East End itself, but also for wealthier families in the West End. By the middle of the century the Irish population in the East End already included several generations. Lynn Lees (1979: 153) shows that by 1851 30 per cent of her sample of five different areas of London was second- or third-generation Irish, increasing to 40 per cent in 1861. She demonstrated that clustering was associated with high levels of intermarriage between different generations so that apparently English-born partners were usually of Irish descent.

> The London Irish generally married within their own ethnic group; there was little intermarriage with people of English ancestry or with continental Roman Catholics. While 24 per cent of the sampled families listed in the 1851 census and 20 per cent of those in the 1861 census contained one English-born and one Irish-born partner, virtually all of the technically English spouses were second- or third-generation Irish. The 'English' men had Irish names and had been born in London; marriage registers from the Catholic churches serving my sample parishes show that most of the maiden names of women marrying Irish-born men were also Irish. First- and second-generation Irish would seem therefore to have intermarried freely.

Out-marriage increased in the early years of the 20th century, for example linking with members of the Jewish community, despite apparently strong religious differences. But the Irish continued as a distinctive presence, often one side of a mixed family tree. Awareness of Irish ancestry remained strong and difference was reinforced by Catholic religious adherence, bringing children from similar backgrounds together in schools. The persistence of Catholic rituals in the public sphere, and their incorporation into local tradition, is recorded by Gilda O'Neill in her collection of local memories entitled *Our East End: Memories of Life in Cockney London.* One interviewee commented on children's games involving building 'grottoes'.

> When you'd made your grotto – it could have anything on it from old postcards to a bunch of weeds in a jam jar, anything a bit attractive – you'd shield it, with your arm round it, so no one got a free look. I'm not sure why they were called grottoes, but the idea probably came from the shrines that the mums from Catholic families used to set up by their street doorstep when it was the day of the local Catholic church's parade. (1999: 102)

The support of Irish workers for Jewish residents targeted by fascists in the 1930s is often noted. In the so-called 'Battle of Cable Street' in 1936, when demonstrators succeeded in halting Oswald Mosley's march despite its police support, many observers commented on the strong Irish Catholic presence. Bill Fishman noted

> I heard this loudspeaker say "They are going to Cable Street". Suddenly a barricade was erected there and they put an old lorry in the middle of the road and old mattresses. The people up the top of the flats, mainly Irish Catholic women, were throwing rubbish on the police. We were all side by side. I was moved to tears to see bearded Jews and Irish Catholic dockers standing up to stop Mosley. (Fishman: undated)

A sharp change took place after the Second World War. Within the space of twenty years recognition of an Irish presence in the East End had faded. The white working classes had become implicitly 'English' and indeed no mention of Irish backgrounds was made in the influential sociological study *Family and Kinship in East London* published in 1963 although it emphasised neighbourhood stability (Walter, 2014). A number of reasons could explain this loss. It was part of a consolidation of 'whiteness' as a symbol of a wider national identity embedded in the welfare state, as well as differentiation from new 'black' immigrant arrivals from the Caribbean and South Asia. It could also have been an unacknowledged element in the desire to hide the ascribed inferiority of 'slum' dwelling. O'Neill commented on attitudes associated with moves to the suburbs in the 1950s:

> The cockney identity, which was once carefully hidden by those who considered themselves fortunate to leave the slums of their childhood, but is now more often acknowledged as a source of great pride. Where once people would have been wary of discussing their working class roots, with mothers telling their children to *talk proper* and to ape the ways of their *betters*, they are now more likely to celebrate such memorable beginnings. (1999: xiii)

The continued salience of fourth-, fifth- and sixth-generation Irish backgrounds is retained in individual memories and claimed identities. For example, in researching the descendants of the matchwomen who participated in the Bryant and May factory strike of 1888, Louise Raw located and interviewed three grandchildren, each of whom retained memories of stories they had been told when young (Raw, 2011: 208). One was the descendant of striker Mary Driscoll, herself a second-generation woman who had two Irish-born parents. Mary's daughter was described by her own daughter, Joan, as feeling herself to be Irish. Joan, Mary's granddaughter – the fourth generation – said that she herself 'inherited this identity'. Another fourth-generation Irish resident, Ted Johns, was interviewed in 1994 and explained his inherited family political allegiances. He was described as 'leading the fight against Fascism' in the Isle of Dogs (*Irish Post*, 1994):

> Ted knows little about his great-grandfather, who emigrated to England as a coal trimmer. His grandfather, Tom Murphy, was greeted on moving into Limehouse in London's East End with a hail of bricks. 'They put his windows in because locals assumed the Irish would be competing for their jobs but the fact that Tom was active in trades unions overcame that.'

Traces of earlier Irish immigration remain in family memories and in a number of public spheres, including political participation in the Labour Party. They also underlie the significant number of Catholic schools in the East End even though these are now predominantly attended by recent arrivals from other global origins.

Conclusion

The Irish in London are part of the ever-changing mosaic of migrant settlement. There are important continuities, including the association with low-paid work for people leaving Ireland at young ages with few qualifications. However the recent large-scale immigration from Eastern Europe has seriously challenged traditional 'Irish' roles such as work 'on the buildings' (Cowley, 2011). Although the White Irish still had the highest proportion in the lowest socio-economic category 'Routine occupations' (11.4 per cent) in 2011 this was not far above White Other (9.2 per cent), which mainly comprises newer arrivals from Eastern Europe (Ryan et al., 2014: 20). At the same time the presence of these White Others strengthens the claim that 'whiteness' does not preclude ethnic difference.

Unlike many recent arrivals the Irish are deeply embedded in London's population over many generations. They have traditionally settled in areas with other incomers seeking 'unskilled' employment and cheap rented accommodation. This was exemplified in the East End in the nineteenth and early twentieth centuries, and more recently in Brent, the most ethnically mixed borough in London, which also had the highest Irish-born proportion in 2011. The positive contribution of this long-term settled migrant identity to neighbourhood social cohesion was observed in Kilburn and is also evident in the East End, as a critic of *The New East End* points out:

> Whilst there have been serious conflicts between groups within the area, historically the diverse populations have been able to mobilize across internal divisions and oppose fascists in the 1930s, property developers in the 1980s and 1990s and the racism of both the Liberal democrats who controlled Tower Hamlets from 1986 to 1994 and the British National Party (BNP). Even with a superficial and outsider's knowledge of the complexity of Tower Hamlets it is obvious that a simple division into black and white (or Bangladeshi and white) will not do, nor will ungrounded reports of white resentment (Moore, 2008: 351)

Despite such longevity and substantial size the Irish community remains a hidden population, often omitted from academic and policy discussions about migration. This reflects an ongoing ambivalence about the place of the Irish in Britain, embedded in the long history of national political conflict. On the one hand Ireland was part of the United Kingdom until 1922 and retains a 'special relationship', for example in respect of welfare and voting rights on arrival. On the other, memories remain of very recent hostilities involving violent action in London with damaging consequences for the treatment of all Irish people, of which residues remain.

Whilst historians and social scientists can chart key aspects of these processes, perhaps the complexities are captured most closely in the rich London Irish literature of novels, short stories and auto/biographical texts (Murray, 2012; McWilliams, 2013).

> By reading them, we become more aware of the ways in which identities are narrativized between home and away, between the personal and the collective and between facts and fictions. As a consequence, we are better able to appreciate the dynamic interdependence between narrative, diaspora and identity, and how and why migrants and their communities proclaim or disavow various forms of cultural allegiance. (Murray, 2012: 190–91)

Printed 'voices' thus reveal experiences of being Irish in London over generations, which are otherwise invisible. Songs and music offer yet another route into expressions of migrant and diaspora identities. In his chapter 'The Importance of Being (London) Irish: Hybridity, Essentialism and The Pogues', Sean Campbell describes The Pogues' 'innovative impulse, which had staged a second-generation Irish speaking position and installed a London-Irish imaginary' (2011:101).

Language is thus a particularly important signifier of Irishness both in written and spoken forms. The apparent 'sameness' of the native language of Irish migrants and 'indigenous' Londoners, masks ways in which it simultaneously denotes difference. Just as second-generation Irish musicians are often labelled English, so the canon of 'English' literature claims Irish writers, as in the case of the poet Seamus Heaney. At the same time Irish 'accents' are key indicators of ethnic otherness, apparently dividing migrants from descendants. 'London Irish' may be seen as a more inclusive identity which acknowledges the multi-cultural reality of the capital city.

References

Campbell, S. (2011), *'Irish Blood, English Heart': Second-generation Irish Musicians in England*. Cork: Cork University Press.

Cowley, U. (2011), *The Men who Built Britain: A History of the Irish Navvy*, Wexford: Potter's Yard Press.

Department of Foreign Affairs, Dublin (2002), <https://www.dfa.ie/media/dfa/alldfawebsitemedia/.../TaskForceReport.pdf> accessed 18 September 2014.

Department of Foreign Affairs, Dublin (2014), <https://www.dfa.ie/media/dfa/alldfawebsitemedia/ourrolesandpolicies/2014-Overview-Emigrant-Support-Programme.pdf> accessed 20 September 2014.

Devlin Trew, J. (2013), *Leaving the North: Migration and Memory, Northern Ireland 1921–2011*. Liverpool: Liverpool University Press.

Fenton, M. (1997), 'Living in Bethnal Green: together or apart?' in Kershen, A. (ed.) *London: The Promised Land?* Aldershot: Avebury, pp. 128–42.

Fishman, B. <http://www.vam.ac.uk/moc/childrens lives/east endlives/Lifestories/bill fishman/index.html> accessed 18 September 2014.

Greater London Council (1984), *Report on Consultation with the Irish Community*. London: Ethnic Minorities Unit, GLC.

Guardian (2014), 'The Guardian view on Ireland's new abortion law: no choice at all' <http://www.theguardian.com/commentisfree/2014/aug/17/guardian-view-abortion-ireland-no-choice> accessed 18 September 2014.

Harman, V. (2010), 'Experiences of racism and the changing nature of white privilege among lone white mothers of mixed-parentage children in the UK', *Ethnic and Racial Studies*, 33(2): 176–94.

Hickman, M.J. and Walter, B. (1997), *Discrimination and the Irish Community in Britain*. London: Commission for Racial Equality.

Hickman, M.J., Morgan S. and Walter, B. (2001), *Second-generation Irish People in Britain: a Demographic, Socio-economic and Health Profile*. Irish Studies Centre: University of North London.

Hickman, M.J., Morgan S., Walter, B. and Bradley J. (2005), 'The limitations of whiteness and the boundaries of Englishness', *Ethnicities*, 5(2): 160–82.

Hickman, M.J. (2011), 'Census ethnic categories and second-generation identities: a study of the Irish in England and Wales', *Journal of Ethnic and Migration Studies*, 37(1): 79–97.

Hickman, M.J., Mai, N. and Crowley, H. (2012), *Migration and Social Cohesion in the UK*. Basingstoke: Palgrave.

Hickman, M.J. (2014), 'Reflecting on gender, generation and ethnicity in celebrating St Patrick's Day in London', in Macpherson D.A.J. and Hickman, M.J. (eds), *Women and Irish Diaspora Identities*. Manchester: Manchester University Press, pp. 112–29.

Holmes, C. (1997), 'Cosmopolitan London' in Kershen, A. (ed.) *London: The Promised Land?* Aldershot: Avebury, pp. 10–37.

Ifekwunigwe, J. (1999), *Scattered Belongings: Cultural Paradoxes of 'Race', Nation and Gender*. London: Routledge.

Irial, G., Kelly, T. and MacÉinri, P. (2013), *Irish Emigration in an Age of Austerity*. Irish Research Council Report, University College, Cork, Ireland.

Irish Post (1994), 'Fighting back in London's East End', 30 April, p. 7.

Irish Post (2004a), 'Conference tackles "hidden Irish" issue', 8 May, p. 5.

Irish Post (2004b), 'Dion Committee in the spotlight as fund hits £6m', 27 November, p. 6.

Kennedy, L., Lyes. M. and Russell, M. (2014), *Supporting the Next Generation of the Irish Diaspora: Report of a Research Project Funded by the Emigrant Support Programme, Department of Foreign Affairs*. Dublin: University College Dublin Clinton Institute.

Leavey, G., Sembhi, S.and Livingston, G. (2004), 'Older Irish migrants living in London: identity, loss and return', *Journal of Ethnic and Migration Studies* 30(4): 763–79.

Lees, L. (1979), *Exiles of Erin: Irish Migrants in Victorian London*. Manchester: Manchester University Press.

Mac Laughlin, J. (1997), 'The new vanishing Irish: social characteristics of "new wave" Irish emigration', in Mac Laughlin, J. (ed.) *Location and Dislocation in Contemporary Irish Society*. Cork: Cork University Press, pp. 133–57.

MacRaild, D. (1999), *Irish Migrants in Modern Britain, 1750–1922*. Basingstoke: Macmillan.

Malone, M. (2001), 'The health experience of Irish people in a North-West London "community saved"', *Community, Work and Family*, 4(2): 195–213.

Malone, M.E. and Dooley, J. (2006), 'Dwelling in displacement: meanings of "community" and sense of community for two generations of Irish people living in North-West London', *Community, Work and Family*, 9(1): 11–28.

McWilliams, E. (2013), *Women and Exile in Contemporary Irish Fiction*. Basingstoke: Palgrave Macmillan.

Moore, R. (2008), '"Careless talk": a critique of Dench, Gavron and Young's "The New East End"', *Critical Social Policy*, 28(3): 349–60.

Murray, T. (2012), *London Irish Fictions: Narrative, Diaspora and Identity*. Liverpool: Liverpool University Press.

Nagle, J. (2008), 'Multiculturalism's double bind: creating inclusivity, difference and cross-community alliances with the London-Irish', *Ethnicities* 8(2): 177–8.

Nagle, J. (2009), *Multiculturalism's Double Bind: Creating Inclusivity, Cosmopolitanism and Difference*. Farnham: Ashgate.

O'Neill, G. (1999), *My East End*. Harmondsworth: Penguin.

Ralph, D. (2014), 'Always on the move, but going nowhere fast': motivations for 'Euro-commuting' between the Republic of Ireland and other EU states', *Journal of Ethnic and Migration Studies*. DOI:10.1080/1369183X.2014.910447.

Raw, L. (2011), *Striking a Light: The Bryant and May Matchwomen and their Place in History*. London: Bloomsbury.

Rossiter, A. (2009), *Ireland's Hidden Diaspora: the Abortion Trail and the Making of a London-Irish Underground, 1980–2000*. London: LASC Publishing.

Rouse, P. (2003), *Lost Generation* <http://www.rte.ie/archives/exhibitions/1030-emigration-once-again/139200-lost-generation> accessed 20 September 2014.

Ryan, L., D'Angelo, A., Puniskis, M. and Kaye, N. (2014), *Analysis of 2011 Census Data: Irish Community Statistics, England and Selected Areas, Report for London*. Social Policy Research Centre, Middlesex University.

Tilki, M., Ryan, L., D'Angelo, A. and Sales, R. (2009), *The Forgotten Irish: Report of a Research Project Commissioned by the Ireland Fund of Great Britain*. Social Policy Research Centre, Middlesex University.

Twine, F.W. (2004), 'A white side of black Britain: the concept of racial literacy', *Ethnic and Racial Studies*, 27(6): 878–907.

Walls, P. (2005), *Still Leaving: Recent, Vulnerable Irish Emigrants to the UK: Profile, Experiences and Pre-departure Solutions*. Dublin: Emigrant Advice.

Walsh, J. (1999), *The Falling Angels: An Irish Romance*. London: Flamingo.

Walter, B. (1988), *Irish Women in London*. London: London Strategic Policy Unit.

Walter, B. (1998), 'Challenging the black/white binary: the need for an Irish category in the 2001 census', *Patterns of Prejudice*, 32(2): 73–86.

Walter, B. (2005/6), 'English/Irish hybridity', *International Journal of Diversity in Organisations, Communities and Nations*, 5.

Walter, B. (2008), 'From "flood" to "trickle": Irish migration to Britain 1987–2006', *Irish Geography*, 41(2): 181–94.

Walter, B. (2013), 'Transnational networks across generations: childhood visits to Ireland by the second generation in England', in Gilmartin, M. and White, A. (eds), *Migrations: Ireland in a Global World*. Manchester: Manchester University Press, pp. 17–35.

Walter, B. (2014), '"England people very nice": Multi-generational Irish Identities in the Multi-cultural East End', *Socialist History*, 45: 78–102.

Weindling, D. and Colloms, M. (2002), 'The Irish in Kilburn: myth and reality', *British Association for Local History*, May: 118–31.

Chapter 9

London as an Informal and Individualistic Paradise? Transnationalism as a Form of Anti-State Resistance by Polish Migrants in London

Michał P. Garapich

Among the many meanings of transnationalism(s), the political significance of transnational action from the perspective of individual migrants does not always gain enough attention. It is usually framed as a way transnational migration processes affect the state, how social movements formed in the diaspora compete for a stake in the home country or, how a particular state manages its diaspora through various policy means. This chapter calls for a more actor-centred approach in which individuals' choices and strategic decisions have an anti-state frame of reference dominating their individualised agendas and norms of behaviour. These are not overtly political, thus falling outside a typical political science lens, but follow what James Scott refers to as 'small scale resistance' or 'weapons of the weak' of structurally subordinate groups (Scott, 1990). In the case of the Polish migrants I discuss below, this follows a long tradition of contestation of the state normative and institutional structures, its surveillance, migration regimes and ways institutions aim to control human actions. With the advent of increased mobility within the European Union due to EU integration processes these patterns of behaviour and cultural attitudes gain particular prominence, offering a variety of means and opportunities to manoeuvre between structural constraints, contest and at times even change them to individual advantage. The context of that resistance is however crucial, with London's global, neoliberal and dynamic face a perfect ground for anti-state resistance and the power of informal contestation of hegemonic national discursive frameworks.

Introduction

In the context of immigration from the EU being one of the factors of increasing British hostility towards the European integration project, to the extent that UK exit from the EU is considered as a real possibility, the question of whether it is really the accumulated decision of a couple of million migrants from Central and Eastern Europe that can trigger such a political earthquake should be taken seriously. This chapter, drawing on several studies, as well as years of observation of Polish migrants in the UK and London in particular, calls for increased attention on human agency potentially having a deep impact on institutional structures. As a result attention is drawn to the migrant as a transnational political actor, who can, *en masse*, have a significant impact on the nation state. Leaving structural determinants – such the EU integration process and rise of global structures of mobility – aside, I argue that these actions result from a fundamental anti-state, and anti-institutional, frame of reference these migrants exhibit; morally justifying resisting, and also breaking institutional-legal rules and, in consequence, searching for a post-national environment, which a global city like London can provide. In order to understand these developments and the interplay between institutional structures on city, state and European level and migrants' agency who, through their actions, are negotiating these, this chapter firstly will discuss the development of the migration system between Poland and the West since the early 1990s until the present day and how people contributed to the development of it, from the perspective of individual migrants. It will then present several case studies which illustrate how the collective action of Polish migrants has shaped several institutional frameworks in various domains – legal, political and institutional. In discussing these I am adopting an anthropological perspective to examine how Polish migrants, equipped with their culturally functional and historically developed anti-state habitus, have influenced the debates over the place of Great Britain in the European Union, the relationship between the citizen and the state and the future of the welfare state. In conclusion, attention is drawn towards the migrants' perception of the city – London in this case – as a place where one can resist hegemonic nation-state frames of reference, while at the same time retaining strong ethnic affiliations along the culture–blood lines.

The literature on migration from Poland is currently undergoing a massive boom with at least a dozen published articles a year as well as special issues, books and conferences. There seems to be gap however in linking the pre-2004 flows with current ones, despite the fact that several studies point to continuity rather than sudden change between these flows (Garapich 2008; Burrell, 2003). What is often omitted is recognition that the pre-2004 flows have strongly contributed to the facilitation and development of further mobility patterns. This in turn, as I will argue, stems not just from a tradition of Polish migration culture (Garapich, 2013; Okólski and Jaźwińska, 2001) being the result of the economic and social transformation of the Polish economy after the collapse of socialism, but from a specific set of norms and values that Polish society has developed over a longer time perspective. The dynamism and massive flow of people in the last decade, should not be solely attributed to the institutional and economic conditions in Poland and the EU, but also to specific habitus in which the state and its legal-institutional framework is perceived, acted upon and negotiated by individual migrants and their households. This habitus rests on a deeply entrenched perception of the state and the legal system as hostile, alien, unfriendly and made to restrict freedoms rather than facilitate human development. Although unfriendly, it is also not all-powerful and it is possible to negotiate its rules through human creativity and stubbornness – values necessary to overcome state rules but also to emphasise one's humanity through gaining social autonomy. In other words, individual freedom is gained through negating the power of the state to restrict it. This anti-state attitude is of course a generalisation, but in order to see the Polish migration system in a different light, linking institutional structures and individual behaviour we need to recognise it as a social force *per se* that is similarly powerful and important to grasp the complexity of the development of the migration system and its future directions. Furthermore, the anti-state values reflected by Polish migrants are strongly linked to their class position, with the working and rural class particularly prone to regard institutional shifts as just another step in history without qualitative change in their position versus the dominant classes, powers they represent and processes they trigger. As Buchowski notes in his study of a Polish rural community in the transformation period: 'What appears to scholars as systemic transformation, for rural people it is just a link in the chain of history'(2004: 174). This means that the practices of anti-institutionalism, anti-stateism and the frequently emphasised division between 'us masses' and 'those elites' have long been familiar to large sections of Polish society caught in the modernisation process often resulting in increased inequality and class tension, especially with the neoliberal project of Polish post-communist modernisation being the main game in town. Current migration dynamics and the creation of transnational social fields between the UK and Poland are just another reflection of these phenomena on a European scale. In that anti-state cultural outlook, an increased role of other political forms of organisation gains prominence – the global city such as London offering a way out of the nation-state discourse replacing it with notions of individual freedom, informality, liberalism and anonymity.

The analysis of resistance to national and global forces working class migrants exercise has been termed as 'transnationalism from below' (Smith and Guarnizo, 1998). Studies point to many examples of the empowering nature of transnationalism (Bhabha, 1990; Kearney, 1991; Basch et al., 1994) allowing migrants to escape the scrutinising gaze of the nation state, its control over regimes of mobility or essentialist identity discourses. Smith and Guarnizo however point out that: 'The totalising emancipatory character of transnationalism in these discourses is questionable' (1998: 5), since they do not have to be resistant to global power relations at all, and sometimes even actively reproduce particular hegemonic discourses. In addition, most of the 'transnationalism from below' research agenda, is focused on the US context, where continuing hardening of the migration regime triggers appropriate and predictable responses from migrants – mainly Latin American (Massey and Pren, 2012). This chapter however, points to a different direction in transnational studies, documenting a particular development where structural conditions, along with cultural meanings individuals construct, result in a significant weakening of the power of the nation state to control, dictate and shape individual lives. Resistance in that sense refers to the sum of everyday actions of individuals and the complex way of constructing cultural meanings contesting hegemonic discourses. A similar approach is used by Glick Schiller and Karagiannis (2006) in their analysis of Pentecostal migrants in Germany, demonstrating how their religious ritual and symbolism resist the German state-orchestrated prescriptions over meanings of integration, assimilation and national belonging. This chapter focuses on a particular migration regime sphere where freedom of movement within the EU has opened up increased opportunities for contesting the power of the state and looks at how this has been done through the eyes of individual migrants.

Anti-State Polish Habitus

Despite common ideological underpinning, communism in Poland was quite specific, in comparison with its mutations in countries such as East Germany, Czechoslovakia or the Soviet Union. It needed to adjust to local circumstances and despite the usage in common parlance of the label 'communist' there were huge variations in time and space between countries and periods. Buchowski, Conte and Ziółkowski remind us that 'Europe east of Elbe river was not simply red, but colourful and diversified, even if the red pigment was manifest everywhere' (2001: 9). One of the most important aspects in the case of Poland was the relative freedom of some civil, non-state institutions. First, after the Stalinist era of oppression, the Polish Catholic Church – in contrast to the Church in Czechoslovakia or Eastern Germany – emerged as an important political actor, keeping control over some of its assets, institutions, publications, education provision, international connections and what is vital – peoples' minds, collective imagery and symbols. Linked to that, Polish communists – in the face of massive opposition from the rural population – gave up quite early one of the central communist ideas of collectivisation of food production. This had effectively acknowledged a certain level of independence of the rural class from the state, although throughout the communist period the pressure to control the rural population was considerable. The main paradox, as observed by Caroline Nagengast (1991) was that the actions of the state and relative farmers' independence and resistance led to the emergence of a specific capitalist, or proto-capitalist, culture of production and social relations recreating a specific class dynamics between the rural and urban populations. She emphasises the role of the anti-state resistance, in particular the black economy, – dating back to previous years of German occupation during World War II and anti-colonial resistance in the 19th century – which eventually led to increased inequalities within rural class. The vital outcome is that the anti-state and strongly traditional outlook of Polish rural communities needs be seen in a longer term perspective and their fight with feudal, communist and now capitalist economic conditions as one continuous chain of struggle for survival and independence from state interference. This anti-state attitude of the Polish rural class seems to be entrenched in a long tradition and is often identified as one of the obstacles in the successful modernisation of its economy, seen by some prominent social thinkers as a 'hang-over' from the communist past and the persistence of the '*homo sovieticus*' syndrome, characterised by anti-state attitudes, welfare dependency, lack of initiative and mistrust or lack of social capital (Sztompka, 1993). If farmers were often regarded by the official Polish communist propaganda as the *bête noire* of the system, it was the working class whose status has been raised to levels unseen before, in terms of economic privilege but also social prestige. Skilled workers, especially in heavy industry, mining, mills and shipyards were seen as the future and soul of the communist nation. With status went along concessions and also a strong political voice – as proved by the August 1980 Solidarity revolution. Ironically, the class mostly cherished by the communist state, turned out to be not only the class that organised the main anti-state strikes which led to the collapse of the system triggering the end of the Cold War, but also, the one that emerged as one of the biggest losers of the post-1989 transformation period. A number of scholars and historians have noted the paradox summarised by Zygmunt Bauman that 'the social forces which led to the downfall of the communist power ... [were] not those that [would] eventually benefit from the construction of the new system' (1994: 33). As Karol Modzelewski, one of most influential Polish dissidents observed in his recent autobiography (2014), Polish transformation was a bitter success, as those who led the revolution ended up being laid off, unemployed and socially degraded. These historical and cultural factors resulted in the displacement of a quite specific set of values, norms and embedded practices in the everyday life of Poles – whatever their class background, but one of most important ones in the context of my argument, is the strengthening and rooting of anti-state and anti-elite attitudes of the vast majority of Polish society. As Ziółkowski notes:

> In Poland, traditional authority – traditional values, religion and family – are much more important than in any other post-communist state, while the rational-legal authority of the state is not held in very high esteem. The state in Poland is not a fully legitimised institution, it is perceived mainly as a welfare state, the agent of the security net. (2001: 169)

It is not a surprise then, that for hundreds of thousands Polish families impoverished by the collapse of the industrial base and dismantlement of the welfare state in the 1990s, migration seemed to be the only option for survival, often seen as another example of the old truth that the state and elites are far removed from what real Poles undergo and the split between the ruling class and impoverished classes. Despite the dominant nationalists' discourse constructing emigration as a 'moral issue' (Erdmans, 1994) where patriotic collectivistic obligation constructed by the elites equated migration with an egoistic and materialistic mind-set (Garapich, 2008a), millions headed west, aided by a tradition of rural-urban mobility stemming from communist under-urbanisation (Okólski and Jaźwińska 2001). Although western countries were increasingly concerned about the 'hordes' from the East (Iglicka, 2007) these millions found their way to the European labour markets. I argue that there is a clear connection between the anti-state resistance tradition and ability of people to find their own way in the West. As Morawska notes (1998) for instance, the set of post-communist attitudes and values, worked in favour of undocumented and informal migration to Germany. The same can be said of migration flows to the UK (Jordan and Düvell, 2002) in which navigating hostile migration regimes, the rules of entry and everyday behaviour of Polish migrants was marked by a common understanding that in order to make it in the UK, one needed to bend the rules, stretch the law, break it and – most importantly – regard it is as your right, not as something morally wrong (Jordan and Düvell 2002, see also Irek, 2011). Throughout my numerous fieldwork studies, Polish migrants I spoke to who had an experience of coming to the UK prior to 2004 frequently spoke about the ways in which they circumvented official regulations, sometimes through illegal means. Most importantly, they often spoke about these endeavours with a sense of pride and achievement. Resistance to state control clearly built on people's experience of the communist system back in Poland where 'beat the system' attitude was morally justified as not just a necessary skill of survival but a proof of one's worth and position in social strata (Wedel, 1986). Crucially, Polish migrants saw nothing wrong in breaking immigration laws and regarded movement within the EU as their fundamental right. A similar attitude was also noted by other scholars of pre-2004 flows who observed:

> Poles seek to earn, to pay for cars or deposit on flats. They assert their economic value to the host society and justify their undocumented, informal and shadow activities as legitimate labour market behaviour. On their accounts, the immigration restrictions that they violate by working when on "tourist" visits should not exist; there should be free movement for them all over Europe. Their actions could, therefore, be taken as a kind of protest or resistance against present border controls and regulations. (Jordan, 2002)

From the perspective of how individual social actors shape state policies and are a driving force of innovation this attitude of Polish migrants is of vital importance and needs to be decoded further. For if we treat citizenship as something more than just membership of a one state system, but rather as the tool by which people negotiate their place in contemporary Europe in using their rights and pushing for the rights they believe they *should* have, the evasion of border controls and restrictions on the labour market can be treated as a form of civil disobedience and strategy to make the set of rights removed from a specific nation-state framework. A good example of this uneasy relationship between state dominance and individual agency is Bogdan, who when interviewed in 2006 was living in London after migrating from Sokółka, a town in the north-eastern part of Poland close to Białystok. Sokółka experienced mass unemployment and poverty in the aftermath of the collapse of the socialist command economy. Like many others from this area, Bogdan had been a migrant for a long time. During the 1970s and 1980s he had travelled to Germany where he was employed as an undocumented worker in farms and factories. Then, in the 1990s, he spent several years as an undocumented worker in Brussels. He had unpleasant memories of police controls, immigration officials, harassment and restrictions and the elaborate disciplining, policing and restricting of what he saw as his basic right – to work in order to sustain his family – were often dressed in his speech in a historical narrative of continuing inequality between parts of Europe. He clearly saw himself as being at the front of that injustice. Bogdan was very often full of bitter remarks about how the East-West divide was maintained through policing him despite the hype about a unified Europe. He spoke about being forced to board a plane from Brussels to Warsaw in handcuffs – 'just because I wanted to work there'. Eventually, through the help of his friends – and diffusion of information on how to navigate and dodge the migration regimes is crucial here – he migrated to Britain in late 1990s and at the time of interview in 2007 run a successful construction company. 'And what the f... they were wasting their energy on? You see, for decades I fought for my dignity, and now, thanks to all this [freedom of movement] I have it, but I don't feel it was given, I suffered my part too' – was his comment on the long and lost battle of Western Europe migration regimes to keep him out of the gates.

Adam, a carpenter from Piwniczna region, a mountainous area in the south of the country had also been coming to London since the mid-1990s and described the strategies which his clients had pursued in order to avoid the questioning of immigration officers. Between 1993 and 2004 the most common practice was to cite a family visit and his clients usually 'adopted' him for this purpose – he was a cousin on a short visit. A letter from a relative or a telephone number for someone, who could confirm the invitation, was a crucial and well known tool to facilitate entry into the UK. It is impossible to underestimate the scale of social capital involved in these practices, the number of strong networks established and the way in which having someone 'out there' was an important source of prestige and power but also potential employment. The network of support facilitating entry involved both British citizens, Polish migrants from previous cohorts, businesses, employers and so on. The myriad of shadowy practices, which Polish migrants undertook before 2004, have become the stuff of urban legends frequently recalled during my conversations with Polish migrants, most often with a sense of pride. Information about the strategies of British immigration controls towards different groups spread quite quickly among migrants and their communities back in Poland. At one stage in the early 2000s, for instance, someone discovered that it was fairly easy to enter Britain through pre-paid package tours by bus to London. Rumours spread fast that immigration officers waved these buses through without asking questions. According to one story the strategy was so established and well known that after entering Britain the tour guides announced through the loudspeaker: 'Ok, so who *really* goes to the National Gallery tomorrow?' and the tour usually returned half-empty. Another strategy took advantage of religious officials not being questioned on entry. This resulted in one grotesque occasion when a nun was stopped after immigration officers discovered that she was seven months pregnant.[1] These stories and anecdotes are now treated with a historical nostalgia, but they were very often recalled on various occasions – Poles passing for Polish Roma (in order to get entry as an asylum-seeker), Poles passing for Danish, French, German citizens in order to get work without question asked, migrants paying for a facilitator of entry (someone who would confirm that he or her is a close family member), forging documents facilitating employment, sale of British passports,[2] entry through lesser known ports in the North of England, false language schools, non-existent employers, fake cousins, family members, spouses and so on. Looking at individuals' migration experiences, it is important to keep these practices in mind precisely because being migrants themselves, they were treated as common place, a norm, an accepted way of finding its way in London and – most importantly, as Jordan points out – as an assertion of their own individual rights. Adam asked about this, was as straightforward as Bogdan was: 'I honestly don't know why did they make life so difficult then. In particular, since all the restrictions clearly didn't work. We Poles, just stuck together in this, sure by illegal means, but we simply wanted some work …'.

These skills, resources and capital, which Polish migrants displayed when circumventing British immigration restrictions and regulations, have sometimes been explained in terms of values developed during the communist period and the 'beat the system' attitude which did help people to be innovative but also ready to break the rule of law. Many social scientists refer to this set of attitudes towards the law as the *homo sovieticus* syndrome. People preferred backstage dealings and encouraged a 'Robin Hood' ethos of gaining fame by successfully beating the system through shady deals or *kombinacje* (surviving, being smart, cheating, getting to know the system and how to beat it). This cultural practice and its meaning and consequence have implicitly or explicitly been normatively valued rather negatively. For many (Sztompka, 1993) it was seen as impeding Polish modernisation and as an obstacle in post-socialist transition. It was treated as a factor undermining trust in institutions, which many scholars in Poland claim to be the lowest in all Europe. Morawska, on the other hand, takes a less normative approach, linking it with the migratory practices of post-transition Polish working class and argues that today: 'Capitalism based on transnational, decentralised, flexible production of consumer services in areas/sectors of the economy unregulated by legal-institutional frameworks renders some features of the accustomed *homo sovieticus* syndrome into effective strategies of economic action in the new situation' (1998). In discussion of the syndrome in the case of Polish homeless men (Garapich, 2013), I too, call for seeing it as a resistance mechanism, the so-called by James Scott (1990) 'weapon of the weak', a tool subordinate groups employ in order to gain some social and cultural autonomy in

---

1   An anecdote recalled in 2004 by then Polish Consul General (Fieldwork notes).

2   In 2003 an advert on a corner shop in West London proclaimed: 'British passport for sale. Photo can be changed'.

a hostile environment, in particular, the legal-rational environment created by the state.

With time, this 'weapon of the weak' in the case of migration flows to the UK, proved to be rather strong. It facilitated the flow of hundreds of thousands of people into the UK in the few years before 2004. The role of pre-accession networks is emphasised by a rapid growth of a sector of commercial activity, which in scholarship is often referred to as the 'migration industry' (Hernandez, Leo 2005; Garapich, 2008). When the accession states and EU members signed the Associate Members Agreement in 1993, nationals from the Associate Members acquired the right to establish businesses in EU states. The right was interpreted differently in each country, but in Britain it helped Polish migrants to enter the labour market relatively easily from the late 1990s (Düvell, 2004). The process of establishing a business took a considerable amount of time and bureaucratic obstacles had to be overcome, so with market forces at work, a group of immigration advisors emerged – mainly in London – responding to a need for specific services for would-be migrants or migrants needing to prolong their stay. Between 2000 and 2004 this group, to some extent, transformed the behaviour of migrants in their ethnic economic niche. Most of these advisors began as low key, back-door, one-person businesses and they often used a single telephone number and relied on private visits. They were not really professional immigration lawyers but people who had seized an opportunity by helping others to fill out the forms and follow the procedures – for a fee, of course. Within a couple of years some of them emerged as very important social brokers, employers and leaders active in the local Polish public sphere (Garapich, 2008). Research on Poles in London during this period predicted correctly that the self-employment schemes would contribute to the 'deepening of the infrastructure of Polish social relations in London' (Düvell, 2004: 25). Indeed, in the early 2000s around 40 immigration advice offices sprang up in the metropolis. The process had its drawbacks, however, since the migration industry could also exploit newcomers, after all the whole sector was based on an unequal relationship between experts in law and those in need (Miller, Castles, 1993: 26). Some of the Polish advisors quickly developed respectable businesses but others were involved in human smuggling or provided migrants with false documents and broken promises. Clients were often cheated and a significant number of advisors were investigated by New Scotland Yard or the Office of Immigration Service Commission. Some advisors changed venues and businesses names in order to attract new customers when things went wrong.[3]

Between 2001 and 2004 tens of thousands of Polish migrants obtained the so-called 'self-employed visa', which allowed them to legalise their presence, work, pay taxes, take out mortgages, and be freer to participate in Britain's social and

---

3   In late 2003, for example, the Home Office asked the Polish Consulate to accept around three thousand Polish passports that had been submitted with an application for a self-employment visa but could not be processed because the advisor did not have a license or had disappeared (Fieldwork notes).

economic life. The popularity of this avenue for migration is reflected in the Home Office 2003 Immigration Statistics report stating: '2003 saw an increase of 151 per cent in the number of persons granted an extension as a person of independent means or as businessmen to 24,800 … Significant increases occurred in nationals from Poland (up 156 per cent to 9,410)' (Home Office, 2003: 15).

This mixture of informal ties and formal business practices in economies occupied by a foreign labour force is not new, of course. Here, however, advisors were easing the passage from a grey economy into the formal one. From the ambiguous position of being tourists/illegal immigrants/visitors, migrants were entering the legal status of self-employed entrepreneurs. Stretching the rules, negotiating the law and creating precedence were integral to this process. For instance, thousands of identical business plans were produced; the occupations were often fictitious and advisors explicitly shared with the clients the fiction behind the whole scheme, winking every time Home Office was mentioned.[4]

This system was eventually attacked by the right-wing press and Conservative politicians as various scams were uncovered in March 2004, which led to the downfall of the then Minister for Immigration, Beverly Hughes. The scams, described in the press, concerned the practice of acquiring the same visa in Bulgaria, but essentially the technicalities of bending the rules was the same. The situation was not helped by some Polish advisors boasting about doing things which were technically impossible under British law. One of them advertised his ability to 'legalise illegals' in the local Polish press – a sharp shock for any Home Office official, who may have read it. Despite this high degree of informality and rule bending, for this group of immigrant entrepreneurs the system worked rather well. Millions of pounds were generated through a £500 charge for the visa, together with such extras as arranging National Insurance enrolment, setting up a bank account and registering with the Inland Revenue – things that were free for those in the know of course.

In order to understand the cultural dimension of that aspect of the migration process, which involved the creation of transnational migration networks and numerous transnational social fields resisting institutional state actions – in this case restriction on Polish nationals to work and settle – it is crucial to realise that the door to the UK was partly open well before May 2004. Polish nationals were able to enter Britain after 1993 without acquiring a visa prior to leaving. They were normally granted a six-month tourist visa at the port of entry as long as they were able to present a justification for stay and indicate the means of supporting themselves – a practice, which was notoriously stretched and negotiated with a 'beat the system' attitude positively valuing an ability to outmanoeuvre the British immigration authorities. In theory it was enough to have a kin, friend, family member whose name was given to the immigration authorities or a formal

---

4   For example, my own business plan for self-employment visa application was made from a template of a construction worker and the sole change consisted of changing the category of 'builder' into 'journalist'.

invitation from language school. In practice, it meant that entering Britain was relatively easy, at least for those with the right 'connections' or knowledge of the system. In 2002, according to immigration statistics, around 298,000 Poles were allowed entry (Home Office, 2002: 53) and although 147,000 said that they were coming as visitors, the vast majority appeared to end up as undocumented workers. In the year just before the accession, in 2003, the Polish influx further increased, rising to 360,000 (Home Office, 2003: 30). Home Office officials acknowledged that Poles were the most determined in their attempts to come to Britain for employment purposes despite the formal restrictions based on tourist visas and limited employment and social rights. As Franck Düvell notes (2004): 'Polish nationals currently have either been identified by the Immigration Service Enforcement Directorate for its illegal strategies ... . In 1996, Polish nationals came third amongst those being identified for illegal entry'. In 2002 Poles constituted the largest group of foreign nationals, who were refused entry at British ports – 11,670 compared with Jamaicans (6,285) and Filipinos (3,960) (Home Office 2002: 53). These statistics show not only their tremendous stubbornness and innovation but also that, in practice, the British government adopted a laissez-faire attitude towards these flows prior to enlargement. This is why, the decision to open the labour market after May 2004 amounted to a *de facto* regularisation of previously clandestine movements.

Interestingly these flows were also noticed by British policy makers and were crucial in their decision making. According to Jonathan Portes, the then Chief Economist at the Department of Work and Pensions, who advised the British government on the decision whether to open the labour market fully in May 2004, or impose temporal restrictions, the decision was based partially on the fact that Poles would come using the business visa scheme anyway, and that registering them as businessmen would involve much higher administrative costs, so it is better to let them in freely rather than create obstacles which will be costly to manage and which would not prevent them from working and accessing welfare provision anyway.[5] So, what Portes admitted is in fact a victory for Polish migrants breaking the law, that seemed unfair to them and unmanageable to the British state, in other words, *en masse*, Polish migrants managed to shape the institutional framework they were operating in. If one needs a proof of the ability of migrants' agency to influence state actions, we need to look no further. Anti-state resistance not only worked but clearly paid out.

Outmanoeuvring the Taxman

Another example comes from my fieldwork and is embodied in the actions of an entrepreneur I encountered and interviewed several times. He started as someone

---

5   Jonathan Portes made this comment at the Polish Embassy conference 'Labour Mobility in the EU', 4 March 2014, during a Q&A session.

providing business visas back in the early 2000s, and turned into a tax advisor later on. With around a thousand clients on his list, mainly Poles working in the construction industry, he did not hide his willingness to bend the rules as much as possible. When I talked to Robert, he often stressed that the new, post-2004 legal environment offered tremendous possibilities for transnational operations aimed at aiding individuals but not the state. For example, he began to offer small firms based in Poland the possibility to register their legal base in the UK. Small companies in Poland are required to pay tax regardless of whether they make a profit or not and the possibility to register in the UK had strong advantages. Recently this has become a huge issue, as observed by the Polish business press with headlines such as 'Polish business run away from Poland'.[6] One of the directors of companies providing relocations for Polish companies to the UK gave an interview to the Polish press addressing the issue of the ethical implications of his business. Asked whether his actions were not unpatriotic and whether his business contributed to smaller inland revenues for the state, the owner replied:

> I admit that sometimes I am called unpatriotic or a traitor. But we live in united and free Europe and this is what provides such opportunities. The aim of business is to profit and in times of increased competition and high taxes you can only achieve this through lowering the costs. And besides, the businessmen that we help leave the saved money in Poland. They spend it on consumption or investment. I know it may be painful for someone that this money is not helping to build and maintain the grand buildings of ZUS (the Polish Inland Revenue) or clerks' salaries. But is this what the businessmen have to work for?[7]

According to the media, who call the phenomena 'the silent protest of the small business' there are hundreds of companies in Poland offering similar services.[8] Robert has the same attitude towards the state, maybe dressed in less diplomatic language. In fact, disdain for the Polish bureaucracy and ZUS runs deep and Polish migrants often point to its existence as the main reason why they decided to leave (see for example, Iglicka, 2009). In seeking the best of both worlds however, Robert recently moved back to Poland and does the main bulk of his work via the internet. He advises Polish firms to move to the UK and also does tax returns for Polish clients based in the UK. Although there is nothing illegal in what he does, his operations take advantage of European law to the extent that transnationalism becomes not just 'connecting two or more nation states' as traditional literature on transnationalism would have it, but operating in a sphere where contesting and outmanoeuvring nation states legislation becomes the norm and the *rationale* for

---

6   <http://biznesmen.co.uk/index.php/aktualne-wydanie>

7   <http://akademia-internetu.pl/prawo-w-internecie/polskie-biznesy-uciekaja-do-uk-wywiad-z-markiem-niedzwiedziem/>

8   <http://gospodarka.dziennik.pl/news/artykuly/301763,firmy-uciekaja-z-polski-do-anglii.html>

his economic behaviour. Looking at the web, the number of companies in Poland offering similar services is truly massive, prompting the Polish Inland Revenue (ZUS) to speed up the implementation of the 2011/16/UE directive which in effect enables the Polish state to invigilate and control companies run by Polish citizens in other EU states.[9] Judging from the reactions on UK based Polish internet forums, this is widely seen as an attempt by the Polish state to reach for the hard-earned money of Polish migrants. One of the comments (without expletives) for example states: 'so we will have long queues across the EU in front of the naturalisation offices [i.e. Poles changing citizenship]... to drop the chains of this useless citizenship [i.e. Polish one].[10] Describing the relationship between the state and individual in the language of war, battle and unjust harassment of the weak by the powerful is very common in Polish discourse. In this case however, migration and the resulting transnational lifestyle and economic activity becomes one of the very few 'weapons of the weak', individuals can employ in order to stay afloat and retain some form of control over their lives and social autonomy of action. In the last decade, there are two quite potent examples of this weapon being more institutionally mobilised in order to gain an upper hand.

The protest of Polish migrants against double taxation between Poland and the UK is one of the best examples. After some campaigning over the net, the mobilisation moved to the street with a demonstration in front of the Polish Consulate in 2006 (Garapich, 2008), petitions to Polish, British and EU politicians and constant pressure from the media. The issue became quite politicised and Polish migrants engaged in the protest were skilled in using it to their advantage, for example grilling Polish politicians, who came to the UK in their campaign trail before the 2007 parliamentary elections, over the issue.[11] In effect, with surprising speed for Polish legislature, the new legislation has been drafted, debated and voted in.[12] The success of the campaign remains one of the very few examples of mass mobilisation of Polish post-2004 migrants, particularly in the light of general political apathy with regards to engagement in the political process of sending or receiving states (see Driver and Garapich, 2013; Iglicka, 2009; Garapich, 2013; Fiń et al., 2013). The second example involves the legal fight between migrants returning from the UK and the Polish state over the registration of 'Anglicy', which stands for cars with the right-hand steering wheels.[13] The Polish Ministry of Infrastructure prohibited these cars from being registered in

---

9   <http://polemi.co.uk/informacje/finanse-podatki/polski-urzad-skarbowy-chce-szpiegowac-polakow-za-granica-6817>

10   <http://polemi.co.uk/informacje/finanse-podatki/polski-urzad-skarbowy-chce-szpiegowac-polakow-za-granica-6817>

11   <http://www.mojawyspa.co.uk/modules.php?name=News&file=article&sid=20146>

12   <http://glasgow24.pl/?show=full&id=83>

13   <http://regiomoto.pl/portal/aktualnosci/skandal-ze-nie-mozna-rejestrowac-samochodow-z-wielkiej-brytanii>

Poland which prompted the beginning of what is known as the Grzegorz Dorobek case (from the name of Polish migrant who returned to Poland and in 2008 wanted his car registered – case number: C-639/11), an appeal to the European Court of Justice, and the European Commission. In March 2014 the Court decided that the Polish state actions were in breach of the principle of free movement of goods[14] and instructed the Polish government to reverse its decision and allow the car to be registered.[15] The case has been closely watched by the Polish press in the UK[16] along with campaigns, petitions and the collective mobilisation of Polish migrants.[17] Although the Polish state contests that verdict, it is clearly another victory for Polish migrants. This time, it is the involvement of a supranational legal framework that worked to their advantage.

London as Paradise for Informal and Anti-State Resistance

Migrants from Poland are far from unique in navigating through state restrictions and hostile migration regimes and, in fact, there is nothing essentially 'Polish' in using transnational positionality in furthering individual goals. As numerous studies document, transnational migration has a potential to disrupt and contest hegemonic discourses on the nation, the state, integration and assimilation (see above). Previous scholarship has focused on more overt and collective forms of contestation (see for example, Smith and Guarnizo, 1998) which omits the individualised, disorganised and leaderless forms of resistance. But as shown above, migrants from Poland through a combination of historically developed habitus and structural shifts in institutional arrangements granting them freedom to move within the EU – effectively weakening the nation state ability to control mobility – not only took full advantage of that moment of history, but strongly contributed to its embedment in the British social, political and economic landscape. But – and it is an important but – we must not forget this is also an urban landscape. Although migration flows from Poland have been known for their spread all over the UK (Drinkwater et al., 2009), their development in the late 1990s is firmly anchored in London. Crucial for our understanding, is that the main industry employing migrants from Poland was, and still is, around construction and housing services (cleaning, decorating, demolition) not only an industry constantly on the rise and the economic powerhouse of the capital, but importantly, for my argument – one that is notoriously known for operating to some extent in the shadow economy worth around 10 per cent of British GDP (Schneider and Williams, 2013). In other words, Polish, as well as other migrant workers present in the construction industry

---

14   <http://curia.europa.eu/juris/documents.jsf?critereEcli=ECLI:EU:C:2014:173>

15   <http://europa.eu/rapid/press-release_CJE-14-37_en.htm>

16   <http://www.mojawyspa.co.uk/artykuly/23828/Polacy-walcza-o-rejestracje-anglikow>

17   <http://www.polishexpress.co.uk/batalia-o-rejestracje-anglikow/>

in London are not as 'popular' as builders due to their perceived 'hard work ethic' but rather, the industry's flexible attitude to migration and tax regulations regarding self-employment, registration and whole institutional apparatus of the British labour market. It is 'easy' to fit into that industry without formalisation of ones' status. This feature has already been noted by Jordan and Düvell, contrasting it with the more rigid and bureaucratic environment of the German labour market, but it also is a strong feature in the numerous interviews with Polish migrants that I conducted. The attractiveness of British liberal tax and legal regulations Poles praise, usually come up when contrasting with the Polish ones, which are seen as a burden on individual entrepreneurship. Consider for example this self-employed builder asked for a comment on the differences between the Polish and British state attitudes to doing business:

> In making business? Totally different. [...] In Poland people do not understand that to have business flourishing there has to be tolerance to taxes, to the grey area, to bankruptcy and all that ... if they would put these restrictions as are in Poland in the UK, this country would die quickly ... UK understand that it is the middle class of businessmen that oils the wheels of the whole economy and you have to be tolerant towards their actions ...[18]

In his words, tolerance to the 'grey area' in small business is key for the economy to flourish. And the construction industry, where Poles are so much present (both in real numbers as well as in popular imagery of the 'Polish plumber' or the 'Polish builder') in that sense is a perfect site where migrants' perception of London as a neoliberal, free, individualised paradise in which neither the state, nor regulations constrain individual entrepreneurship is made meaningful and practically applied.

Conclusions: From Nation to City

I began the discussion with the anthropological understanding of anti-state resistance Polish migrants are engaged in, mainly manifesting itself as everyday, disorganised ways individuals and their family contest the normatively grounded hegemonic state regulations (related to tax, mobility, labour market). It is not a coincidence that I end with a spatial focus on London, its housing industry tied to the capital's place as the financial global powerhouse, being perceived by many migrants as the idealised place where the state has a limited influence and they can lead their transnational lives away – relatively speaking – from the gaze of the state and taxman. It is tempting thus, to remind ourselves that the city always, historically speaking, gave refuge and means of contestation of the hegemonic structures of oppression – be it slavery, feudalism or nationalism (Flanagan,

18   Interview 36 from ESRC-funded project, Eade J., Drinkwater, S. and Garapich, M. (2006) 'Class and ethnicity: Polish migrants in London'. RES-000-22-1294.

1999). In modern times, the city re-enters important debates on citizenship and belonging. As Rogers notes:

> Current debates on citizenship raise questions about the relationship between membership in some form of community and the formal aspects of citizenship; cities are the sites of the most profound questions of belonging and identity. The assumption of shared community and culture as the basis for citizenship becomes most problematic in the city. Liberal and universalistic formulations face their strongest challenge from communitarian, neo-republican and identity politics formulations of citizenship. It is in the city that the contradictions between universal and differentiated conceptions of citizenship become most evident. (Rogers, 2001: 286)

In the light of my argument, migrants who navigate and contest various forms of structural constraints find London as the place where membership and citizenship are far from categorical prescriptions defining their rights and obligations to a larger collective. Through their transnationally embedded and transnational mode of consciousness (Vertovec, 1999) actions they are able to not just bend the institutional landscape but influence it in a significant way. London with its strong neo-liberal and de-regularised economy and labour market, as well as diversity, allows for maintaining a degree of economic, social and cultural autonomy these migrants crave. This is not to say, they are, in effect, free from structural constraint. Far from it, the inequality, wage disparity, discrimination and increasing anti-European and anti-immigrant political discourse form new frames of limitations people are faced with. However, armed with their habitus, one cannot claim that they are defenceless. It is tempting therefore to position Polish migrants as a new kind of 'counter-national' migrants, who as opposed to the dichotomy used by Bauman of 'global elites and local poor' (1998) or the 'eurostars' crisscrossing Europe (Favell, 2008) successfully use structures provided partially because they have always regarded the state not just in republican terms as a necessary evil, but in almost anarchic terms, as something one can do without, particularly a Polish one. Being able to influence the British migration regime, Polish tax system, laws regarding registration of cars with right-hand drive, and successfully enter and dominate the London construction industry, should not be seen as solely using legal opportunities provided by European integration, but a way social actors use their culturally functional tools to widen their social autonomy versus the state. In that sense, whether Polish migrants will, in the light of potential British exit from the EU, opportunistically begin to apply for British citizenship *en masse*, or engage in more elaborate strategies to hide their earnings from Polish tax payers remains to be seen, but it would be reasonable to expect that they have the skills and attitudes that will help them to do so.

References

Basch, L., Schiller N. and Szanton-Blanc, C. (1994), *Nations Unbound: Transnational Projects, Postcolonial Predicaments and Deterritorialized Nation-States*. Amsterdam: Gordon and Breach.

Bauman, Z. (1994), 'After the patronage state: a model in search of class interests' in Bryan, C.G.A. and Mokrzycki, E. (eds), *The New Great Transformation? Change and Continuity in East-Central Europe*. London and New York: Routledge.

Bauman, Z. (1998), *Globalization: The Human Consequences*. New York: Columbia University Press.

Bhabha, H.K. (1990), 'DissemiNation: Time, Narrative and the Margins of the Modern Nation', Homi K. Bhabha (ed.), *Nation and Narration*. New York: Routledge, pp. 291–322.

Buchowski M., Conte, E. and Ziółkowski, M. (2001), 'Post-war Poland: a presentation', in *Poland beyond Communism. "Transition" in Critical Perspective*. Fribourg: University Press, pp. 9–10.

Buchowski, M. (2004), 'Redefining Work in a Local Community in Poland. Transformation and Class, Culture and Work', in Procoli, A. (ed.) *Workers and Narratives of Survival in Europe: The Management of Precariousness at the End of the Twentieth Century*. Albany: State University of New York Press.

Burrell, K. (2003), 'Small-scale Transnationalism: Homeland Connections and the Polish "Community" in Leicester', *International Journal of Population Geography*, (9)4: 323–35.

Drinkwater S., Eade, J. and Garapich, M. (2009), 'Poles Apart? EU Enlargement and the Labour Market Outcomes of Immigrants in the UK', *International Migration*, 47(1): 161–90.

Düvell, F. (2004), *Highly skilled, self-employed and illegal immigrants from Poland in United Kingdom*. Working Papers, Centre for Migration Studies, Warsaw, <http://www.migracje.uw.edu.pl/obm/pix/054.pdf>

Eade, J., Drinkwater, S. and Garapich, M. (2006), *Class and ethnicity: Polish migrants in London*. RES-000-22-1294 ESRC Project.

Erdmans, M.P. (1992), 'The Social Construction of Emigration as a Moral Issue', *Polish American Studies*, 49(1): 5–25.

Favell, A. (2008), *Eurostars and Eurocities: Free Movement and Mobility in an Integrating Europe*. New Jersey: Wiley-Blackwell.

Fiń A., Legut A., Mazurek K., Nowak W., Nowosielski M. and Schöll-Mazurek K. (2013), *Polityka polonijna w ocenie jej wykonawców i adresatów*. Poznań: Instytut Zachodni.

Flanagan, W. (1999), *Urban Sociology: Images and Structures*. Boston, MA: Allyn and Bacon.

Garapich, M. (2012), *Between Cooperation and Hostility – Constructions of Ethnicity and Social Class among Polish Migrants in London*. Kraków: Studia Sociologica.

Garapich, M. (2008), 'The Migration Industry and Civil Society: Polish Immigrants in the United Kingdom Before and After EU Enlargement', *Journal of Ethnic and Migration Studies*, 34(5): 735–52.

Garapich, M. (2008a), 'Odyssean Refugees, Migrants and Power: Construction of the "Other" within the Polish Community in the United Kingdom', in Reed-Danahay, D. and Brettell, C. (eds), *Citizenship, Political Engagement and Belonging: Immigrants in Europe and the United States*. New Brunswick: Rutgers University Press, pp. 124–44.

Garapich, M. (2013), 'Polska kultura migracyjna po 2004 roku – między zmianą a tradycją', in Lesińska, M. and Okólski, M. (eds), *Współczesne polskie migracje: strategie – skutki społeczne – reakcja państwa*. Warszaw: Studia Migracyjne, WUW, pp. 17–35.

Garapich, M. (2014), '*Homo sovieticus* revisited – anti-institutionalism, alcohol and resistance among Polish homeless men in London', *International Migration*, 52(1), pp. 100–117.

Glick Schiller, N. and Karagiannis, E. (2006), 'Contesting Claims to the Land: Pentecostalism as a Challenge to Migration Theory and Policy', *Sociologus* 36(2).

Home Office (2002), 'Control of Immigration Statistics'. London: The Stationery Office.

Home Office (2003), 'Control of Immigration Statistics'. London: The Stationery Office.

Irek, M. (2011), 'The Myth of 'Weak Ties' and the Ghost of the Polish Peasant: Informal Networks of Polish Post-Transition Migrants in the UK and Germany'. COMPASS Working Paper, No. 87. Oxford: University of Oxford <https://www.compas.ox.ac.uk/fileadmin/files/Publications/working_papers/WP_2011/WP1187%20Irek.pdf>

Iglicka, K (2007), 'Introduction' in Kicinger, A. and Weinar, A. (eds), *State of the art of the migration research in Poland*. Central European Forum for Migration and Population Research CEFMR Working Paper 1/2007.

Iglicka, K. (2009), *Kontrasty migracyjne Polski*. Warsaw: Wydawnictwo Naukowe Scholar.

Jaźwińska, E. and Okólski, M. (2001), (eds), *Ludzie na huśtawce. Migracje między peryferiami Polski a Zachodu*. Warsaw: Scholar.

Jordan, B. and Düvell, F. (1999), 'Undocumented Migrants in London'. Full Research Report; Economic and Social Research Council R000236838: <http://www.esrcsocietytoday.ac.uk/esrcinfocentre/viewawardpage.aspx?awardnumber=R000236838>

Jordan, B. (2002), *Migrant Polish Workers in London: Mobility, Labour Market and the Prospects for Democratic Development*. Paper given at the conference 'Beyond Transition: Development Perspectives and Dilemmas'. Warsaw 12–13 April 2002.

Massey, D. and Pren, K. (2012), 'Unintended Consequences of US Immigration Policy: Explaining the Post-1965 Surge from Latin America', *Population Development Review*, 38(1): 1–29.

Miller, M. and Castles, S. (1993), *The Age of Migration: International Population Movements in the Contemporary World*. London: Macmillan, p. 26.

Modzelewski, K. (2014), *Zajeździmy kobyłę historii. Wyznania poobijanego jeźdźca.* Warsaw: Iskry.

Morawska, E. (1998), 'The Malleable *Homo Sovieticus*: Transnational Entrepreneurs in Post-Communist East Europe'. EUI Working Papers. RSC No 98/53. Badia Fiesolana, San Domenico 1998.

Nagengast, C. (1991), *Reluctant Socialists, Rural Entrepreneurs: Class, Culture and the Polish State.* Boulder, CO: Westview Press.

Rogers A. (2001), 'Citizenship, Multiculturalism and the Multicultural European City', in Bridge, G. and Watson, E. (eds), *A Companion to the City.* London: Blackwell.

Schneider, F. and Williams C. (2013), *The Shadow Economy*. London: The Institute of Economic Affairs.

Scott, J.C. (1990), *Domination and the Art of Resistance: Hidden Transcripts.* New Haven, CT: Yale University Press.

Smith, M.P. and Guarnizo, L.E. (1998), 'Transnationalism From Below', *Comparative Urban and Community Research, Volume 6.* New Brunswick: Transaction Publishers.

Sztompka, P. (1993), 'Civilizational Incompetence: The Trap of Post-Communist Societies', in *Zeitschrift fur Soziologie*, 2: 85–95.

Vertovec, S. (1999) 'Migrant Transnationalism and Modes of Transformation', *International Migration Review*, 38(3): 970–1001.

Wedel, J. (1986), *The Private Poland: An Anthropological Look at Everyday Life.* New York: Columbia University Press.

Ziółkowski, M. (2001), 'Changes of Interests and Values of Polish Society', in *Poland Beyond Communism: "Transition" in Critical Perspective*, pp. 161–79.

Chapter 10

Latin London: Negotiating Invisibility among Latin Americans in London

Cathy McIlwaine

Introduction

It has long been recognised that a multicultural city such as London comprises complex and dynamic cartographies underpinned by waves of migration that fashion the nature, function and boundaries of the city in economic, political, cultural and social ways. The ways in which those living in the city are at once visible and invisible are mutable. Global cities in particular both welcome and reject arrivals in ways that influence the visibility of new migrant groups (as well as more established ethnic minorities). This chapter explores the experiences of one of London's newest and fastest growing migrant groups in the city. Although Latin Americans have been arriving for several decades, since 2000 they have emerged as an important new population that make-up a substantial element of 'super-diverse' London. The discussion engages with conceptualisations of visibility among migrants, in part because the research on which the chapter is based draws on a report entitled *No Longer Invisible* (McIlwaine et al., 2011), and also because visibility has become an important dimension of the nomenclature for migrants and ethnic minority groups in the city more widely. In particular, it examines the ambiguities surrounding the presence of Latin Americans where on the one hand, they need and demand to be recognised, yet on the other hand, it is often in their interests to remain invisible, especially in cases where they are irregular. It examines the ways in which the community has been constructed over time, as well as the range of invisibility practices developed from below by Latin Americans before concluding with a brief discussion of the ethnic recognition campaign.

Exploring (In)visibility and Migration in the City

It has long been acknowledged that the city has provided a home for the 'unknowable' and the 'stranger' who are often migrants or recent arrivals (Keith, 2005: 15). In turn, the notion of visibility has been attributed to migrant populations in various ways in different places and over time. In the British and North American contexts, invisibility was originally mainly linked with race relations debates and especially as a way of outlining patterns and processes of marginalisation among black populations (see Bryce-Laporte, 1972 on the US; Macdonald and Macdonald, 1972 on Great Britain). Subsequently, the term has broadened to include a wide range of nationality groups such as Italians in the UK (Fortier, 2006) and Syrians in Lebanon (Chalcraft, 2009) and groups of nationalities such as Arabs in the US (Naber, 2010). As well as immigration status and race, invisibility has also been used to describe female migrants in general (Kofman, 1999) and in specific situations (Ghorashi, 2010 on Islamic women in the Netherlands). In turn, invisible migrants have been denoted as 'non-European refugees, European minority refugees (such as Roma), internally displaced persons, self-settled refugees, and urban refugees in Africa' (Polzer and Hammond, 2008: 419).

Therefore, which migrants are invisible varies considerably according to nationality, race gender, sexuality and other intersecting social identities. Yet, certain migrants are invisible to some and not to others and in diverse ways depending on the context. It is thus important to ask why migrants have been cast as invisible and the role that such invisibility plays in their lives especially in relation to wellbeing. As such, visibility reflects not just a particular situation but rather is the result of a dynamic process whereby invisibility can be enforced from above or invoked from below in complex and intersecting ways. Indeed, drawing on Foucault's notion of disciplinary power exercised through invisibility, Polzer and Hammond (2008: 418) argue that power relations underpin invisibility because it is created and maintained by those who control resources in a given society. This means that visibility can be withheld by those with power for a range of reasons that might include visibility as threat where certain populations might be viewed as threatening the status quo or notions of racial or ethnic harmony by highlighting their presence (Keith, 2005: 78–9 on the black population in London). In addition, limiting visibility can also act to potentially reduce demands for services on those who control them. Accommodations around visibility can also be made between states and migrants in what Pugh (2011) in relation to Colombian refugees in Ecuador calls an 'invisibility bargain'. This is where refugees are allowed to stay in the country in return for social and political invisibility, even if this effectively means that their rights are ignored.

The extent to which the invisible can claim some rights to visibility can also be seen through various resistance and protest strategies that have been important in ensuring recognition through a range of means, whether collective and/or individual. In relation to Palestinians, Feldman (2008), maps the creation of their 'visibility field' (p. 508) that comprises the evolution of material objects into symbols of visibility such as keys to houses still owned on Palestinian land from which they have been displaced that are then projected as powerful images during protest demonstrations and the use of humanitarian documents such as ration cards to mark visibility and also to make claims to nationhood. While these types of practices can be used to promote visibility in a positive way, they can also simultaneously exploit and bring shame to the invisible.

The ambivalence surrounding visibility is perhaps most clearly illustrated in terms of migrants with irregular immigration status. Not only is the categorisation of migrants according to how they have entered a country heavily contested, but those without official authorisation to reside are invariably criminalised and denied their rights (Anderson and Ruhs, 2010). While terms used include 'irregular', 'undocumented', 'illegal' and 'unauthorised', a key dimension of descriptions of these types of migrants relates to visibility. Some terms imply invisibility such as 'non-status' (Goldring, Berinstein, and Bernhard, 2009), while others are more explicit such as Coutin's (2000: 30) suggestion that these migrants live in a situation of 'nonexistence' that entails a social space of 'forced invisibility, exclusion, subjugation, and repression' (see also De Genova, 2002). For irregular migrants in particular, their invisibility is necessary and useful in order to ensure that they can not only enter a country but that they can continue to reside there under the radar of the authorities (McIlwaine, 2015).

Immigration status is also not the only form of social categorisation that influences which migrants are constructed as invisible or not. While it has long been acknowledged that such categories are socially constructed representations of a certain reality (Anthias, 1998), some migrants will be more visible than others depending on their gender, race, nationality, as noted above. In turn, it feeds into the politics of representation in terms of how data about migrants is constructed, how group claims are made and how the notion of community is manipulated (Polzer, 2008). Indeed, migrant communities which are themselves rarely homogenous and cohesive in themselves will unevenly exclude or invisibilise some potential members and include others from the same nationality or ethnic group. Such ethnic spaces comprising migrants with some shared characteristics therefore have porous boundaries and often high levels of discord within them (Werbner, 2002). These spaces and places will also have strangers in their midst who may be visible at some points in time or in some spaces and invisible in others (Calhoun, 2002).

These conceptualisations around invisibility as paradoxical are especially pertinent to the Latin American population in London. As a recent, yet fast-growing group, Latin Americans are emerging as an important population who are on the one hand, demanding visibility in a range of ways, yet on whom visibility has sometimes been imposed and sometimes been chosen. The discussion now turns to explore these issues in relation to the empirical realities of the population drawing on a range of sources and projects.[1]

---

1 The main project on which this chapter draws entailed a survey of 1,041 questionnaires with a wide range of different Latin American nationalities from across the socio-economic spectrum as well as 50 in-depth interviews, 3 focus groups and a series of 15 interviews with community representatives. The project was conducted between 2009 and 2010 (McIlwaine et al., 2011). It also refers to an earlier project that comprised in-depth interviews conducted with 28 Colombians, 22 Ecuadorians and 20 Bolivians in London together with 3 focus groups and 10 interviews with community representatives between 2006 and 2007 (McIlwaine, 2007).

Constructing a Latin American Community in London

As noted briefly above, Latin Americans effectively represent one of London's 'new migrant groups' who have contributed to London's marked 'super-diversity' (Vertovec, 2007). This super-diversity has been aptly characterised as resulting in a move away from large-scale migration from Commonwealth nations towards the migration of people from a more diverse range of countries. In turn, these migrants are usually ethnically and linguistically varied with diverse immigration statuses and often with few previous ties with the UK. They are also transnationally constituted through a wide array of financial, social and cultural ties back home (ibid.). Of particular importance in relation to Latin Americans is that as a group or community they are internally super-diverse in relation to nationality, year of arrival, immigration status and class position. This in turn, has created a stratified community with uneven patterns of cohesion and levels of integration, the latter conceptualised according to the British government's notion of citizenship attainment and English language skills (McIlwaine, 2011).

Despite this internal diversity, Latin Americans as a group have slowly become a visible presence in the city, especially since the 1980s. However, the history of the Latin American population in the city has been much longer. At various historical junctures since the independence struggles in Spanish America, London has provided refuge for liberation leaders, diplomats, writers, artists, political exiles and commercial traders from many Latin American countries as well as a temporary home for the elites in pursuit of education and leisure (Decho and Diamond, 1998). But it was only from the 1970s onwards that Latin Americans, and specifically Colombians arrived in any numbers. The latter arrived to work in catering and cleaning, first with work permits and subsequently through a range of routes including family reunion, as students and claiming asylum as a result of the armed conflict that worsened markedly in the 1990s. Another important but smaller flow that was initiated in the 1970s comprised political exiles mainly from Chile, but also from Uruguay, Argentina, and Colombia. Although the proportion of exiles included in the research was limited, seven per cent identified political factors as being the main reason they left Latin America. For example, the proportion leaving for political reasons is much lower (seven per cent) and is concentrated among Chileans, Colombians and Ecuadorians. For example, Consuela who was 61 years old and had been living in the UK for 34 years recalled:

> I had a quiet life, I worked, I looked after my girls, I had a normal life until the military coup in Chile in 1973 when everything changed completely. After that my personal life and that of my children and ex-husband changed completely and we had to come to England in 1975 to flee persecution.

Since the 1990s, increasing numbers of Ecuadorians, Peruvians and Argentineans arrived and more recently since 2000, Bolivians and Brazilians. This was mainly for economic reasons, but was also linked with political and social factors. The closure of many routes to the United States after 9/11 in 2001 coupled with increasing levels of inequality and poverty linked with neoliberal economic policies across the region has also contributed to Latin Americans searching for alternative destinations. While those migrating for economic reasons are often concentrated in the lower socio-economic groups, there has also been an increase in student and professional migration, linked partly with the introduction of managed migration policies focused on skilled migration. Indeed, the main reasons cited in the survey research as to why Latin Americans left their homeland was lack of economic or professional opportunities at home and/or the prospect of better opportunities abroad (43 per cent). For example, Viviana, a 47-year-old from Colombia who had lived in London since 1978 working as a teacher complained that she could barely get by back home economically:

> I worked three shifts as a teacher. I left my house at 6 in the morning and I got home at 11 at night, every day. The shifts were really hard and we also worked Saturdays. I did this because in every school that I worked they only paid the minimum ... So I said to myself: "with my abilities in another country I will be paid a dignified wage and I'm going to live well and also not have to beg someone for a letter of recommendation".

Education and language acquisition were also important in that more than one-fifth left Latin America for educational reasons (22 per cent), either to learn English or to pursue further studies, and was especially related with those who worked in professional and managerial jobs. In addition, social or family reasons prompted 16 per cent to migrate, mainly to join other family members or to join friends or relatives who had already migrated but also due to family conflict. For example, Serafina, 40 years old and from Ecuador had lived in London since 1996. Although Serafina's parents had migrated to England in 1990 for economic reasons, she never planned to leave Ecuador. However, she and her husband began to have marital problems and she saw migration as a way of dealing with their personal problems (McIlwaine et al., 2011).

Onward migration of Latin Americans moving from other southern European countries has also been extremely important since 2008 as a result of the global economic downturn that has markedly affected these nations' economies. More than a third (36.5 per cent) of Latin Americans had previous experience of migration before arriving in the UK, with most arriving from Spain (38 per cent). This was especially important for Ecuadorian and Colombian migrants; almost three-quarters of Ecuadorians and half of Colombians who had resided elsewhere before travelling to the UK had previously lived in Spain. This reflects wider migration processes in Spain which has a very large Latin American migrant population, a large proportion of whom have become EU citizens through length of residency as well as a series of regularisation programmes throughout the 2000s. While flows from Spain to the UK were firmly established before the economic downturn, they accelerated markedly as the crisis led to unemployment and widespread dissatisfaction with working conditions in construction and agriculture for men and care work and domestic service for women which in turn, was further exacerbated by a perception of racism against Latin Americans. For instance, Ana from Ecuador noted:

> In Spain if you are *latino*, if you are foreign you are excluded a little more; they don't look at the quality of your work, but rather the appearance of it. I think that there, it's hard for *latinos* to get on; the majority work in construction and cleaning and it's very hard to work in an office or a bank. There is too much discrimination.

Migration via Italy was also an important gateway to the UK, especially for Brazilians and Argentinians who could apply for European passports on the basis of their Italian ancestry (which is relatively easy to establish). Yaritza, for example, was 45 and arrived in London in 2008 after spending 3 months in Italy applying for an Italian passport. She was not keen to stay in Italy as there were few job opportunities and she was not interested in having to learn Italian; instead, she wanted to learn English which she felt was more useful. She had been working as a cleaner earning the minimum wage since she arrived (see McIlwaine 2012 for further discussion; also below).

While these flows effectively created the Latin American population in London, the issue of visibility and size has been more contested. From the mid-2000s onwards, a series of estimates about the size of the community were published, few of which were based on empirical reality. Instead, a series of guesses initially identified by community activists who were keen to ensure that Latin Americans were recognised as an important population became enshrined in more official documents. For example, a Foreign and Commonwealth Office (FCO, 2007: 5) report that suggested that there were between 700,000 and 1,000,000 was based on an online article by an oral historian who openly admitted that she was guessing the numbers (McIlwaine 2007). According to the census, there were just over 4,000 Latin Americans in England and Wales in 1951 with an increase to 17,000 in 1991 (Miller, 1998: 8). In 2001, there were 46,325 and by 2011, a total of 138,197 were recorded of which 82,771 or 60 per cent were living in London. While this shows a clear growth in the population, it is also widely acknowledged that the census is an underestimate of the actual size mainly on the basis of under-recording of irregular populations, albeit not to the extent suggested by the FCO and acknowledging that the 2001 census officially accounts for those without regular status. Related with this, the *No Longer Invisible* report attempted the first robust estimate that included regular, irregular and second generation Latin Americans in London. Based on the Annual Population Survey for 2008, this identified 113,578 Latin Americans in London including 17,100 irregular migrants and 17,182 second generation based on 2008 figures. This made them roughly the same size as the Polish and ethnic Chinese in London at the time and represents 61 per cent of the British Latin American population as a whole which was estimated at 186,500 (McIlwaine et al. 2011: 15).

In terms of the geographies of invisibility as to where Latin Americans live in London, residence tends to be dispersed despite concentrations in Southwark, Lambeth and Haringey. Indeed, Latin Americans in London are effectively a 'community without propinquity' (Webber 1964 cited in Zelinsky and Lee, 1998: 288) characterised by heterolocalism (ibid.; Winders, 2012). This affects their visibility in that they do not congregate overwhelmingly in a specific ethnic neighbourhood, a situation not uncommon in London where multicultural communities are more likely the norm (Keith, 2005). None the less, Latin Americans have increasingly created a series of institutions, spaces and services that specifically serve their community and which often have marked physical presences in the boroughs mentioned above. However, it is also important to recognise that the construction of a community among Latin Americans has been complex and contested. As noted above, Latin Americans comprise a stratified and super-diverse group who at times represent a unified front in relation to such issues as ethnic recognition, while at others emerge as a community riven with divisions and conflicts. Yet despite not being universally homogenous or cohesive, they can still be referred to as a community in terms of comprising people who originate from the same continent, share a language (with the exception of Brazilians) and a loose set of cultural and social affinities (see Kivisto, 2001 for a conceptual discussion).

As an emergent ethnic group, Latin Americans have constructed what Cock (2011) in relation to the Colombian community in London refers to as a series of 'ethnic publics' which are effectively ethnic spaces that often but not always translate as territory and locality but which are predominantly predicated on social networks and relations (Werbner, 2002). For instance, from the 1980s onwards, a range of civil society organisations serving Latin Americans emerged. Although most current migrant organisations were first established to campaign against military dictatorships in Latin America they have subsequently evolved into service-providers for those residing in London. These included the Campaign Against Repression in Latin America which became Carila, Latin American Welfare Group, the Chile Democrático group that became Indo-American Migrant and Refugee Organisation (IRMO), the Latin American Women's Rights Service as well as the Latin American Advisory Committee which was important in the creation of Latin American House (Cock, 2009). At the same time, other spaces also emerged such as the football pitch in Clapham Common, which became a meeting point for the community. Nightclubs, cafes and shops were increasingly established and became more common during this period and into the 1990s (McIlwaine et al., 2011).

Since then, Latin American organisations, businesses, media and events have burgeoned in London. Today there are commercial hubs for Brazilians in the Willesden area and for Spanish speaking Latin Americans in Elephant and Castle and in Seven Sisters (even if both of the latter are under threat from developers). There are several media outlets in the form of newspapers in both Spanish (*Express News*, *Extra*) and Portuguese (*Brazilian News*, *Leros*) and large scale events such as the Carnaval del Pueblo which is a Latin summer carnival held in Burgess Park in South London and which is reported to be the largest Latin American festival in Europe which has been running for 16 years. Arguably these places, spaces and institutions have been central in the creation of the Latin American community especially in terms of encouraging the emergence of an ethnic discourse and identity as well as establishing the visibility of the community in the urban landscape.

Yet, these spaces are often zones of conflict and ambivalence as well as support, again highlighting the contradictions inherent in processes of visibilising a migrant community. For example, although there is widespread participation in Latin American cultural events such as carnivals with almost two-thirds attending the summer carnivals such as the Carnaval del Pueblo (63 per cent), they tended to be more likely to be attended by those lower down the socio-economic ladder (see also McIlwaine and Bermudez, 2011). In addition, levels of use of commercial spaces was very high (85 per cent) with most accessing cafes or restaurants, buying food and ingredients, sending money home or using hairdressers. Consuela from Chile said that these places were really important for people: 'Well, it's important for the community to maintain their products, their customs'. This is reflected in the fact that shopping centres also played a social function for Latin Americans with community meetings and events being held there. Yet others held much more ambivalent perspectives in terms of fearing the risk of exposure to deportation among irregular migrants or being subject to gossip (see also below). For example, Rosa from Bolivia stated:

> I don't go to Latin places because I'm afraid that they'll do something to me. I never go to Latin restaurants or clubs, I practically don't leave my house except to go shopping ... Places like Elephant and Castle are full of immigration these days and they are detaining and deporting people who go there ... I've had very bad experiences with Latin people because of envy, people trying to take my job, they like to gossip about illegals.

Thus people related to these spaces and places with varying levels of intensity and approbation that was dependent on social identity and immigration status in particular. While Rosa's words highlight the plight of irregular migrants, those from higher social class positions were often disparaging about the 'popular' characteristics of many commercial spaces and engaged only sporadically and instrumentally with them (Cock, 2011). Nationality also played a part with some spaces more associated with certain nationalities more than others. While Colombians and Ecuadorians often vied for control over some spaces as two most numerous Spanish-speaking nationality groups, Brazilians often disassociated themselves from being Latin Americans in the first place. For example, only 44 per cent of Brazilians identified as Latin American, compared with over 70 per cent among all Spanish-speaking nationalities. They were also the least likely to celebrate any of the cultural activities with only one-third attending summer carnivals. This is also reflected in the fact that there tends to be different organisations serving each set of language groups and different commercial and cultural outlets. In a focus group of six Brazilians, one person noted:

> I don't know if I feel [like a Latin American], I also think it is more to do with accepting it than feeling it. For instance, if I have to tick a box about my profile and I see 'British' and all the others, and also 'Latino', then I'll tick this box, but I think it is important to note that I have let this happen to me, I know very little about the countries in South America, I have never visited, I feel there is little integration amongst us.

Other Brazilians stated that they felt that Latin American was a derogatory term, as noted by Sandra: 'it is because of the status of the region, when you talk about Latin American the first thing that always comes to my mind is Colombia, yes I think of their dress, the ponchos, the hats'. Indeed, Brazilian women in particular were more likely to reject their Latin American identity and assert being Brazilian, partly because they were more likely to be working in professional occupations than their male counterparts who accepted their marginalised status more readily (Datta and McIlwaine, 2014).

All these ambiguities serve to highlight the contested nature of the community and also how the visibility of migrant groups in the city can be negotiated and played out in different, often contradictory ways. This is especially marked when entering the country in the first instance and through regularisation practices to which the chapter now turns.

Practising Invisibility through Entry and Settlement

Reflecting Polzer and Hammond's (2007) point about invisibility being both imposed from above and emerging from below with gains and losses accrued to those in control and to the powerless, for some migrants invisibility provides a useful way of manipulating increasingly punitive migration regimes. In the case of the UK, immigration policy has been restrictive since the 1960s as attempts were made to curb Commonwealth immigration even if the reality has been relatively large scale migration, permitted mainly due to labour shortages. More recently though, ever more draconian measures have been put in place which have also led to an increase in irregular migration to the UK (Bloch, Sigona and Zetter 2011; Wills et al., 2010). As noted above, irregular migrants are not only invisible in national accounting and statistics, but such migrants themselves negotiate their invisibility as a means to enter and to remain in the country in complex ways. However, as I have argued elsewhere (McIlwaine, 2015), this negotiation entails the creation of webs of regularity and irregularity that challenge binary and hierarchical understandings of legality that are underpinned by invisibility. Migrants can move in and out of regularity, sometimes because of impositions from above in terms of changing immigration legislation but also because of complex practices enacted by migrants themselves in ways that reflect the exercise of their agency (Cvajner and Sciortino, 2010). These practices or 'tactics' act as mechanisms to avoid risk and/or deal with exclusion (Datta et al., 2007) as well as reflecting forms of resistance and protest (Ellerman 2010). While much research to date has focused on the practices of irregular migrants in particular (Broeders and Engbersen, 2007), it is important to include migrants across the spectrum of regularity for the reasons relating to the dynamism and complexity of what being irregular really means. Drawing on a typology I have outlined elsewhere (McIlwaine, 2015), I argue that entry and regularisation of migrants revolve around a series of spatial, economic and social invisibility practices. Although I have previously foregrounded the mutability of immigration status and the creation of webs over hierarchies, here, I highlight the role of invisibility as foundational for how these practices function in the case of Latin Americans in London or what I refer to as 'practising invisibility'.

Practising Invisible Entry

Among Latin Americans in the London, the vast majority (97 per cent) entered the UK with valid documentation. Almost two-thirds entered with a tourist or student visa or their home country passport and no visa. One-fifth entered with papers that allowed them to settle, such as EU passports (17 per cent). Importantly in relation to the notion of super-diversity noted above, there were marked variations by country of birth in how people entered. For instance, Bolivians were the most likely to enter as tourists or visitors (75 per cent), whereas Colombians were the most likely to arrive with student visas (32 per cent). In turn, Brazilians and Ecuadorians were the most likely to enter the UK with EU passports (a quarter in each case). In terms of actual immigration status, 19 per cent admitted to having no valid documents with a quarter having British passports, and another 19 per cent holding EU passports. Again, this varied according to nationality with Brazilians and Bolivians being the most likely to be irregular (38 per cent and 36.5 per cent) while Colombians were the least likely (6 per cent). In addition, Peruvians and Colombians were most likely to hold British passports (38 per cent and 37 per cent) while Brazilians had the highest levels of EU passport ownership (31 per cent). There were also important gender differences in immigration status in that women were more likely to have British citizenship (30 per cent of all women compared with 20 per cent of men) whereas men were more likely than women to be irregular (22 per cent of men compared with 16 per cent of women) (McIlwaine et al., 2011; also McIlwaine, 2010 on gender issues).

It is therefore clear that negotiating immigration status as well as visibility is strongly differentiated by nationality among Latin Americans. This also intersects with the histories and geographies of the migration regime in the UK which has over time gradually introduced visa restrictions as the government recognised the arrival of significant flows from particular countries, as well as with a range of other social identities. From an historical perspective, the issue of visibility in the

1970s and 1980s pertained mainly to the fact that Latin Americans were a small population group with a very low profile in the city. The majority entered legally with work permits or through asylum claims and it was only in the 1990s that visibility and invisibility became an issue for the community. On the one hand, they became more visible through their burgeoning presence (see above), but on the other, the channels of entry that were possible to transform relatively easily into settlement declined dramatically requiring migrants to develop practices of invisibility and concealment.

Indeed, in relation to the latter, migrants often had to literally learn how to practice invisibility as their own immigration status changed, often over relatively short time periods. For example, Juliana was 50 years old and from Bolivia. She had migrated to London in 2005 with her husband in order to provide for the education of their six children. After being advised by a travel agency in Bolivia to go to London, they arrived with tourist visas after which Juliana's husband secured a student visa that permitted her to be his dependent. However, in 2007, the government tightened entry requirements for migrants in general preventing entry on tourist visas and conversion into student permits, with entry visas for Bolivians specifically being imposed in 2009. As a result of these processes, Juliana and her husband became overstayers and therefore irregular. From 2007 onwards, they had to live and work (as cleaners) illegally and ultimately invisibly.

Some Latin Americans developed entry practices of concealment of identity that took on two main forms linked with onward or 'transit migration' (Collyer, Düvell and De Haas, 2010). At a general level, the large and growing flows arriving with EU passports, mainly from Spain but also from Italy and Portugal mean that it is increasingly difficult to identify Latin Americans unless they state their country of birth because they arrive as European citizens.[2] Many arrived legally through legitimate regularisation programmes while others arrived in a more clandestine manner. In terms of the former, 47-year-old Ronaldo from Ecuador had lived in Spain for 10 years before moving to London in 2008. He first left Ecuador because he separated from his wife entering Spain with a tourist visa and subsequently living in an irregular situation. However, the boss of the factory where he worked in Zaragoza sorted out his regularisation papers and he managed to obtain a Spanish passport which he then used to move to London.

Others arrived through a range of illegitimate networks as part of the 'foggy social structures' that facilitate entry of migrants without detection and rendering them invisible (Broeders and Engbersen, 2007). This entailed purchasing false passports for between US$800 and $2000 and were those of naturalised Latin Americans which allowed people to 'manipulate their identity' (Engbersen, 2001).

---

2   Confusion and obfuscation between country of birth and nationality is exacerbated by the fact that some official statistics such as the International Passenger Survey and the Labour Force Survey use nationality to denote origin while the census and the Annual Population Survey use country of birth (and nationality in the case of the census) (McIlwaine, et al., 2011).

Sometimes, passports were bought permanently, at others they were 'rented' for one entry only. For example, Manolo who was 42 years old and from Colombia bought a false Spanish passport during a two-week stay in Madrid on his way to London. He noted how he bought it from an Ecuadorian in Barcelona who gave him the passport and bus tickets that took him to Belgium after which he arrived in the UK on the Eurostar train.

A smaller but important minority were more explicitly smuggled into the country, arriving completely invisibly. Clara from Colombia recalled how although she managed to enter the UK with a false Spanish passport, her boyfriend was queried trying to use one at Madrid airport after which he panicked and fled the airport. After waiting for two months in Spain, Clara reported how he paid a smuggler who arranged for his entry in the back of a lorry via France. She remembered how 'he was smuggled in. He said it was horrible, he could hear the police sniffer dogs outside the lorry. When he got here he cried from happiness and from nerves'.

Also important is that visibility is mutable and intersects closely with changes in immigration status. As such, some migrants might arrive in an invisible manner but they become more visible as they negotiate their settlement and regularisation. Edilma from Colombia, for example, discussed how she and her husband recruited a smuggler in Bogotá after they had their visa applications turned down and who sold them false passports which facilitated their entry via Spain. While their entry was concealed and invisible, they had managed to become British citizens via making an asylum claim that was eventually granted through the family amnesty in 2002 with the help of a migrant organisation.[3] Indeed, negotiating regularity in some form and hence practising invisibility was experienced by a large proportion of Latin Americans. For instance, although 43 per cent entered on a tourist visa, only 20 (two per cent) reported having one at the time of survey. Similarly, while only 3 per cent entered without valid documents, 19 per cent ended up without them.

Practising Invisible Settlement

Both regular and irregular migrants negotiate various forms of isolation, invisibility and identity manipulation after they enter and attempt to settle through a series of 'residence strategies' (Engbersen, 2001). These entail various forms of 'everyday politics of mystification' (Broeders and Engbersen, 2007) and 'identity-stripping' (Ellerman, 2010) that revolve around spatial, economic and social invisibility practices.

---

3   The Family Amnesty programme of 2002 gave asylum claimants with at least one dependent child in the UK and who had claimed before 2 October 2002 the right to apply for Indefinite Leave to Remain subsequently giving them full rights to remain and work in the UK.

For Latin Americans in London, the main invisibility practice adopted by irregular migrants was to limit spatial mobility in order to maintain a low profile by the immigration authorities. These invariably involved staying close to home, limiting use of public transport, and avoiding places where the authorities were known to frequent such as the various markets (Elephant and Castle and Seven Sisters) (see also Roman-Velasquez, 2009). Alba's case illustrates this; she arrived in London from Bolivia in 2005 with a tourist visa for herself and her two children to join her husband who migrated a year before (he had already obtained British citizenship). Alba's tourist visa expired leaving her and her children in an irregular position. This has severe psycho-social effects as she commented: 'I am ill from nerves, I'm very stressed, everything gets to me, and unfortunately I can't go to the doctor because I'm illegal … I'm so scared that I'll be caught and arrested and deported'. As a result, Alba was too afraid to travel anywhere beyond her children's local primary school, she never used public transport and said she felt like a prisoner in her home which was a hostel room.

Economic invisibility practices were mobilised among irregular migrants in order to access the labour market. A host of unorthodox mechanisms were developed to negotiate an increasingly restrictive labour market. These included the purchase of false working visas or passports and false National Insurance (social security) numbers which could be purchased, borrowed or rented. In addition, irregular migrants sometimes worked under the names of regular workers who had since left employment, with deals often done around sharing bank accounts (see also Datta, 2012). These economic invisibility practices also reflect how irregularity is functional to the wider economy in that such processes maintain a flexible, low-paid labour force that underpins what has been identified as the 'migrant division of labour' (Wills et al., 2010) where migrants end-up being concentrated in the lower echelons of the labour market in jobs that others are unwilling to do. Furthermore, these invisible irregular migrants also invariably contribute tax and National Insurance as they work in the formal economy despite being unrecognised (three-quarters of all Latin Americans pay tax and National Insurance regardless of their immigration status).

Indeed, the notion of visibility is important for all Latin Americans in London in relation to their important economic contributions more widely. Not only do they have very high rates of employment (85 per cent) which is much higher than for the population as a whole or for the foreign-born population as a whole, but almost half of all working Latin American migrants work in elementary occupations (47 per cent) such as in cleaning, catering, hotels and as security guards. This often reflects a process of dramatic downward occupational mobility in that a very small proportion of Latin Americans worked in elementary jobs in their home countries, yet on arrival, 70 per cent ended-up employed in such activities. This was also linked with the fact that Latin Americans are very well-educated with 70 per cent having achieved some form of education beyond secondary level. Therefore, their education and qualifications invariably remain invisible to employers because of immigration status or lack of English language proficiency.

The nature of the work that many Latin Americans undertake in London's labour market is also highly invisible, especially among those working in the cleaning sector. Many worked on a part-time basis (one-third overall but half of those in personal service and cleaning). Moreover, Latin Americans are effectively an invisible workforce in that cleaners in particular usually work for 3–4 hours at a time and at unsociable hours in the early morning and evenings. Wilson from Ecuador, for example, had three cleaning jobs – one for three hours 4–7am, another full-time job 9–5 and another in the evening from 7–10pm, all in office cleaning. Wilson spoke of having to travel for up to an hour on the bus between jobs although he said that this allowed him to catch-up on his sleep. While being invisible in this way was useful for some such as irregular migrants, for others, it reflected a deep neglect and lack of recognition of their contribution to the functioning of London's economy.

Social invisibility practices were also enacted in a range of ways by regular and irregular Latin Americans and which intersected with various spatial and economic mechanisms discussed above. Social relations and trust among Latin Americans were somewhat ambivalent in that on one hand, social networks were crucial for facilitating various types of assistance, yet on the other hand, many spoke of social isolation and mistrust (see also Menjívar's 2006 'mistrustful solidarity'). The survey evidence highlights that more than half (53 per cent) of Latin Americans trusted their compatriots. This trust was linked with assistance on first arrival in terms of accommodation and finding jobs. For example, Soraya, a 28-year-old from Bolivia who worked as a cleaner stated:

> When there is a problem, people communicate by text message and tell someone else trying to find help for them. I'm not sure what happens with Ecuadorians and Colombians, but in the Bolivians case if someone needs something or they are suffering in some way, we try and contact someone to help either economically or with other support.

Among the 47 per cent who stated that Latin Americans did not trust one another the most important issue was a sense of individualism (identified by 27 per cent) or envy (cited by 24 per cent). As well as competition in accessing jobs, immigration status emerged as one of the most significant factors that created resentments. In some cases, this involved denouncements to the Home Office as a form of control and power within disputes among friends, neighbours and even between husband and wife. Associated with this were small friendship circles dominated by their own nationality or other Latin Americans. One of the most common statements in relation to friendships was: '*yo no soy muy amiguera/o*' (I'm not a very friendly person) due mainly to a fear of gossip as Ximena from Colombia noted: 'I'm not very friendly, I like to be alone, I don't have people knocking on my door ... I like to prevent any gossip'. However, social fragmentation appeared to be changing as the community matured and social networks were built in more sustainable ways over time. Patricio from Peru who arrived in 1992 noted:

> I think the community is united and it's getting more united every day, it's getting much better. There seems to be more understanding now than before ... I like Latin American places, they're really nice, and they remind me of my culture.

In turn, religion provided an important, if paradoxical, form of social glue for Latin Americans. Almost 70 per cent attended church services every week (35.5 per cent) or sometimes (31.5 per cent), with most attending Roman Catholic services (67 per cent) yet with more than a quarter going to Evangelical Protestant services. Churches provide essential access to a range of welfare advice as well as spiritual guidance. They also provide essential social and psychological support to help people to cope with life in London. For instance, 44-year-old Francisco from Bolivia who went to a Catholic church noted: 'I go to church every Sunday and I go to prayer groups. I think the church helps us to keep going and it gives us strength to deal with what we need to do here, our work, loneliness'. By the same token, others were antagonistic towards the churches, mainly because of the demands for economic donations of around ten per cent of their incomes. Edilberto from Colombia actively did not attend church for this reason: 'I think it's very false to make people give money and then tell them – I will help you if you are a brother, I will help you if you donate, I will only help you if you are in my church.'

On balance, however, social relations among Latin Americans are fairly robust in the sense of creating a range of 'ethnic publics' as indicated above. While not everyone engages with other Latin Americans or with organisations or commercial spaces in sustained and consistent ways, there is a general sense that people are part of some wider collective, albeit in somewhat ambivalent ways. However, the issue of invisibility in wider London society is also significant in that several people complained that Latin Americans were introverted as a community and needed to integrate more explicitly and fully as Reynaldo from Colombia noted: 'They close themselves in the Latin community, they only go to Latin places, they only eat Latin food, they only read Latin newspapers, they are not interested in learning about the new culture'. Arguably, this self-imposed invisibility is linked with wider processes of exclusion and discrimination. Indeed, it is significant that almost 70 per cent identified some form of discrimination, especially in the workplace and in relation to stereotyping. The latter was especially marked among Colombians as Luis reported: 'There is a stigmatisation of those of Latin American origin. They think that we are not capable of some things. In addition, they think that Colombians sell and grow drugs'. Indeed, this led some Colombians to tell British people that they were Spanish, regardless of their immigration status and whether they held a Spanish passport.

Therefore, while some practices are negotiated by Latin Americans in order to maintain invisibility for their benefit, other forms of invisibility are imposed from above and favour the wider society or economy more widely as in the case of their economic contributions. Moreover, it is important to remember that many Latin Americans experience widespread marginalisation such that maintaining their 'community' as invisible can act as a buttress against exclusion. However, on the whole there has been a marked shift towards engendering greater recognition of the role of Latin Americans in London and the UK more generally, evidenced not only by the *No Longer Invisible* research, but also by the ethnic recognition campaign.

Ethnic Recognition and Political Visibility

One of the key recommendations from the *No Longer Invisible* report was the need for ethnic recognition

> to include a 'Latin American' category as well as improving recording of other large ethnic communities in the capital. This is particularly important for the Greater London Authority, other London-wide public agencies and local and health authorities with significant Latin American communities, in order to support their inclusion in relevant policies, strategies and in service planning and delivery. (McIlwaine et al. 2011: 132)

This recommendation (among others) has been taken forward by the Coalition of Latin American Organisations in the UK (CLAUK) and draws on an earlier history of mobilising through the Ibero-American Alliance (who focus on Spanish and Portuguese language and extend beyond Latin America) and the Latin American Recognition Campaign (who were formed in response to the former in order to re-focus on Latin America alone). With Latin Americans often only able to identify as 'other' in ethnic monitoring, CLAUK argues that information on specific Latin American ethnicity will allow local authorities to improve services, address exclusion and distribute resources more fairly.[4] To date, only two local boroughs with large concentrations have recognised Latin Americans in their ethnic monitoring forms: Southwark (in 2012) and Lambeth (2013). This is an explicit attempt to put Latin Americans on the political map and to explicitly address their invisibility. However, returning to the issue of community building, it is also about the creation of a collective endeavour around which people can mobilise and around which the super-diversity within the population can overcome their internal differences. Indeed, it is telling that in the survey, only 17 per cent identified as Latin American, with 40 per cent stating their racial and ethnic origin as *mestizo* (mixed race) and 29 per cent as white. However, among the 52 second generation Latin Americans, 44 per cent stated they were British Latino suggesting a move towards a collective identity over time. The importance of ethnic recognition is especially important for this generation as Felipe, who was 17 years old and at college, and of Colombian descent stated:

> When I'm asked what ethnicity I am, there is no box. It seems that there are not enough Latin Americans to make a box, this is wrong. We do not have political

---

4   See <http://www.clauk.org.uk/recognition/> (accessed 5 December 2014).

leaders. I feel I have an identity crisis. I feel British Colombian. Before I had more in common with blacks, but now I have more in common with whites.

Therefore, rather than the individual negotiations over visibility discussed above whereby invisibility was often sought and valued as a way of facilitating entry and settlement for migrants, ethnic recognition was a positive and collective endeavour for Latin Americans to ensure that their needs as a population were met and also that their presence and contributions were recognised.

Conclusion

Drawing on a conceptualisation of invisibility as being important for migrant groups as they incrementally secure their place in the nation in general and in the city in particular, this chapter has traced the emergence and settlement of one of London's fastest growing new migrant populations. In outlining how the 'community' has been created, especially since the 1970s, it has highlighted not only the super-diversity within the population, especially on grounds of nationality, but also the ambiguities surrounding their presence (and absence) from various spaces and places in the city. By arguing that the notion of visibility for migrants is deeply imbued with power relations, the chapter shows how visibility can be a powerful tool of negotiation for some migrants in their quest for entry into the UK as well as in their settlement practices. As such, the creation of entry as well as spatial, economic and social invisibility practices among Latin Americans accords them a degree of agency in the context of an increasingly restrictive immigration regime. However, it also highlights that invisibility can also mean neglect, exploitation and discrimination, especially for those with irregular immigration status, by those with power and control over resources in wider society. In the face of the latter, the chapter has shown that it is necessary to mobilise collectively in ways which call for recognition, which in this case, entails an ethnic recognition campaign.

London comprises many invisible groups, whether they be migrants from a specific nationality group or set of nationalities or those identified by a range of specific social identities. Many are involved in the contested visibility processes identified here in relation to Latin Americans as they build their communities. As such, it is hoped that this chapter has shed some light on the increasingly more visible Latin American community in London and how their (in)visibilities have emerged in ambiguous ways over time and space, but also that the notion of invisibility practices will be useful in analysing other marginalised population groups in the city.

Acknowledgements

I would like to thank the Latin American Women's Rights Service, the Trust for London and the Leverhulme Trust (grant no. RF/7/2006/0080) for funding this research as well as Carila Latin America Welfare Group, Juan Camilo Cock, Brian Linneker, Carolina Velasquez and the team of community researchers.

References

Anderson, B. and M. Ruhs. (2010). 'Guest editorial: researching illegality and labour migration', *Population, Space and Place*, 16: 175–9.

Anthias, F. (1998), 'Evaluating 'diaspora': beyond ethnicity?', *Sociology*, 32(3): 557–80.

Bloch, B., Sigona, N. and Zetter, R. (2011), 'Migration routes and strategies of young undocumented migrants in England: a qualitative perspective', *Ethnic and Racial Studies*, 34(8): 1286–1302.

Broeders, D. and Engbersen, G.B.M. (2007), 'The fight against illegal migration. Identification policies and immigrants' counter strategies', *American Behavioral Scientist*, 50(12), 1592–1609.

Bryce-Laporte, R.S. (1972), 'Black immigrants: the experience of invisibility and inequality', *Journal of Black Studies*, 3(1), 29–56.

Calhoun, C. (2002), 'Imagining solidarity: cosmopolitanism, constitutional patriotism, and the public sphere', *Public Culture*, 14(1), 147–71.

Chalcraft, J. (2009), *The Invisible Cage: Syrian Migrant Workers in Lebanon*. Stanford, CA: Stanford University Press.

Cock, J.C. (2009), Colombian Migrants, Latin American Publics: Ethnicity and Transnational Practices among Colombian Migrants in London, unpublished PhD thesis. London: School of Geography, Queen Mary, University of London.

Cock, J.C. (2011), 'Latin American commercial spaces and the formation of ethnic publics in London: the case of the Elephant and Castle', in C. McIlwaine (ed.), *Cross-Border Migration among Latin Americans*. New York: Palgrave Macmillan, pp. 175–96.

Collyer, M., Düvell, F. and de Haas. H. (2010), 'Critical approaches to transit migration', *Population, Space and Place*, 18, 407–14.

Coutin, S.B. (2000), *Legalizing Moves: Salvadoran Immigrants' Struggle for U.S. Residency*. Ann Arbor: University Michigan Press.

Cvajner, M. and Sciortino, G. (2010), 'Theorizing irregular migration: the control of spatial mobility in differentiated societies', *European Journal of Social Theory*, 13(3), 389–404.

Datta, K., McIlwaine, C., Evans, Y., Herbert, J., May, J. and Wills. J. (2007), 'From coping strategies to tactics: London's low-pay economy and migrant labour', *British Journal of Industrial Relations*, 45(2), 409–38.

Datta, K. and McIlwaine, C. (2014), 'Negotiating masculinised migrant rights and everyday citizenship in a global city: Brazilian men in London', in Gorman-Murray, A. and Hopkins, P. (eds), *Masculinities and Place*. Aldershot: Ashgate, pp. 93–108.

Datta, K. (2012), *Migrants and their Money: Surviving Financial Exclusion in London*. Bristol: Policy Press.

Decho, P. and Diamond, C. (1998), *Latin Americans in London: A Select List of Prominent Latin Americans in London c. 1800–1996*. London: Institute of Latin American Studies.

De Genova (2002), 'Migrant "illegality" and deportability in everyday life'. *Annual Review of Anthropology*, 31: 419–47.

Ellerman, A. (2010), 'Undocumented migrants and resistance in the liberal state. *Politics and Society*, 38(3): 408–29.

Engbersen, G. (2001), 'The unanticipated consequences of panopticon Europe: residence strategies of illegal immigrants', in Guiraudon, V. and Joppke, C. (eds), *Controlling a New Migration World*. London: Routledge, pp. 222–46.

Feldman, I. (2008), 'Refusing invisibility: documentation and memorialization in Palestinian refugee claims', *Journal of Refugee Studies*, 21(4), 498–516.

Foreign and Commonwealth Office (2007), *Latin America to 2020: A UK Public Strategy Paper*. London: FCO.

Fortier, A. (2006), 'Global migranthood, whiteness and the anxieties of (in) visbility: Italians in London', in Harzig, C., Juteau D. and Schmitt, I. (eds), *The Social Construction of Diversity*. New York and Oxford: Berghahn, pp. 227–48.

Ghorashi, H. (2010), 'From absolute invisibility to extreme visibility: emancipation trajectory of migrant women in the Netherlands'. *Feminist Review*, 94: 75–92.

Goldring, L., Berinstein, C. and Bernhard, J.K. (2009, 'Institutionalizing precarious migratory status in Canada', *Citizenship Studies*, 13(3), 239–65.

Keith, M. (2005), *After the Cosmopolitan? Multicultural cities and the future of racism*. London and New York: Routledge.

Kivisto, P. (2001), 'Theorizing transnational immigration: a critical review of current efforts', *Ethnic and Racial Studies*, 24(4): 549–77.

Kofman, E. (1999), 'Female 'birds of passage' a decade later: Gender and immigration in the European Union'. *International Migration Review*, 33(2): 269–99.

MacDonald J.S. and MacDonald, L.D. (1972), *Invisible Immigrants*. London: Runnymede Trust.

McIlwaine, C. (2007), *Living in Latin London: How Latin American Migrants Survive in the City*. London: Department of Geography, Queen Mary, University of London. Available at: <http://www.geog.qmul.ac.uk/docs/staff/4400.pdf>

McIlwaine, C, (2010), 'Migrant machismos: exploring gender ideologies and practices among LatinAmerican migrants in London from a multi-scalar perspective', *Gender, Place and Culture*, 17(3) 281–300.

McIlwaine, C. (2011), 'Super-diversity, multiculturalism and integration: an overview of the Latin American population in London, UK', in McIlwaine, C. (ed.), *Cross-Border Migration among Latin Americans*. New York: Palgrave Macmillan, pp. 93–117.

McIlwaine, C. (2012), 'Constructing transnational social spaces among Latin American migrants in Europe: perspectives from the UK'. *Cambridge Journal of Regions, Economy and Society*, 5(2): 271–88.

McIlwaine, C. (2015), 'Legal Latins: creating webs and practices of immigration status among Latin American migrants in London', *Journal of Ethnic and Migration Studies*, 41(3): 493–511.

McIlwaine, C., Cock, J.C. and Linneker, B. (2011), *No Longer Invisible: The Latin American Community in London*. London: Trust for London.

McIlwaine, C. and Bermudez, A. (2011), 'The gendering of political and civic participation among Colombian migrants in London', *Environment and Planning A*, 43, 1499–1513.

Menjívar, C. (2006), 'Liminal legality: Salvadoran and Guatemalan immigrants' lives in the United States', *American Journal of Sociology*, 111(4), 999–1037.

Miller, R. (1998), 'Introduction', in *Latin Americans in London: A Select List of Prominent Latin Americans in London c. 1800–1996* compiled by P. Decho and C. Diamond. London: Institute of Latin American Studies.

Naber, N. (2000), 'Ambiguous insiders: an investigation of Arab American invisibility'. *Ethnic and Racial Studies*, 23(1), 37–61.

Polzer, T. (2008), 'Invisible integration: how bureaucratic, academic and social categories obscure integrated refugees', *Journal of Refugee Studies*, 21(4): 476–97.

Polzer, T. and Hammond, L. (2008), 'Editorial introduction: invisible displacement'. *Journal of Refugee Studies*, 21(4): 417–31.

Pugh, J. (2011), UNCHR rights and protection in Ecuador: the effects of non-state institutional innovation on peace-building and human security. APSA 2011 Annual Meeting Paper. Available at: <http://ssrn.com/abstract=1900446>

Roman-Velasquez, P. (2009), 'Latin Americans in London and the dynamics of diasporic identities', in Keown, M., Murphy, D. and Proctor, J. (eds), *Comparing Postcolonial Diasporas*. Basingstoke: Palgrave Macmillan, pp. 104–24.

Vertovec, S. (2007), 'Super-diversity and its implications', *Ethnic and Racial Studies*, 30(6): 1024–54.

Werbner, P. (2002), *Imagined Diasporas among Manchester Muslims: The Public Performance of Pakistani Transnational Identity Politics*. Oxford: James Currey.

Wills, J., Datta, K., Evans, Y., Herbert, J., May, J. and McIlwaine, C. (2010), *Global Cities at Work: New Migrant Divisions of Labour*. London: Pluto Press.

Winders, J. (2012), 'Seeing immigrants: institutional visibility and immigrant incorporation in new immigrant destinations'. *The ANNALS of the American Academy of Political and Social Science*, 641: 58–78.

Zelinsky, W. and Lee, B.A. (1998), 'Heterolocalism: an alternative model of the sociospatial behaviour of immigrant ethnic communities', *International Journal of Population Geography*, 4: 281–98.

Chapter 11

Ethnicity and Culture in 21st Century Medicine

Veronica L.C. White

The author of this chapter is a consultant respiratory physician with a specialist interest in tuberculosis (TB). I undertook my undergraduate studies at the London Hospital Medical College, Whitechapel, London, UK, which is in the heart of London's 'East End'. During my postgraduate training I studied for a full-time Master's degree in Medical Anthropology and subsequently wrote my doctoral thesis on 'Cultural Barriers to the treatment of tuberculosis (TB) in the Bangladeshi Community of East London, UK'. I am currently clinical lead for the Tuberculosis (TB) service at Barts Health NHS Trust, which serves a community of one million in East London. The service treats over 600 cases of active TB per year and is one of the largest TB services in Western Europe.[1]

At the end of the 1990s I was working in the East End. At that time, there was concern in the local TB clinic that patients from different ethnic and cultural backgrounds were not presenting to their general practitioners or TB clinic for treatment because they were seeking medical advice elsewhere in the community, possibly with traditional healers. My research at that time aimed to look at the cultural health beliefs in the East London Bangladeshi community in relation to TB and to understand if there were any traditional beliefs or cultural myths that either prevented people presenting with the disease or inhibited them from taking medication. Patients from South Asian heritage made up, and continue to make up, the majority of TB patients in our local TB clinics.

This chapter highlights the ways in which ethnicity and culture are major factors which have to be taken into account when treating patients who are either immigrants or second and third generation residents of the UK. Although focusing predominantly on the care of patients with TB, it takes a wider view in order to appreciate the problems encountered when treating immigrants from a diversity of backgrounds, many of whom have little or no English, or

---

1 In 2013 there were 7,892 cases of active TB in the UK, which is an incidence of 12.3/100,000; 38 per cent of cases were in London (total of 2,985), with 335 cases in the Borough of Newham – a slight reduction on the previous year and 100 cases in the London Borough of Tower Hamlets. See <www.gov.uk/government/uploads/system/uploads/attachment_data/file/385823/2014_10_30_TB_London_2013_data__1_.pdf> data on Tower Hamlets and Newham and general (accessed 6 January 2015).

understanding of the working of the UK health system. It also examines the impact on practitioners of the changing nature of the migrant population, using East London and its Bangladeshi population as the spatial focus for this study.

Ethnicity and Culture in 21st Century Medicine

Over the past two hundred years modern medicine has developed rapidly; many diseases that went undiagnosed or untreated in the 19th century can now be recognised early, treated and cured. This has led to a dramatic increase in life expectancy, as well as in the expectations of those seeking treatment. An entirely new culture of medicine has developed with its own language and beliefs.

Prior to such developments, most people relied on folk knowledge of medicine, herbal medication and their religious faith to treat their ailments. Many of these beliefs were passed down from generation to generation and in some cases, both in the Western world and elsewhere, continue to influence health seeking behaviour.

Whilst the so call 'first world' developed countries, such as those in North America and Western Europe, have in general been served well by medical progress the developing world has lagged behind with poorly developed medical facilities and poor access to essential drug treatment. Access to care can sometimes depend on wealth and status and can be difficult to obtain. A contemporary example of this would be the recent Ebola outbreak in West Africa where there is a clear divide between the care available in that part of the world and that given to returning ex-patriot medical staff repatriated to the UK and USA (BBC, 2014).

Folk beliefs continue, as does reliance on herbal medication; many people, from all backgrounds, turn to their religious beliefs in times of illness and often seek divine intervention. When individuals migrate to more affluent countries, their cultural and religious upbringing can influence their health seeking behaviour.

At the same time modern medicine may have achieved much, but it comes with its own set of rules. As students, doctors and nurses learn a new language from their medical textbooks and rapidly forget the lay terms for problems such as high blood pressure (hypertension) and heart attacks (myocardial infarction); the collar bone becomes the 'clavicle' and the glands become the 'lymph nodes'. Many disease entities are expected to present with a particular set of symptoms such as chest pain or breathlessness. The practitioner is then at a loss when a patient presents saying, 'I feel queer', or 'I'm off colour, doc', or *'Mal de fois'*.

In the UK, the NHS was founded in 1948 which brought free healthcare to all. Services can be crudely divided into community (physiotherapy, health visitors, community matron), primary care (GPs) and secondary care (hospitals). However the cash strapped NHS is not an easy system to navigate even to those born into it and access to healthcare for the newly arrived migrant can be both difficult and confusing.

East London and Healthcare

The East End of London has been a destination for émigrés for many centuries. The Huguenots, Eastern European Jews and latterly the Bangladeshi community have sequentially made the area their home and each wave of settlers has brought its own unique culture. The Bangladeshi community of East London is the largest outside Bangladesh and most of its members' heritage can be traced back to the Sylhet province of Bangladesh in the North East of the country (Eade, 1997a, Waterman, 1997). Part of the Borough of Tower Hamlets, is now known as 'Bangla Town' where Bangladeshi supermarkets, corner shops and cafes predominate; there is also a large mosque and Islamic centre in Whitechapel which is a focus of worship and community life.

In the 2011 census, Tower Hamlets was found to have the fastest growing population of any local authority in the UK over the previous ten years, with the Bangladeshi community making up 32 per cent of the Borough (London Borough of Tower Hamlets, 2013). Some of this growth is due to continued migration although the community is in general a settled one, with many second and third generation British born members. Some of older generation travel regularly between the UK and Bangladesh, staying in Bangladesh for several months in the UK winter. Large families with extended families living together are still the norm. This has led to marked overcrowding, where it is not unusual to find two or three young families living in, for example, a two-bedroom apartment meant for only one. Whilst educational and employment opportunities 20 years ago were relatively poor, the standards of local schools has recently risen dramatically leading to a rise in career aspirations and university education, some schools staying open during the holidays to allow pupils a quiet place to study for exams.

A wander around East London testifies to successive healthcare structures: old Victorian dispensaries which are now restaurants, Jewish lying-in homes converted to student residences and now a modern state of the art 16-storey tower block that makes up the local hospital, the Royal London Hospital, part of Barts Health NHS Trust, the largest hospital trust in Europe. It serves not only the local community as a 'district general' style hospital, but is also a specialist trauma, stroke and cardiac centre. The Bangladeshi community has high rates of heart disease, diabetes and stroke. This is highlighted by a report published in 2012 by Public Health England (PHE) which showed that Tower Hamlets was one of the London boroughs with the highest premature mortality rates in the UK (PHE, 2012).

Culture and Ethnicity

What is culture? It is the social, ethnic and religious background and 'cultural' milieu within which an individual is born, brought up and continues to live. The author would argue that culture can be considered unique to everyone. However, most of us have particular 'cultural' traits. We may all be doctors and trained within a particular medical tradition. We may have been born in, for example, the Irish community of Manhattan and be a fierce supporter of Irish traditions whilst still considering ourselves a true US citizen. We may have been born in Bangladesh and moved to London at the age of one and view ourselves as a British Bangladeshi, or a Londoner, or a devout Muslim, or actually all three (Eade, 1997b, Eade 1998).

Both our upbringing and our cultural background, as well as our current milieu, dictate how we react in times of ill health, our response and our health seeking behaviour. This can be described as our 'explanatory model' of illness which may vary considerably from patient to patient, even within the same family (Kleinman, 1986)). For example, a sore knee may simply bother a biology teacher or academic, but be of great alarm to an athlete, thus changing both their reaction and health seeking behaviour to a similar problem (Loustaunau and Sobo, 1997). Together with this is a patient's cultural interpretation of symptoms: in mainstream Western medicine the complaint of chest pain is often a great cause for concern as it may be due to a heart attack or is related to a serious lung problem; in some cultures describing chest pain may not refer to the physical sensation of pain, but rather the psychological symptoms of loss or sadness, 'My heart is broken', 'I am depressed' (Good and Good, 1980).

Seeking Medical Treatment

Where do people go when they feel unwell? For most people who have been born and bred in the UK, their local general practitioner (GP) tends to be their first port of call. However, where do you go if you are new to the system, and even if you are registered with a GP and have an NHS number, how do you navigate the system? If you do not speak English making an appointment maybe your first challenge or even working out how you make an appointment.

It can therefore be easier to choose another alternative: simply showing up at the local Accident and Emergency Department may be an option, but is not always well received if the health problem is not an emergency. In response to the growth of new immigrant communities a number of 'foreign' doctors have arrived to service people from their own countries, this is noticeable amongst the London Polish and Spanish speaking population. Thus some people will attend doctors in their community who speak their language, even though some may not be registered in the UK system or indeed have a recognised primary medical qualification. Others will book appointments at local private hospitals only to find that they do not have the funds to continue in the private system. Still others may go to private registered practitioners via company health schemes and then be referred on to the NHS system. Others will simply fly home and seek help in a system they understand with the support of both family and local finances. This is particularly true of those from Europe and the more affluent incomers. In East London there is now a clinic set up by an international organisation called, *Doctors of the World*, who provide health care to clients who are not entitled to

NHS care, including undocumented migrants (Doctors of the World, 2014). In addition at least one of the local GP practices is funded to look after homeless patients (NHS, 2014).

The current situation has been made more complicated by the recent introduction of the Immigration Act 2014 which brings in financial charges for recent and irregular migrants for certain primary care and emergency medicine services. This is likely to deter migrants from accessing healthcare services, although the full impact will not become clear for some time after the imposition of the act.[2]

Language

For many people who have come to live in the UK, English is not their first language, and particularly in older patients, they may not read or write in their first language. Navigating GP or hospital appointments can be a real challenge for both patient and their medical team. Many patients will be accompanied by relatives who help to translate, however, this can be beset with difficulties. It is not unusual for children to be taken out of school in order to help translate for their family members at GP surgeries or hospital appointments.[3] Many lay people do not understand medical terms and there is concern about the accuracy of their translating; there are major issues about medical confidentiality and whether more sensitive issues such as gynaecological problems become very difficult to explore, particularly if a male relative is translating (Green et al., 2005, MacFarlane et al., 2009; Kale, 2010).[4]

---

2 <www.legislation.gov.uk/ukpga/2014/22/part/3/chapter/2/crossheading/national-health-service/enacted> (accessed 6 January 2015).

3 One community worker told the author about a woman with urethral thrush who went to her GP on three consecutive days. Each time she took her ten-year-old daughter out of school in order to accompany her to the doctor's surgery. Each time she went she could not tell the GP about the thrush, as she was too embarrassed to mention the problem in front of her daughter. She instead complained about a variety of other symptoms. Finally she discussed her problem with community workers. They visibly shuddered when she told them that she had been so desperate to sort out the problem that she had tried washing herself with Dettol, when this did not help she tried using her husband's aftershave. She said to them, 'I thought that "Doomsday" had come, as it hurt so much!' (White, 1999).

4 The author saw a patient with asthma whose 11-year-old daughter was translating. The patient complained of 'blackouts'; after five minutes of confusing conversation, I asked what they meant by blackouts – the daughter admitted that it was a term used by their GP and she did not understand what it meant. The author requested the help of a Bengali advocate, who happened to be female. The consultation resumed without the daughter present: the patient then admitted that her husband was being abusive and that she was hyperventilating (over breathing) to the point of becoming unconscious.

Some hospitals have dedicated medical translators, sometimes called health advocates, trained in medical vernacular. This is easier where there are larger ethnic communities. The name comes from the need not just to provide accurate medical translation but for translators to 'advocate' on behalf of the patient to allow medical staff to understand, not just their words, but their feelings, concerns and in some cases the 'cultural context' or cultural sensitivities around a medical problem. The author would also argue that the advocates 'advocate' for the medical staff as well. For example, a patient may refuse urgent surgery because of fears around having a general anaesthetic, maybe due to prior experiences; a skilled health advocate can assist the medical team in explaining the pros and cons of modern anaesthetic agents and helping ease anxieties. There are also telephone translating services such as Language Line where the practitioner can dial in to a central controller and ask for a given language (White, 1999; El Ansari, 2009; Withycombe et al., 2013).

However, the use of advocates has been shown to be sporadic and often dependent on the experience of medical staff in using translators together with the willingness of staff to request the service. Some authors argue that training on the use of advocates should go hand in hand with cultural competency training for healthcare professions (El Ansari, 2009; Kale, 2010, Withycombe et al., 2013).

Gender and Culturally Sensitive Care

Men and women have different health needs and mechanisms for coping with health issues, on occasion very different health problems, for example breast cancer versus prostate cancer, and are known to access healthcare in different ways. Women tend to visit their general practitioners more often, not always for themselves, but for their children. Many female patients prefer to see a female practitioner; this is not unique to Muslim patients, but is particularly relevant when working within a large Muslim community. There are numerous stories of women avoiding seeking medical care when they knew that they would not see a female doctor or patients seeking medical attention too embarrassed to explain the problem once in the surgery. Mixed hospital wards were until fairly recently common, for many migrants these are also culturally and religiously unacceptable and the author once found a Bengali woman crying outside a hospital ward because she was so traumatised at being placed in a bay with male patients.

The opposite can also be true, and is often forgotten, that male patients prefer a practitioner of the same gender. Again this is not unique to any particular religious groups but is often overlooked in the busy milieu of a GP surgery or NHS ward. Key departments such as gynaecology, breast clinics, male urology clinics and sexually transmitted disease (STD) clinics now try provide same sex practitioners, as well as same sex translators/advocates.

Other issues include the provision of appropriate food, for example halal, kosher or vegan meals, as well as prayer facilities, with many hospitals now having a multi-faith prayer room instead of, or as well as, a traditional Christian chapel, or a separate Muslim prayer room and washing facilities. Visiting a sick relative or friend when they are unwell is a Muslim obligation and can mean that some patients have large numbers of visitors, some arriving simply holding a piece of paper with a record of their ward and bed number written, but not necessarily knowing their full name. Ward staff as well as other patients can become frustrated, leading to tensions between staff and community, and negotiations may have to take place to regulate numbers at the bedside (White, 1999).

Cultural and religious practices around death are also sensitive issues, with both Jewish and Islamic faiths requiring burial within 24 hours; this often requires medical practitioners to ensure that documentation such as death certificates are completed quickly and can lead to frustration and sometimes anger if the coroner needs to be involved or a postmortem is required. There is a trend towards postmortem MRI scans being performed for certain religious groups rather than traditional postmortems, although families can often be required to pay for this service if it is their preference (*The Telegraph*, 2009).

Culture and Tuberculosis

Tuberculosis is an infectious disease. It basically has two forms: active disease which primarily affects the lungs, but can cause disease in any part of the body, including the heart, abdomen, brain, spine and skin, and latent or dormant disease. This occurs when the TB bacteria linger in the body, 'sleeping' and not causing harm or pathological disease, but with risk of reactivating or 'waking up' later in the person's life. The main symptoms of TB are cough, coughing up blood (haemoptysis), fevers, night sweats and weight loss. However, the disease, particularly outside the lung, can develop insidiously with non-specific symptoms that go unrecognised by patients and their doctors and they subsequently present later on in their illness and are often, therefore, much sicker and with a poorer prognosis (Davies et al., 2014, TB Alert, 2014).

There has been a cure for TB since the 1940s and a robust treatment regimen since the 1970s which, ironically, has not changed much since then. In developed countries, such as in Western Europe and North America, where there has been access to reliable TB healthcare and treatment, rates of active TB cases have dropped dramatically.[5] However many developing countries, such as Bangladesh, have suffered from decades of either non-existent or under resourcing of healthcare and at the same time poor access to cheaper, less effective, TB drug therapy. Bangladesh only gained independence from West Pakistan at the end of 1971,

---

5   A decrease in rates of TB has not been simply due to a reliable drug treatment regime. Improved living standards, with better diet, less over crowding and improved health education, together with mass vaccination programmes, including the BCG for TB prevention, have all contributed to the decrease in number of cases.

and one of the aims of the young country was to provide healthcare for the whole community and to ensure that each Thana (district) had its own health complex. In 1993, a National TB Programme was implemented based on World Health Organisation (WHO) guidelines which provides free medical care and treatment for TB (White, 2000).

Unlike HIV and AIDs which has attracted widespread media attention and the patronage of a number of famous people, TB is still perceived as a poor person's disease, a dirty disease, which does not affect well educated, middle class individuals, when in fact it can affect anyone, of any background. Until the last decade, most people in the UK thought that TB had disappeared; it is only due to a number of well documented cases in the popular press and the advent of a new TB charity in the UK, TB Alert, that TB is back in the public consciousness (*Metro*, 2012, Potter, 2014).

North East London[6] has some of the highest rates of TB in Western Europe with over 700 cases per annum. At least 80 per cent of patients are born abroad, with over half of these from Indian subcontinent (India, Pakistan and Bangladesh). More established patients might be familiar with the UK health system and seek medical attention earlier in their disease whilst new migrants may struggle to do so. TB patients tend to be young (aged less than 35 years), and fortunately, otherwise fit. However, some still present very late in the disease and there is still a significant death rate from TB in the UK.

My research focused on cultural barriers to the management of TB in the Bangladeshi Community of East London, looking specifically at recognition of symptoms, stigma attached to the disease, traditional health beliefs and practices and attitudes to medication. I rapidly sensed that the cultural issues that surrounded the disease could have been replicated in other cultural groups where the responses may have been somewhat different, but the sentiments and fear surrounding the diagnosis would have drawn a common thread across the groups (White, 2005). The quotes in the following text are from the patients and lay community (all of Bangladeshi heritage) and health workers enrolled in the study.

Symptoms and Signs of Tuberculosis

Cough and haemoptysis (coughing up blood) are recognised symptoms of TB and part of the messaged delivered by health education programmes in Bangladesh,

---

6   The author's TB service includes the London boroughs of Tower Hamlets, Newham and Waltham Forest; in 2013: Hackney, Barking, Dagenham and Havering local authorities also make up the North East London Group of TB services. Newham had the highest rates of TB in the UK, with 335 cases, at 107/100,000. This was a reduction of the 2012 number, when 436 patients in the UK died of TB or TB was related to the cause of death (PHE, 2014b). <www.gov.uk/government/uploads/system/uploads/attachment_data/file/385823/2014_10_30_TB_London_2013_data_1_.pdf> and PHE (2014a).

where the symptoms of lung TB are promoted along WHO guidelines (White, 2000). Haemoptysis, in particular, generated anxiety and prompted action to seek medical attention. Generalised symptoms, particularly sweats and fevers, were less well understood. 'I thought I had 'flu', 'I did have night sweats for several months', were frequently used explanations for such problems and a number of patients waited many months before they sought medical attention or indeed the symptoms were recognised by their medical practitioners. 'Lots of people in Bangladesh get unwell with symptoms like fever, sweats and 'flu ... so getting night sweats is not unusual.'

Patients tended to 'normalise' their symptoms and put them down to common illnesses such as colds and flu. Zola (1973), describes this in his work with people becoming quite unwell before a 'trigger' precipitated their decision to seek medical care as well as needing their illness to be 'sanctioned' either by friends, family or a medical practitioner. Furthermore there were a group of patients who presented to their East London GPs on a number of occasions before they were referred to the TB clinic.

There was also a lack of understanding that TB does not just affect the lungs, but any organ in the body. 'I was surprised [that I had TB] because I had no cough and was not coughing up blood.' Another patient with lymph node TB was very suspicious of the diagnosis: 'I still think that it's just a boil, a *boron*.[7] TB is only in the chest.' Another patient with TB in the spine: '[I have had] back pain for one year.' There was sometimes a striking delay between symptoms occurring and a diagnosis being made, with a number of patients having had many months of fevers before seeking medical attention.

Failure to recognise symptoms, rather than being related to cultural or geographic interpretation may have been associated with latent denial. This may have been for several reasons: firstly, and particularly in young people where time off work equated with lost wages, a feeling of invulnerability to being unwell, and secondly, given the stigma surrounding the disease which will be described below, a subconscious dismissal that they could possibly be suffering from TB, a disease whose very name filled them with dread.

Patients were also asked how they thought they had got TB. Some of our patients and community members thought TB was caused by smoking, others because they had worked in dusty environments. Some thought it was inherited, and the disease was passed in families, however, they could not tell us how: was it 'bad' blood, or 'dodgy' genes? Together with members of our local TB team, I realised that TB clinics perpetuated this myth by inviting family members of patients to clinic to be screened for TB to ensure they had not caught the disease. Rather than simply screening household members, we were of course often screening family members and the route of transmission of the disease, if not clearly explained, became entrenched in mythology.

---

7   *Boron*, Bengali word for 'boil'.

Stigma and TB

> To display or not to display: to tell or not to tell; to lie or not to lie: and in each
> case, to whom how, when and where. (Goffman, 1963)

Even in the 21st century, 50 years after an effective cure was found for TB, stigma was a major issue and the research revealed that the fear and misunderstanding surrounding the disease has a major influence on the reaction of their family, friends, and community together with health professionals. The fear was almost palpable. TB was very much seen as a dirty disease, a poor person problem. 'I can't have TB, I've led a good life, it's a dirty disease' (Health professional with active TB).

TB was generally regarded as a highly contagious illness that could not be cured, despite treatment. '[you] must not touch them [TB patients]; whatever you do, whatever you touch, you're contagious.' Remembrance of sick friends and relatives, images from health education films and public hearsay all fuelled concern about 'jokka',[8] 'the patient is rotten inside'. However, some patients appeared more worried about the social problems and the processes that might arise from the diagnosis than the health consequences. They were afraid of the effect that it might have on their immediate and long-term relationships and their community's attitude towards them. A word that was used on a number of occasions was *ginnaiba*, meaning 'to hate' or to 'be repelled' or 'be disgusted.' 'People may hate me, *ginnaiba* and they may stay away. They may worry about getting infected.' Previous literature reports similar phases being used in relation to TB (Khan et al., 2000).

The major factor was the fear of contagion. TB, even when the concept of bacteria was not understood, was known to be 'infectious' and therefore those suffering from the disease needed to be avoided. 'It's contagious, I'm worried for my children, that I've passed it onto them.' Very few laymen knew that TB could affect parts of the body other than the lungs, and those that did were not aware that extra-pulmonary TB was not infectious. Furthermore both patients and their acquaintances were sometimes left confused by the actions of medical staff who were themselves seen as being uncomfortable with the illness. The isolation of TB patients in hospital side rooms with the insistence that visitors, even those living closely with the patient throughout their illness, needed to wear masks to protect themselves often confused and promoted anxiety. One medical professional said, 'The use of the mask ... haunted me in this job.'

The diagnosis of TB clearly creates very real fear and can lead to social isolation. However stigma is often perceived by the patient rather than being real, and when they tell their close family and friends, they are surprised about the degree of support that they are given and this has been reflected in previous studies (Liefooghe et al., 1997; Nair et al., 1997). The fear about TB

---

8   Bengali word for 'tuberculosis'.

alters behaviour: one patient would not return to Bangladesh until he completed treatment; others would not tell the medical team who they lived with in order to offer contact tracing. In the sub-Saharan African community a diagnosis of TB can be directly associated with a diagnosis of HIV and AIDS and the two are often thought to go hand in hand.

Stigma is not exclusive to older patients who might be considered less educated than their offspring, whilst increasing age was perceived by the younger generation as being associated with outdated views about TB, it did bring, in general, added security and respect. Indeed elders will often be 'protected' by their status in the community. They were sick and their families were expected to look after them, 'My family has no choice, they have to be supportive!', (43-year-old man). Young patients felt that they fared less well and worried about its effect on their social standing: the diagnosis of TB was a social death trap and their marriage prospects ruined. No one wanted to marry their son to a girl who had TB. She obviously had 'bad' genes, or 'bad' blood. Younger patients did not trust the older generation with the news about diagnosis and preferred to keep it to themselves, afraid of the myth that TB was somehow passed from one generation to the next, 'The older generation are different, they don't understand that it can be treated, they still think that it's a killer.' Others were much more pragmatic about their illness. 'People of my age do not think anything of it – they know it's curable.' 'I've told people. I'm not worried. It's a God-given disease.'

Employment was an issue which the author wished she had explored in more detail. Many of the patients were chefs or waiters in Indian restaurants;[9] 'Some of the restaurants that I've worked in wouldn't take me back.' Some stopped working when they were unwell, which in some cases was understandable, but, in hindsight, may have been due to their employers finding out about the diagnosis and quietly dismissing them. One patient worked as a 'temp' in a call centre; she had lymph node TB (non-infectious). As soon as she told her manager the diagnosis, she was asked to leave.

TB patients were also asked about the image of TB and reaction to the diagnosis: what did they see when they shut their eyes and thought of TB. Many patients remembered being taken aback. 'I was shocked', 'I was surprised', were common phrases. The fear that was detected in these initial reactions as reflected in the patients' images of the disease: 'It is dark, and serious and sinister.' 'I think of a skeleton face.' 'The patient is rotten inside.' 'Someone coughed and coughed and coughed and had to be kept away.' Researcher: 'If you had a friend with TB, how would you feel?' Patient: 'I would feel disgusted; I would stay away from them.'

---

9 Many worked in restaurants in towns and cities all over the South of England; it is very common for restaurant workers to live quite literally 'above the shop', with 3–4 waiters sharing a bedroom above an establishment, often in overcrowded conditions and returning to see their families on their day off. Such overcrowding only helps to spread infectious TB.

Traditional Practices

The Bangladeshi community in East London is predominately, but not exclusively, Muslim and a large proportion come from, or can trace their heritage back to, the Sylhet District of Bangladesh, in the north east of the country. Their birthright brings with it their religious beliefs and also folk beliefs that stem from the village or area that they originated from. As with many communities, religious and Bengali folk beliefs have become intertwined over many centuries and it can be difficult to separate one from the other and their magico-religious beliefs in black magic, jinn and ghosts are complex. Particularly in conversation, people will use the terms 'jinn' and 'ghosts' (*bhut*) interchangeably, although religious purists will point out distinct differences between them. Jinn are Islamic ghosts that have a chapter dedicated to them in the Koran; ghosts and magic are considered evil and un-Islamic, although many people admit being convinced by their existence and power. Both magic and bad jinn are thought to cause ill health (Islam, 1985; Gardner, 1995: White, 1999; Dein et al., 2005).

There are many mosques scattered over East London, many of them independent from each other and run by individual mullahs or imams. There is a larger religious centre in Whitechapel, the East London mosque, with an associated Islamic centre and school. As with many communities, people vary in their devoutness and there is enormous religious heterogeneity within the community, but many often turn to their faith in time of illness, 'Even I pray more often when I'm sick!'.

This often involves visiting a religious leader: some will simply provide spiritual support in the form of prayers and Sura (religious texts), to bring Allah's blessing. Others will offer more magico-religious explanations for illness and offer exorcism of jinn or ghosts or amulets known as *tabiz* which contain verses from the Koran. Others will blow on the affected individual, a practice known as *foo* or *jhar phook*, or provide blessed water which is ingested like a tonic or blessed oil used as an ointment. These practices go back many hundreds of years.

What was also reported amongst more outspoken and often better educated Muslims was that there was a large number of 'fake' healers in the community in East London as well as in Bangladesh, taking money from a community which was already deprived. Their popularity spread by word of mouth, although the basis of their healing skills may be quite questionable. There was also a number of 'homeopathic' practitioners or herbalists in the Bangladeshi community. Some were medically trained and known as 'professors.' Others used recipes passed down from generation to generation and saw their skills as a gift from Allah to be used wisely and without profits.

One of the concerns that we had in the TB clinic before the research began was that patients were seeking health advice from traditional healers for some time before they reached a western-trained practitioner. This was based around the case of the young man with the disease who refused to believe his clinical diagnosis and was convinced that his ill health was due to being possessed by evil spirits; he disappeared from our clinic. We believe he returned to Bangladesh to seek further traditional remedies.

However, in general, our concerns, at least in our local Bangladeshi community, appear to be unfounded. Whilst some patients had visited traditional healers or religious leaders, this did not stop them seeking more mainstream medical advice. What often delayed making a diagnosis was their lack of recognition of symptoms or indeed lack of recognition by medical practitioners rather than faith in traditional methods.

One form of traditional medicine that has become more popular within the Bangladeshi community in East London over the last decade is cupping. Cupping is the technique of placing hot glass cups or jars on an individual's back with a view to drawing out any impurities in the body. Sometimes a small cut is made in the skin under the area where the cup is placed in order to draw out impurities in the blood. Cupping is discussed in the *Hadith* (word of the Prophet) and is a tradition of the Prophet Mohammed who is recorded as having cupping done on himself on a regular basis and recommended it for health and religious purposes. The practice appears not to be necessarily for health issues, but as a form of purification or detoxification and heighten sense of spiritualisation. Use of the practice and where to have it performed is spread by word of mouth; in theory, as a religious practice, it should be offered for free with individuals making a gift to the practitioner in return for the procedure, although in reality some pay up to £200.

What was clear is that for some people Western medical care and traditional practices work in synergy to look after them and most were quite capable of pluralistic health beliefs. For example, some of our patients were diagnosed with TB in our clinics and took appropriate medication to kill bacteria while simultaneously visiting their mullahs for religious blessing, possibly receiving blessed seeds to ingest or blessed oil to rub on the offending part of the body. As one community member commented on traditional methods, 'It's mainly psychological' and 'It's like a placebo effect'.

Medication

Undergoing a course of antituberculous therapy can be difficult for patients. It could be described as a clumsy but necessary regimen. Active TB infection requires treatment with at least three or four drugs, for a minimum of six months. The tablets are often large, can taste unpleasant and have numerous undesirable side effects, including nausea and vomiting.[10] We had had a theory at the beginning of the research that patients from the Indian subcontinent preferred being treated with

---

10   The standard UK standard regimen of isonaizid, rifampicin, pyrazinamide and ethambutol is most commonly used; most patients need to take at least 8–11 tablets per day for two months, followed by two a day for a further four months.

injections rather that tablets. However, our patients were much more pragmatic: they wanted the best treatment for the problem. Their complaint about treatment was that of all our TB patients: 'Too many tablets, for too long'.

Patients from all backgrounds respond to explanation: rather than medical practitioners being dismissive of a patient with a viral cold wanting antibiotics, an explanation that antibiotics do not treat viruses can help to allay anxieties. Similarly with TB: the tuberculosis bacteria is a lazy one, it takes a long time to grow and cause disease and in equal measure takes a long time to kill, with at least six months of a cocktail of antibiotics. The bacteria are good at remodelling and one antibiotic will not do as the bacteria can mutate and drug resistance develops, making it even more difficult to treat. At the same time, side effects of medication clearly need to be addressed and discussed with patients, otherwise they may discontinue therapy.

However TB kills, maims and makes people very unwell, and an individual's desire to retain good health often overcomes many barriers: 'It is essential for policy makers and programme managers to recognise that patients strive to get well and endeavour to complete their treatment, and yet are thwarted by the failure of the health care system to meet their needs' (Ogden et al., 1999).

What was clear was that the patient support structure was crucial and many acknowledged the support of medical staff in their recovery (TB nurse = key worker) as well as the significant help of loyal friends and family which supported them both psychologically and practically. Adherence to medication did not appear to correlate with educational achievement or levels of literacy, indeed some of the illiterate patients were the most enthusiastic about their care, particularly as they appeared to have felt well supported by their families and medical carers. Other patients appear to work on a 'hierarchy of needs', where they gave attention to their health when they felt unwell, but once they felt better other issues in their lifer took precedence and the importance of their medical care diminished.

During Ramadan many patients continued to fast despite religious dispensation for those on essential medication. The TB team worked with them to adjust times for tablets to be taken during fasting: 'Culturally sensitive care can affect patient compliance, satisfaction, comfort and attitude towards the medical establishment' (Loustaunau and Sobo, 1997).

Impact on Practitioners

Treating patients from different cultural backgrounds can be both interesting and challenging. It is important for medical practitioners to have an understanding of the local community in which they work in relation to diet, family structure, living arrangements, religious obligations and language. One local hospital that serves a large orthodox Jewish community gives new employees information about Jewish customs and the community itself has good relations with the Trust.

Understanding cultural nuances of expressions of illness can be more difficult, particularly when working in an area serving multiple ethnic groups. Expression of illness and explanatory models have already been discussed, together with language. Giving high quality care in an environment where translators may not be readily available can be frustrating with a fear that they may miss an accurate diagnosis or are missing an important point in the medical history which leads to missing a diagnosis and the potential consequences. Translation services, however, are expensive and as with all services are often rationed. Likewise, without any background understanding of the customs of a minority community, it is difficult to develop an understanding of patients' explanatory model of their illness, their traditional beliefs or indeed their previous experiences of healthcare.

Knowledge about traditional medicine in our study was virtually non-existent amongst most practitioners and is not routinely discussed at staff induction. This can lead to both misunderstanding and suspicion about 'alternative' practices and can lead to a breakdown in professional relationships if patients feel their religious or traditional beliefs are somehow being undermined by patronising medical staff. The concept of pluralistic beliefs working side by side is likely to surprise many staff, although if they look closely at their own communities they are likely to see widespread examples. Cultural Competency training has been developed at some institutions to help improve the awareness of staff as well as clinical outcomes and the patient experience of healthcare (Owiti et al., 2014).

Discussion

This chapter illustrates the overlap between traditional medicine, cultural and religious beliefs and modern medicine. Their interaction can be complex, varying both between individuals and communities. Their relationship is, in some cases, symbiotic and mutually harmonious or, on the other hand, there can be a 'cultural' clash of ideas and beliefs which can affect both illness behaviour and patient care. Their significance can become intertwined and it can sometimes become difficult to unravel whether health issues are related to culture, practical issues or education of either patients or health workers. There is also a danger that where by concentrating on the cultural requirements of certain minority groups, the needs of the often 'silent' majority community, may be forgotten.

Whether we take our local Bangladeshi community or, for example, a White Irish community, understanding their 'alternative' health beliefs is important. A Roman Catholic may also visit their religious leaders, priest, in times of illness; they may receive a blessing or list of appropriate prayers; a friend may give them a bottle of holy water to use. For other religious groups, including Christian ones, there are beliefs that illness is caused by evil spirits, witchcraft or demons and elaborate exorcism ceremonies may be organised to 'cure' the afflicted.

The importance of studying how ethnicity and culture can affect patients' access and utilisation of health care services, as well as the way in which they are treated by the service, has been reviewed in previous studies (Ahmed, 1993; Hillier and Kelleher, 1996; Samje and LeGrand, 1997; Blakemore, 2000, Smith et al., 2000; Hillier, 2003). Such work suggests that understanding cultural issues helps us tailor services to meet the needs of individuals or groups and that traditional therapies need to be understood rather than marginalised. However, at the same time researchers need to be mindful that not all health inequalities amongst ethnic minority groups may result from ethnic difference but from social economic disadvantage, lack of employment opportunities and poor housing that continues to affect many migrant groups even those who have been settled for a long time.

In general in the UK, the NHS and Western medical practice, whilst not always seen as perfect in its delivery and suffering from the funding issues that affect all public services, is recognised by most patients as providing effective modern medicine. However religious and traditional beliefs do influence individual's images of, and attitudes to, their illness and can therefore affect their outlook on treatment, as well as their interaction with medical staff.

This chapter focused on issues related to TB in the Bangladeshi community of East London, looking at four main themes. As far as patients' interpretation of symptoms of the disease were concerned, patients often appeared to try to 'normalise' their symptoms and continue with their busy daily lives and, despite some previous experiences or health education, did not always associate their symptoms with TB. Such findings are not unique to ethnic communities or culturally based and have been shown to be a common reaction to non-specific symptoms with a strong desire to continue with everyday life, regardless of feeling unwell. Patients often needed a precipitating factor, such as coughing up blood or being unable to work and earn an income, in order to seek medical attention (Helman, 1973; Zola, 1973; Scambler, 2003).

Stigma, however, was a major issue, with vast amounts of confusion, mythology and fear being associated with the disease. Lay health education is a crucial intervention, but needs to be culturally sensitive and to target effected communities e.g sickle cell disease in patients of Black African and Caribbean descent. Health education programmes via the churches, mosques, temples and local community centres can be very effective together with local newspapers, radio and television channels which are often in both locally used languages as well as English. Involving community groups and their leadership is also key with the development of peer support, either on an individual basis or in groups, recruiting those who have already experienced an illness to support those with new diagnoses. TB Alert has a patient group called the TB action group (TBAG) and are funding the set up of more local support groups (TB Alert, 2014b).

There was also concern that traditional and religious practices might adversely affect patients' presentation and treatment. The simple answer from the author's work was, 'in general, they appear not to.' It also highlights the importance of not assuming that a particular cultural or social group hold an homogeneous set of beliefs, and revealed the capacity of patients to cope with pluralistic health beliefs. Indigenous healers can help provide a bridge between Western medicine and traditional beliefs by using culturally familiar rituals and symbolism. They may not just provide a healing role in the conventional sense, they are not necessarily attempting to heal, for example, the infectious process of TB. They also serve to address more social and emotional matters. By providing a listening ear and culturally and religiously acceptable management, they may well be answering the psychological and spiritual needs of a patient whilst the Western trained practitioner cures the illness. In many respects it could be argued that a religious faith and, in other cases, the use of traditional healing methods, provide individuals with a firm spiritual and psychological foundation that sustains them through treatment with conventional therapies. In addition the strong cultural emphasis that exists in many smaller communities of mutual family support gives many patients a firm social base which supports them through their illness.

Undergoing a course of TB therapy did not appear to have been affected by ethnic issues. In the words of Sumartojo (1993), 'The reasons for poor adherence are not only multi-faceted and complex, but range from characteristics of the individual patient to qualities of the social and economic environment that influences all tuberculosis prevention and control activities.' Cultural acceptability of treatment was important and has been discussed together with the importance of family and professional support structures.

None of the issues discussed in this chapter are easy to address. Some of them are practical problems which require funding and organisation tailored to the local community: public transport to local health centres and hospitals, translation or advocacy services, provision of multi-faith prayer rooms, staff access to death certificates out of hours to assist in religious requirements around death, the provision of halal, kosher or vegan meals. In most London hospitals it would now be considered unusual not to have a multi-faith chaplaincy or varied menus to suit most types of diet.

Access to healthcare is an issue; Primary care is often the gateway to the UK health system and simply registering with a General Practitioner can be complex and beset with difficulties. Furthermore, NHS services, such as outpatient care, X-rays and phlebotomy, that often operate Monday to Friday and can be difficult to attend, especially for those in full-time education or employment.

Language both in the vernacular, local expression of disease and colloquialisms affects medical care. The issues surrounding patients unable to speak English or having English as their second or third language have been outlined above. Language, however, is not just about expressing yourself in the local or national lingo; it is also about expression of illness: most people have not read a medical textbook and do not discuss their cardiomyopathy, arthroplasty or beclomethasone inhaler; they talk about their 'heart problem' their 'knee problem' or 'brown inhaler'. In order to empower patients, healthcare professionals need to both provide them with information but also understand *their* expressions of disease without becoming frustrated that their understanding is not the same as ours.

Gender issues are also complex. On the one hand society is trying to become more equitable and non-discriminatory; whilst at the same time there needs to be consideration of religious and personal preferences, both of which are sometimes ignored in the organisation of healthcare. Single sex bays are now mandatory across the NHS in England and have certainly improved the situation locally and there is also greater provision of gender-sensitive care in some specialties.

The knowledge and attitudes of health professionals can also have a major impact on the patient experience. In the author's research, professionals appeared to have little experience of religious or traditional beliefs and did not always consider it necessary information that might help them in their medical practice. In the author's study, a health professional commented: 'They [the local community] tend to stick to us.' 'No, it doesn't happen ... it's not an issue here', apparently unaware that their patients may also be consulting traditional healers in addition to themselves. Certainly an understanding that a synergy can exist between modern medicine and traditional beliefs appears to be lacking and fear and mistrust about these beliefs are more likely to have a negative impact on the doctor-patient relationship, rather than a considered understanding.

Staff education about the communities that they work in is therefore crucial and developing an appreciation that traditional beliefs can sit side by side with modern medicine and not detract from care and treatment is essential. The term 'cultural competency' has recently been coined to encompass training in cultural issues and it could be argued that teaching institutions should include such training in their curricula. However, as Kleinman and Benson (2006), point out, what do we mean by 'cultural' and is that always the root of the problem? Sometimes it is not ethnic or religious beliefs that inhibit medical care, but straight forward practical issues such as getting time off work or paying the bus fare to the hospital.

A recent paper about asthma from the University of Leicester shows that there was 'a disconnect between traditional "one size fits all" approach of the NHS to the needs of the ethnic minority community that they cared for' (Asthma UK, 2014). The lead researcher stated that 'we need a different way of working with the communities that we care for, and that involves working in partnership. We need to go back to the community and find out what the issues are, for example, there is no word for "asthma" in South Asian languages.' (Lakhaipaul et al., 2013)

In many respects, modern medicine is providing 21st century care in 21st century language, but often fails to realise that the communities it serves, regardless of ethnicity, culture and religious backgrounds have a different understanding of illness, unique ways of interpreting and expressing symptoms and therefore present at diverse stages of their disease process. Individual beliefs may then affect attitudes to treatment too.

How then do we provide culturally sensitive and culturally appropriate care? Kleinman (2006) recommends that we focus on the patient as an individual not as a cultural stereotype and take not just a medical history but if possible an ethnography, the patient's whole story. Whilst an enormous challenge in the milieu of a busy NHS clinic, this was certainly the experience of the author: beware our own cultural assumptions and treat all patients as individuals, look beyond and behind the medical issues and discover the person behind the patient.

References

Ahmad, W.I.U. (1993), 'Making black people sick: "race", ideology and health research', in Ahmad, W.I.U. (ed.) *'Race' and Health in Contemporary Britain* Buckingham: Open University Press, pp. 11–33.

Asthma UK (2014), 'UK South Asian families with asthma need more help' <www.asthma.org.uk/Blog/research-south-asian-families-need-more-help> accessed 7 July 2015.

BBC (2014), 'UK Ebola survivor William Pooley tells of virus "horror."' <http://www.bbc.co.uk/news/uk-29456849> accessed 7 July 2015.

Blackmore, K. (2000), 'Health and social care needs in the minority communities: an over-problematized issue?' In *Health and Social Care in the Community* 8(1): 22–30.

Daily Telegraph (2009), 'Muslims and Jews to be allowed to have different post mortems'. <www.telegraph.co.uk/news/religion/5195466/Muslims-and-Jews-to-be-allowed-to-have-different-post-mortems.html> accessed 7 July 2015.

Davies, P.D.O., Gordon, S.B., Davies, G., (2014) (eds), *Clinical Tuberculosis*. London: Hodder Arnold Publications.

Dein, S., Alexander, M., Napier, A.D. (2008), 'Jinn, Psychiatry and contested notions of Misfortune among East London Bangladeshis', *Transcultural Psychiatry* 45(1): 31–55.

Doctors of the World (2014), <www.doctorsoftheworld.org.uk/pages/london-clinic> accessed 7 July 2015.

Eade, J. (1997a), 'Keeping the options open: Bangladeshis in a global city', in Kershen, A.J. (ed.), *London, The Promised Land? The Migrant Experience of a Capital City*. Aldershot: Avebury, pp. 91–109.

Eade, J. (1997b), 'Identity, nation and religion: educated young Bangladeshis', in London's East End', in Eade, J. (ed.) *Living the Global City*. London: Routledge, pp. 377–94.

Eade, J. (1998), 'The search for wholeness: the construction of national and Islamic identities among British Bangladeshis', in Kershen, A.J. (ed.) *A Question of Identity*. Aldershot: Ashgate, pp. 136–59.

El Ansari, W., Newbigging, K., Roth, C., Malik, F. (2009), 'The role of advocacy and interpretative services in the delivery of healthcare to diverse minority communities in London', *Social Care in the Community*, 17(6): 636–46.

Hillier, S. (2003), 'The health and health care of ethnic minority groups', in Scambler, G. (ed.), *Sociology as Applied to Medicine*. London: Saunders.

Hillier, S. and Kelleher, D. (1996), 'Considering culture, ethnicity and the politics of health', in Kelleher, D. and Hillier, S. (eds), *Researching Cultural Difference in Health*. London: Routledge.

Gardner, K. (1995), *Global Migrants, Local Lives*. Oxford: Clarendon Press.

Goffman, E. (1963), *Stigma: Notes on the Management of Spoiled Identity*. London: Penguin Books.

Good, B.J. and Good, M.J.D. (1980), 'The meaning of symptoms: a cultural hermeneutic model for clinical practice', in Eisenberg, L. and Kleinman, A. (eds), *The Relevance of Social Science for Medicine*. Boston: D. Reidel Publishing Company.

Green, J., Free, C., Bhavnani, V. and Newman, T. (2005), 'Translators and mediators: bilingual young people's accounts of their interpreting work in health care', *Social Science & Medicine*, 60: 2097–2110.

Helman, C.G. (1978), '"Feed a cold, starve a fever": folk models of infection in an English suburban community, and their relation to medical treatment', *Culture, Medicine and Psychiatry*, 2: 107–37.

The Home Office (2013), Immigration Bill Factsheet: Overview of the Bill. London: The Stationery Office.

Islam, M. (1985), 'Women, Health and Culture'. Women for Women: Research and Study Group, Dhaka.

Kale, E. and Syed, H.R. (2010), 'Language barriers and the use of interpreters in the public health services. A questionnaire-based survey', *Patient Education and Counselling*, 81: 187–91.

Khan, A., Walley, J., Newell, J., Imdad, N. (2000), 'Tuberculosis in Pakistan: socio-cultural constraints and opportunities in treatment', *Social Science & Medicine* 50: 247–54.

Kleinman, A. (1986), 'Concepts and a model for the comparison of medical systems as cultural systems', in Currer, C. and Stacey, M. (eds). *Concepts of Health, Illness and Disease*. Leamington Spa: Berg.

Kleinman, A. and Benson, P. (2006), 'Anthropology in the Clinic: The Problem of Cultural Competency and How to Fix It', *PLoS Med* 3(10): e294. DOI:10.1371/journal.pmed.0030294.

Lakhanpaul, M., Bird, D., Culley, L., Hudson, N., Robertson, N., Johal, N., McFeeters, M., Williams, C.H. and Johnson, J. (2013), 'Development of tailored and integrated health-care interventions to reduce inequalities in health outcomes: The Management and Interventions for Asthma' (MIA) project. *The Lancet* 382: S57.

Liefooghe, R., Baliddawa, J.B, Kipruto, E.M., Vermeire, C. and De Munynck, A.O. (1997), 'From their own perspective. A Kenyan community's perception of tuberculosis', *Tropical Medicine and International Health*, 2: 809–21.

London Borough of Tower Hamlets (2013), Population Key Facts, a profile of the population of Tower Hamlets. Research Briefing, 2013–12, December 2013, Tower Hamlets Council.

London Borough of Tower Hamlets (2014), Demography 2014 <http://www.towerhamlets.gov.uk/lgsl/901-950/916_borough_profile/research_and_briefings/demography.aspx> accessed 7 July 2015.

Loustaunau, M.O. and Sobo, E.J. (1997), *The Cultural Context of Health, Illness and Medicine*. Westport, CT: Bergin and Garvey.

MacFarlane, A., Singleton, C. and Green, E. (2009), 'Language barriers in health and social care consultations in the community: A comparative study of responses in Ireland and England', *Health Policy*, 92: 203–10.

Metro (2012), 'Teen Anina Sarag asked if she was lovestruck died of TB' <http: metro.co.uk/2012/05/14/teen-alina-sarag-asked-if-she-was-lovestruck-died-of-tb-424948/> accessed 7 July 2015.

Nair, D.M., George, A. and Chacko, K.T. (1997), 'Tuberculosis in Bombay: new insights from poor urban patients', *Health Policy Planning* 12(1): 77–85.

NHS (2014), 'Health E1 Homeless Medical Centre'. <www.nhs.uk/Services/GP/Overview/DefaultView.aspx?id=40360> accessed 7 July 2015.

Ogden, J., Rangan, S., Uplekar, M., Porter, J., Brugha, R., Zwi, A. and Nyheim, D. (1999), 'Shifting the paradigm in tuberculosis control: illustrations from India', *International Journal of Tuberculosis and Lung Disease*, 3: 588–861.

Owiti, J.A., Ajaz, A., Ascoli, M., De Jongh, B., Palinski, A. and Bhui, K.S. (2014), 'Cultural consultation as a model for training multidisciplinary mental healthcare professionals in cultural competence skills: preliminary results', *Journal of Psychiatric and Mental Health Nursing*, 21: 814–26.

Potter, A. (2014), 'Killer disease is truly global', *Metro*, 24 March, 12–13.

Public Health England (2012), 'Longer Lives'. <www.longerlives.phe.org.uk> accessed 7 July 2015.

Public Health England (2014a), 'Annual TB Update', <https://www.gov.uk/government/publications/tuberculosis-tb-annual-update> accessed 7 July 2015.

Public Health England (2014b), 'Tuberculosis in the UK', 2014 Report. <www.gov.uk/phe> accessed 7 July 2015.

Scambler, G. (2003), 'Health and illness behaviour', in Scambler, G. (ed.), *Sociology as Applied to Medicine*. London: Saunders.

Smaje, C. and LeGrand, J. (1997), 'Ethnicity, equity and the use of the health services in the British NHS', *Social Science & Medicine*, 45: 485–96.

Smith, G.D., Charsley, K., Lambert, H., Paul, S., Fenton, S. and Ahmad, W. (2001), 'Ethnicity, health and the meaning of socio-economic position', in Graham, H. (ed.) *Understanding Health Inequalities*. Buckingham: Open University Press.

Sumartojo, E. (1993), 'When tuberculosis treatment fails', *American Review of Respiratory Disease*, 147: 1311–20.

TB Alert (2014a), 'Symptoms of TB'. <www.tbalert.org/about-tb/what-is-tb/symptoms/> accessed 7 July 2015.

TB Alert (2014b), 'TB Action Group'. <www.tbalert.org/what-we-do/uk/tb-action-group/> accessed 7 July 2015.

Waterman, S. (1997), 'The 'return' of the Jews into London', in Kershen, A.J. (ed.), *London, the Promised Land? The Migrant Experience of a Capital City*. Aldershot: Avebury, pp. 143–60.

White, V.L.C. (1999a), 'Health Advocates in Medicine', in Kershen, A.J. (ed.) *Language, Labour and Migration*. Aldershot: Avebury, pp. 74–90.

White, V.L.C. (1999b), 'Medicine and migration: health beliefs and practices within the Bangladeshi community of East London'. Unpublished MSc dissertation, University College, London.

White, V.L.C. (2000), Unpublished observations and data during visit to Bangladesh, 2000.

White, V.L.C. (2005), 'Cultural Barriers to the management of tuberculosis in the Bangladeshi Community of East London'. Unpublished MD thesis, University of London.

Withycombe, E.C., White, V.L.C. (2013), 'Barriers to the use of medical interpreters'. Unpublished.

Zola, I.K. (1973), 'Pathways to the doctor – from person to patient', *Social Science & Medicine*, 7: 677–89.

Chapter 12

The Presence and Treatment of Infection in the Migrant Population of London

Jane Anderson

Introduction

Although international migration, one of the most emotive subjects in contemporary society is now a consistent and integral part of global existence, it has never been as socioeconomically and politically significant nor accorded such priority as is the case today (Castles, 2013). This is even more pronounced when issues of health, particularly in the context of infectious or contagious conditions such as HIV are juxtaposed with those of migration. In today's world, for those who are diagnosed in time and are able to access high quality care, HIV has the potential to be a long term chronic condition. In England life expectancy for people with HIV has increased dramatically. People living with HIV are ageing and the complications of longevity are impinging on clinical care, increasing the long term costs of the condition. At the same time new infections continue, with more people than ever before living with HIV, requiring new and innovative paradigms of clinical and social care. These shifting epidemiological and clinical aspects of HIV infection are coupled with, high rates of stigma, social deprivation and disproportionately high infection rates amongst marginalised communities, including significant numbers of people born outside the UK, where the intersection of these issues leads to a situation of profound inequality.

The coalition government has radically altered the British health economy with the introduction of the *Health and Social Care Act 2012* (2012) coinciding with a period of considerable economic constraint, which are together impacting on the ways in which HIV prevention, diagnosis and treatment is organised and funded, as well as the lived experience of those with the infection.

There is no shortage of historical examples of responsibility for importing and transmitting infections being attributed to people born elsewhere, along with blame for an array of afflictions and social ills. Confusion about the legal status of migrants, for example the UK social category of asylum seeker is often portrayed as 'undeserving' and separate from 'genuine refugees', further exacerbated by racism and xenophobia (Dodds, Keogh and Chime, 2004), can mean that being both a migrant and living with HIV carries a doubly compromised social identity (Worth, 2006). This combination of migration with a stigmatised, sexually transmissible infection has generated a particularly hostile political and public discourse in many countries. A recent UK example, which prompted a media storm, were the remarks made by the right wing politician Nigel Farage in an interview for *Newsweek* on the topic of inward migration in which he stated that UKIP wished to control the quantity and quality of people who come to Britain. When asked how he defined 'quality people' his reply included the words 'People who do not have HIV, to be frank. That's a good start' (Chalmers, 2014).

The number of international migrants (people residing in a country other than their country of birth for 12 months or more) continues to rise, from about 155 million in 2000 to 214 million in 2010, accounting for approximately three per cent of the world's population, and 8.7 per cent of the total European population (Migration, 2011). New countries have joined the European Union leading to an increase in intra-European mobility, yet simultaneously securitisation across international boundaries makes entry into European states more tightly controlled than ever and migrant access to social support and health care more difficult.

Connections are made between migration and increases in both risk and vulnerabilities for the acquisition and transmission of HIV. It is principally the conditions under which people move and establish themselves that are particularly pertinent to infection and to outcomes (Haour-Knipe and Zalduondo et al., 2014). In many cases, those who migrate do not simply leave their home country and permanently live in another; rather, people come and go, have children and develop extended families in other countries or continents. Migration is a dynamic rather than static process, with the fluctuating moving population confounding statistics (Anderson, 2008). Yet despite the numbers and the complexity of global migration there is little coordinated health policy across national boundaries for migrants (WHO, 2010). Existing approaches tend to either reflect potential risks to the destination society or the vulnerability of the migrant, with only recent attention being paid to considering the more ethical and assets based approach to delivery of coordinated and equitable health related responses (Zimmerman and Kiss et al., 2011). Yet, even in the current climate in which health equity and the wider determinants of health and wellbeing are being given increasing prominence, for example through the ground breaking work of Sir Michael Marmot (Marmot, 2010), attention remains narrowly focused on socioeconomic factors with little consideration of the impact of migration as a key intersecting factor (Ingleby, 2012). Increasingly there is a need for explicit migrant health policies in those countries of Europe that are home to substantial populations of migrants (Keygnaert and Guieu et al., 2014)

What do we know about Migrants and their Health and Wellbeing in the UK?

The 2011 UK census identified approximately 7.6 million people living in the UK who were born outside the country, half of whom came to the UK in the preceding ten years (ONS, 2014). This accounts for approximately 13 per cent of the UK population, an increase from the eight per cent recorded in the 2001 census (ONS, 2012). In 2013, 22,592 applications were received for asylum, representing a rise of 14 per cent over 2012, but an overall fall from the peak of 84,132 in 2002 (ONS, 2013). There are no accurate figures for the numbers of migrants who lack legal status within the UK, with widely varying estimates that range from 525,000 to almost one million (Whyte, Whyte and Hires, 2015).

Although acknowledged as being amongst the most vulnerable people in society, data on the overall health and wellbeing of migrants in the UK is lacking. Legal status and citizenship is a key marker of differentiation of vulnerability and health related risk. Irregular migrants tend to have worse jobs and poorer living conditions, temporary residents frequently face pressure from employers and officialdom. Even for those with secure status, employment rates for people born outside the UK are overall lower than their UK born compatriots (ONS, 2014) and many experience discrimination, and find difficulty accessing the services they need (Castles, 2013).

Getting better at meeting the health and social care needs of vulnerable migrants has been prioritised by the UK Government, via the newly established National Inclusion Health Board, however attempts to deliver on this have stalled due to a paucity of baseline data (Aspinall, 2014), including that on children and families (Glass, 2015). Without data on the particular unmet health needs, driving appropriate service design and development is difficult. (Jayaweera, 2014). Some health conditions are very tightly linked to migration. Hepatitis B and C are increasing in the UK and contributing to the rise in liver disease largely found in people migrating from high endemicity regions (NICE, 2011). The risk profiles for a range of infectious diseases in the UK in 2010 found significant differences between migrants and the indigenous population, with a majority of the cases of TB, HIV in heterosexuals, malaria and enteric fever being diagnosed amongst people who were migrants. The report further emphasised the need to improve data collection, in particular recording of country of birth as a risk factor for infection. (Wagner and Lawrence et al., 2014).

Migrants with particular HIV-related vulnerabilities include sex workers and those belonging to LGBTI (lesbian, gay, bisexual, transgender and intersex) groups who may have elevated HIV-related risks. Differences in sexual health according to migration status have been seen in female sex workers in the UK. A systematic review looking at health differences between migrant and non-migrant female sex workers revealed that migrant women have lower risks in higher income countries (Platt and Grenfell et al., 2013). A London comparison of migrant women sex workers from Eastern Europe with those born in Britain showed migrant women tended to be younger, seeing more clients and less likely to use contraception. Engagement with specialist outreach health workers leads to improved outcomes for women (Platt and Grenfell et al., 2011). Much less is known about male sex workers in the UK, who tend to have poor sexual health. Almost one third of male sex workers in a London based study were migrants, with a majority coming from Brazil (McGrath-Lone and Marsh et al., 2014).

In a number of countries same sex sexual relationships are either considered unacceptable or in some countries, for example Uganda, Nigeria and Russia are illegal. Sexual orientation may be the reason for people to seek a life elsewhere where they can express their sexuality more freely. Migrants in this situation may encounter additional challenges in the UK, facing more extreme social and financial exclusion and greater risk of exploitation than other groups of refugees and migrants (Stuart, 2013). A study of ethnic minority and migrant gay and bisexual men described lived experiences that were more problematic and challenging than those facing White British gay men, who were seen as coming from a more liberal and accepting culture in contrast to their own, which was deemed judiciously policed for anything that diverged from a hetero-normative path (McKeown and Nelson et al., 2010). The accession of ten Central and Eastern European (CEE) countries to the EU in 2004 and 2007 produced a very large influx of new migrants to the UK, including a number of men who have sex with men (MSM). These men appear to be poorly networked, involved in high risk sexual behaviour and hard to reach (Evans and Hart et al., 2011). In an interview based study Eastern European MSM described how extricating themselves from traditional systems of social control in their home societies and having greater access to gay venues in London resulted in their increased sexual activity, and high risk behaviour particularly in the first phase of migration. This activity was further influenced by perceptions of risk in the UK vis-à-vis Central and Eastern Europe. Risk-prevention behaviour depended upon the possession of relevant information, as well as the motivation to use condoms and appropriate behavioural skills, with the latter two factors in particular influenced by social mores in the home country and the UK (Mole and Parutis et al., 2014). Increasing numbers of Latin Americans are coming to the UK including significant numbers of men who have sex with other men or who are bisexual (McIlwaine, 2011).

In an online survey of 991 ethnic minority and migrant MSM and 11,944 white, British born MSM, self-reported HIV seropositivity was low for men of South Asian, Chinese, and 'other Asian' ethnicity (range, 0.0 per cent–5.8 per cent) and for men born in CEE (4.5 per cent) but elevated for men born in South or Central America (18.7 per cent), compared with white British men (13.1 per cent) (P < 0.001). This highlights the importance of health promotion targeting MSM from all ethnic and migrant groups in Britain (Elford and Doerner et al., 2012). 2,648 CEE migrants who were surveyed online reported high rates of risk behaviour for STIs and HIV. Men reported higher rates of partner acquisition, of paying for sex and both men and women had higher levels of injection drug use than the general population. However, CEE migrants reported high levels of consistent condom use and self-reported rates of STIs and HIV were low. In terms of health care access a majority of CEE migrants were not registered with a primary care provider (Burns and Evans et al., 2011). However use of GUM (sexual health clinics) report significant numbers of migrants from CEE countries, women using the facility more than men. Female sex work and paying for sex by men was also widely reported ((Evans and Mercer et al., 2011).

HIV in the UK

Data from 2013 show no evidence of a decline in HIV infection. The proportion of newly diagnosed people who have been recently infected has consistently increased (22 per cent in 2013 as compared to 14 per cent in 2009). Overall HIV diagnosed prevalence among population aged 15–59 years old was 2.41 per 1,000 in England. One in five (66/326) local authorities had a diagnosed prevalence >=2 per 1,000 population aged 15–59 years old (Public Health England, 2014).

The UK HIV epidemic is principally concentrated among gay and bisexual men and other men who have sex with men (referred to above as MSM) and Black African, mainly heterosexual, men and women. In 2013, there were an estimated 107,800 people in the UK living with HIV infection of whom approximately 25 per cent were undiagnosed and unaware of their infection (Public Health England, 2014). In the same year 6,000 people (4,480 men and 1,520 women) were newly diagnosed with HIV in the UK. People born outside the UK carry a disproportionately high burden of the epidemic, although their countries of origin are changing. In 2012, 46 per cent of those newly diagnosed with HIV were born in the UK. Those born elsewhere were predominantly from Africa (28 per cent) Europe (14) per cent and Latin American/Caribbean (5 per cent). There has been a significant change in pattern since 2005, when 35 per cent were born in the UK, 50 per cent in Africa, seven per cent in Europe and less than one per cent Latin American and the Caribbean (Public Health England; Personal Communication, 2015).

Within the UK, London is particularly affected with an HIV rate almost three times that of the England average. In 2013, 41 per cent of the people with HIV in the UK lived in London, one in three of those newly diagnosed was a London resident and almost half of all the new diagnoses made in the UK that year happened in a London based health care facility (Public Health England 2014). The 33,863 people living with diagnosed HIV in London in 2013 represented an increase of four per cent over 2012 and is 78 per cent higher than in 2004 (Public Health England, 2015).

Men who have sex with men have the highest rates of newly diagnosed HIV infection accounting for 54 per cent of new HIV diagnoses across the country, and even higher, at 62 per cent amongst London residents in 2013. The proportion of MSM living in the UK newly diagnosed with HIV who were born abroad increased from 28 per cent in 2004 to 40 per cent in 2013. In 2013, of MSM born abroad, approximately 47 per cent probably acquired their infection while living in the UK. Newer migrant communities include Central and Eastern Europeans and Latin Americans with significant numbers of men who have sex with men, (McIlwaine, 2011). Both CEE and Latin American born migrants have high rates of largely UK acquired HIV relative to the UK background levels. Both populations are over-represented amongst sex workers, and also appear to have poor access to primary care (Granada and Paccoud, 2014).

People who acquired their infection through heterosexual contact accounted for 2,490 (45 per cent) of new HIV diagnoses in the UK in 2013, of which 1,070 were heterosexual men and 1420 were heterosexual women.

People from sub-Saharan Africa continue to account for the majority of people living with heterosexually acquired HIV, although this is changing. The numbers of migrants from Africa newly diagnosed with HIV reached its highest number in 2003 and has since been falling, following global changes in migration patterns. The 2011 UK census reveals that 3.1 per cent of the population of England and Wales identify as Black African (ONS, 2012), yet people of Black African heritage account for 47 per cent of those living with diagnosed HIV in the UK (Public Health England, 2014). A majority are of East African origin, however the proportions of Africans newly diagnosed with HIV that are from West African countries has shown a consistent increase over the past decade. Despite some important overarching similarities (National Aids Trust, 2014), there is no single 'African' or 'migrant identity in the UK and correspondingly there will be diverse experiences and needs. Gender and sexual orientation are critical factors that impact upon the experiences of African people in relation to HIV in the UK (Anderson and Doyal, 2004, Doyal and Anderson, 2005, Doyal, Anderson et al. 2007, Doyal, Anderson et al. 2009). Almost twice as many women from African backgrounds are living with HIV in the UK as men, and African heterosexual men are amongst those with highest rates of late and undiagnosed HIV (Public Health England 2014). The complexity of the lives of African men who have sex with men is particularly pronounced, many keeping their sexual lives secret for fear of reprisals and discrimination from within the community (Doyal, Paparini et al. 2008) The numbers of African men acquiring HIV through sex between men may be underestimated as a result of the reluctance to disclose same sex activity to clinical services (Hué, Brown et al. 2014). Critical factors that impact on how African migrants deal with HIV in the UK include high levels of poverty and unmet social need (Ibrahim, Anderson et al. 2008), the complexities of the migration process (National Aids Trust 2014), eligibility for and access to medical care (Department of Health 2012) (Thomas, Aggleton et al. 2010) as well as HIV associated stigma (Elford, Ibrahim et al. 2007, Chinouya, Hildreth et al. 2014). Not only is it important to recognise the structural issues facing migrants in relation to health and HIV it is also crucial to acknowledge that there may be different understandings about health, wellbeing and illness held by people from different backgrounds and cultures, and that the importance of transnational health networks for both individuals and communities (Thomas 2013).

Testing and Diagnosis

HIV testing is a pivotal intervention for the health and wellbeing of both the individual as well as for prevention and for the wider public health. For those diagnosed in time who are able to access effective therapy HIV has the potential to be a long term chronic medical condition and life expectancy has increased to be almost equivalent to those who are HIV-free ((May, Gompels et al. 2014). Knowledge of HIV status also has an impact on the prevention of HIV transmission and acquisition. Work on transmission dynamics within the epidemic suggest that most new infections are acquired from people with HIV who are undiagnosed and thus unaware of their HIV infectivity risk (Punyacharoensin, Edmunds et al., 2015). People who test HIV positive are able to modify their sexual behaviour and reduce risk of transmission (Marks, Crepaz et al. 2006). Effective antiretroviral therapy markedly reduces infectiousness making the risk of passing HIV on to others is extremely low (Fidler, Anderson et al., 2013). Importantly, people with a negative test have a key opportunity for information and prevention interventions for their future health and wellbeing.

Rates of late diagnosis of HIV, a key Public Health Outcomes Framework (PHOF) indicator, remain unacceptably high across the country, in particular amongst older heterosexual people and those born abroad. That 24 per cent of people with HIV in the UK remain undiagnosed and 45 per cent are only diagnosed when treatment should already have begun, dangerously undermines therapeutic and prevention opportunities, results in preventable morbidity and mortality and represents a critical health inequality.

In London, as in the rest of the UK, heterosexual people (and men more so than women) are those most likely to be both undiagnosed and diagnosed late. For people born outside the UK, particularly those of African origin the figures are far worse. Africans are significantly more likely to present to clinical care with undiagnosed and late diagnosed infection than the white population – 61 per cent and 31 per cent respectively (Public Health England 2014). Laboratory techniques that allow recent HIV infection to be identified (Recent Infection Testing Algorithm – RITA) find less recent infection amongst heterosexual people with HIV born outside the UK (Aghaizu, Murphy et al., 2014), which is entirely consistent with observed rates of late diagnosis amongst this population.

Despite these data there are no migrant-specific HIV testing programmes in the UK, although there is specific work aimed to reach Africans. National guidance recommends that all health professionals should routinely offer and recommend an HIV test to anyone who is known to be from a country of high HIV prevalence and to those who report sexual contact abroad or in the UK with someone from a country of high HIV prevalence (NICE – National Institute for Health and Care Excellence, 2011). There is now a very robust evidence base underpinning the effectiveness of testing in securing best outcomes in both clinical (Public Health England, 2014) and community settings (Thornton, Delpech et al., 2012). Yet existing guidance is neither appropriately nor consistently implemented. Barriers may be either patient or provider related with a lack of awareness by both sides playing a significant role. Many people from countries with widespread epidemics believe that their infection risk in the UK is much lower. A community based survey in 2013 of people of Black African heritage in the UK, 78 per cent of whom were migrants, found that almost three-quarters were unaware of the high

HIV prevalence amongst African people in England and of their personal risk of infection. Of those who had never had an HIV test only half were confident about where to go to get a test. Two-thirds believed they had no reason to think they might be HIV positive (Bourne et al., 2014). Additional barriers to equal access to HIV services have been identified, included language barriers and others bordering on the use of traditional medicine by African migrants, understanding of cultural diversity, awareness of how and where to access HIV services, and getting information about HIV (Shangase and Egbe, 2015).

There is widespread evidence of missed diagnostic opportunities in clinical encounters where staff have failed to offer an HIV test when indicated (Burns, Johnson, et al., 2008; Elmahdi, Gerver, et al., 2014). Programmes of opt out HIV testing in a range of clinical settings have been shown to be successful in making the offer of a test routine (Rayment, Asboe et al., 2014). Routine screening offers to new migrants for a range of health related issues including HIV can be acceptable, however disease-related stigma present in the newly arrived person's own communities and services being perceived as non-migrant friendly are barriers to uptake (Seedat, Hargreaves et al., 2014). Approaches that raise awareness about the benefits of screening together with community-based packages that combine multiple screening tests into a single general health check in primary care may increase acceptability by reducing HIV associated stigma. Low registration rates by migrants with primary care compromise this approach. (Hargreaves, Seedat, et al., 2014) For those who are registered with a general practice rapid point of care tests for HIV incorporated within the new patient health check have been shown to reach African migrants as well as pick up HIV at an earlier stage than conventional testing approaches (Leber, 2013). Opportunistic testing for HIV alone as well as for combinations of infectious agents such as hepatitis B and C in accident and emergency departments and acute medical admissions wards has been shown to successfully reach ethnic minorities and those born outside the UK (Strudwick, 2015). In the case of undocumented migrants living with HIV, securing access to services as part of the asylum process acted as a gateway to health services (Whyte, Whyte, et al., 2015).

Treatment and Outcomes

In England, once the diagnosis has been made, people with HIV are rapidly linked to and largely retained in highly effective medical care with excellent clinical and virological outcomes that are equivalent for all groups of patient, irrespective of sex, ethnicity or country of birth. Markers of wider determinants of care quality are consistently highly rated by patients (Public Health England, 2014). These excellent outcomes reflect the universal nature of freely available NHS HIV care for all those resident in the UK. Importantly, following a change in legislation in 2012, antiretroviral therapy is available in the UK to all who need it without charge, irrespective of immigration status (Department of Health, 2012). Reasons why some people fare less well is complex and multi-factorial. From European studies there is some evidence to suggest that people with HIV living outside their country of birth fare less well than indigenous patients (Nellen, Wit, et al., 2004) (Lima, Fernandes, et al., 2009), with higher rates of treatment failure. Progression to AIDS in people with HIV across the European Union between 1999 and 2006 was noted to be more common amongst migrants from sub-Saharan Africa and from Latin America than in people living in their country of birth (Del Amo, Likatavicius, et al., 2011). This may be a consequence of the higher rates of late presentation associated with migrant communities, and emphasises the need for accessible and appropriate testing and diagnostic pathways for migrants in the UK (Rice, Elford et al., 2014). An association of poorer virological outcomes with socioeconomic deprivation in the UK has been described (Burch, Smith, et al., 2014), circumstances that are particularly likely to be experienced by those born outside the UK.

Tackling the Problem: Prevention

Knowledge and interventions already exist to make new HIV infections completely preventable. Why then is there still an epidemic and why are migrants to the UK at particular risk of both acquisition of HIV and of poorer outcomes? Even though many migrants from high prevalence areas acquire HIV in their country of origin it is clear that substantial numbers of HIV positive people born outside the UK are acquiring HIV infection in the UK, after their arrival. Between a quarter to a third of all HIV-positive Africans currently resident in the UK, nearly half of HIV-positive African men who have sex with men, and about one third of heterosexual Africans born abroad, probably acquired HIV infection whilst in the UK, with the proportion rising year on year (Burns, Arthur, et al., 2009); (Rice, Elford, et al., 2012). Importantly, the estimate of 33 per cent of HIV acquired in the UK through modelling work is three times higher than the 11 per cent estimate that is reported from routine clinical services (Rice, Elford et al., 2012), highlighting potential false assumptions that are made by clinicians about HIV risk for African born people living in the UK.

Effective action on HIV prevention delivers reduced HIV incidence, ensures access to high quality care for all those who are HIV positive, reduces HIV-related health disparities and optimises individual and community health and wellbeing in its widest sense. Although there have been studies exploring the prevention needs of Black Africans in the UK, there is no needs assessment of all migrants in relation to HIV prevention, which represents a significant gap, given the current state of the epidemic in the UK. Awareness raising, promoting increased and innovative approaches to HIV testing and increasing access to condoms underpin the existing National HIV prevention programme, 'It Starts with Me' run by HIV Protection England which has a particular focus on reaching Black Africans and gay men. The programme is commissioned and funded through the Department of Health and a consortium of NGOs delivers the work. The programme is set to run from 2013 to 2015; an evaluation of the programme through a survey of Black African people found that only one third had seen the materials associated with the programme (Bourne et al., 2014).

Is this the right approach? With migration becoming a global norm and a much wider group of migrants being affected by HIV across the UK it is timely to review the best strategic approach to improving the health and wellbeing of migrants in relation to not only HIV but also to the wider determinants of health. Coupling national strategic approaches to tackling HIV with tailored programmes of delivery that are able to translate and implement evidence into action, scaling up interventions that have been shown to work for the right people in the right place at the right time are crucial for effective prevention. At the same time, particularly for migrants to the UK, there is a need to see the bigger picture, ensuring that the social, structural and health system determinants of HIV are properly addressed. Success will require communication and collaboration across many different areas of responsibility, including health, education, employment, the law, housing and social care. This can best be facilitated by an enabling policy environment with clear and consistent commitment, prioritisation and investment to both migrant health and to tackling HIV.

Making it Happen

The passage of the controversial Health and Social Care Act of 2012 into law radically altered the way in which the health economy in England operates. Much of the power and budgetary responsibility previously invested in the Department of Health has now been devolved to a number of new bodies, including NHS England, local authorities and GP-led Clinical Commissioning Groups. Dispersed leadership, local decision making and implementation are key themes, with local politicians taking the lead and being answerable to their local electorate. Based on the premise that local leaders are best placed to secure the best health for their communities and populations, responsibility and much of the budget for Public Health has moved from the NHS into local government, and within the Public Health portfolio are now the responsibilities and finances for a majority of sexual and reproductive health services and activities. As a consequence open access, Sexual Health, Reproductive Health and HIV services, previously integrated as a single system with clinical leadership, governance and accountability all contained within the NHS, have undergone major changes in commissioning and service provision. From April 2013 upper tier and unitary local authorities in England have a mandatory duty to commission comprehensive sexual health services including HIV prevention and diagnosis, at a local level in a way that best meets the needs of their local population. The notable exceptions are the responsibilities and finances for HIV treatment and care and abortion care where responsibilities have remained under NHS commissioning and governance control, albeit within different organisational areas. In practice, for HIV prevention, diagnosis, treatment and care three separate bodies have commissioning responsibilities for separate components of the pathway. With this split in responsibility and in funding comes the risk of fragmentation of what needs to be seamless integrated care. The difficulties facing people with less understanding of the system, those with more complex HIV-related needs and those who are already marginalised are likely to be magnified in this complex environment. It is with local Government that the power lies to make a difference to the social determinants of health and wellbeing that is complementary to the clinical abilities of healthcare providers. Bringing the two more closely together coupled with effective collaboration and joined up commissioning has the potential to improve outcomes. The financial deficit facing the National Health Service in England has led to a full review of how health care could be better managed and organised over the next five years which brings a clear emphasis on building prevention and the social determinants of health into all aspects of care (NHS England, 2014).

How London is Approaching HIV and Migrant Health in the New Landscape

As Lord Darzi in his recent review of health in London noted, the division of responsibilities recognises the complexity of health and health improvement, and the consequent need for coordination to achieve concerted action (Darzi, 2014). The considerable effort and meticulous attention to detail that is required to make the whole HIV, sexual and reproductive health system work, (see the guide 'Making it Work' produced by Public Health England, 2014) is being undertaken in a period of drastic financial pressure both within the NHS and within local government. The existing budgets for Sexual and Reproductive Health Rights and HIV services are not ring-fenced and are being keenly scrutinised by both Local Government and NHS England commissioners. Joining up the costs and the benefits to all involved in the pathway is key. In 2014, £5.6 million was spent in London on HIV prevention activities, yet the lifelong estimated treatment cost for each person who acquires HIV is approximately £370,000. Despite the clear cost effectiveness of preventing HIV infection, the impact of the expenditure and the subsequent saving falls to different parts of the system, as money invested by local government in HIV prevention initiatives will be recouped by savings within the clinical care budgets of NHS.

Although funding for HIV prevention in England exists at both a national and local level there has been a consistent and progressive decline in the amount spent, falling from £55 million in 2001 to approximately £10 million in 2014/15 (National Aids Trust, 2015). Such National funding as remains has been focused on men who have sex with men and people of Black African heritage, without a specific remit for the wider migrant population.

Local authorities, of which there are 33 in London, are now responsible for addressing the prevention needs of their local populations, with financial allocations under the new arrangements built around the historical allocation at the time of transfer of responsibilities. A London wide assessment of the situation in 2013 (Rashbrook 2013) demonstrated a clear need for a coordinated, strategic city-wide approach to HIV prevention in addition to the particular local needs, leading to the London Councils successfully coming together to support and deliver a pan London HIV prevention programme to which each local authority contributes. However, although 32 of the 33 London boroughs are 'high HIV prevalence' areas with a diagnosed prevalence of HIV of more than two per 1000 residents, the population at risk differs, with some areas having higher proportions of people born outside the UK than others. Prioritisation of HIV prevention by, and within, these particular local areas, ideally interwoven with local interventions to reduce inequalities in general, will be a key route into appropriate and effective interventions for migrants. The challenge will be to secure this prioritisation, given that in 2014/15 less than one per cent of the local authority public health allocation in high prevalence local authorities was spent on HIV prevention (National Aids Trust 2015).

Summary

This chapter has highlighted the fact that HIV within the migrant population of the capital is a health issue that continues to deserve special attention. From a general medical point of view, as illustrated in the previous chapter, migrants have particular health needs. Language, cultural differences and the stigma attach to certain diseases – HIV being one of the most stigmatised – are all issues which frequently result in the late presentation of those in need of medical care. The fact that 32 of London's 33 boroughs have a high HIV prevalence emphasises still further the need for health policies and provisions, within and beyond the capital, to be joined up. Health commissioners and providers in London need to recognise that migration into what is a major global city has become the norm. Yet, at the same time they have to be conscious of the fact that the migrant community is now super-diverse and that when considering the needs of the migrant, the appropriate assessment, evaluation, provision and monitoring of the individual, as well as the group, is exercised; in other words provision must be explicitly tailored to specific need.

In order to ensure the best patient outcomes, it is vital that both the health and social care workforce be competent and knowledgeable, not only about the medical needs of the individual and the requirements of tending to those with HIV, in addition, staff must have an understanding of, and respect for, the religious and cultural mores of patients who are migrants. Linguistic and religious/cultural misunderstanding can at times result in unnecessarily delayed treatment for the patient and unnecessary pressure on the health worker.

Finally, there is a need to recognise the geographic necessities of HIV policies in the broader context of the constant movement of migrants within and beyond the European Union. As with healthcare policies in London and the UK, there is a need to develop strategies in Europe which acknowledge the presence of a substantial migrant population within sovereign states and develop explicit and coordinated health policies across the EU.

References

Aghaizu, A., Murphy, G., Tosswill, J., DeAngelis, D., Charlett, A., Gill, O., Ward, H., Lattimore, S., Simmons R. and Delpech V. (2014), 'Recent infection testing algorithm (RITA) applied to new HIV diagnoses in England, Wales and Northern Ireland, 2009 to 2011', *Euro surveillance: bulletin Européen sur les maladies transmissibles* [European communicable disease bulletin], 19(2).

Anderson, J. (2008), 'Coming and going: some aspects of care for migrants with HIV in the UK', *Journal of Infection*, 57(1): 11–15.

Anderson, J. and Doyal, L. (2004), 'Women from Africa living with HIV in London: a descriptive study', *AIDS Care*, 16(1): 95–105.

Aspinall, P. (2014), 'Hidden Needs: Identifying Key Vulnerable Groups in Data Collections: Vulnerable Migrants, Gypsies and Travellers, Homeless People, and Sex Workers', *The Centre for Health Services Studies*, University of Kent.

Bourne, A., Reid, D. and Weatherburn, P. (2014), 'African Health and Sex Survey 2013–14: Headline Findings', London, Sigma Research, London School of Hygiene and Tropical Medicine.

Burch, L., Smith, C., Anderson, J., Sherr, L., Rodger, A., O'Connell, R., Gilson, R., Elford, J., Phillips, A., Speakman, A., Johnson, M. and Lampe, F. (2014), 'Socio-economic factors and virological suppression among people diagnosed with HIV in the United Kingdom: Results from the ASTRA study', *J Int AIDS Soc*, 17(4 Suppl. 3): 19533.

Burns, F.M., Arthur, G., Johnson, A.M., Nazroo, J. and Fenton, K.A. (2009), 'United Kingdom acquisition of HIV infection in African residents in London: more than previously thought', *AIDS*, 23(2): 262–6.

Burns, F.M., Johnson, A.M., Nazroo, J., Ainsworth, J., Anderson, J., Fakoya, A., Fakoya, I., Hughes, A., Jungmann, E., Sadiq, S.T., Sullivan, A.K. and Fenton, K.A. (2008), 'Missed opportunities for earlier HIV diagnosis within primary and secondary healthcare settings in the UK', *AIDS*, 22(1): 115–22.

Castles, S. and Miller, M.J. (2013), *The Age of Migration: International Population Movements in the Modern World*. Basingstoke: Palgrave Macmillan.

Chalmers, R. (2014), 'Inside the Mind of Nigel Farage: "I Want to Be Minister for Europe"', *Newsweek*, 9 October.

Chinouya, M., Hildreth, A., Goodall, D., Aspinall, P. and Hudson, A. (2014), 'Migrants and HIV stigma: findings from the Stigma Index Study (UK)', *Health Soc Care Community*, 23(3).

Darzi, A. (2014), 'Better Health For London', Report of the London Health Commission. London.

Del Amo, J., Likatavicius, G., Perez-Cachafeiro, S., Hernando, V., Gonzalez, C., Jarrin, I., Noori, T., Hamers, F.F. and Bolumar, F. (2011), 'The epidemiology of HIV and AIDS reports in migrants in the 27 European Union countries, Norway and Iceland: 1999–2006', *Eur J Public Health*, 21(5): 620–26.

Department of Health (2012), 'HIV treatment for overseas visitors', </www.gov. uk/government/publications/hiv-treatment-for-overseas-visitors-in-england-from-1-october-2012> accessed 6 January 2015.

Dodds, C., Keogh, P. and Chime, O. (2004), 'Outsider status: stigma and discrimination experienced by gay men and African people with HIV', Sigma Research, <http://www.sigmaresearch.org.uk/downloads/report04f.pdf> accessed 6 January 2015.

Doyal, L., Anderson, J. and Paparini, S. (2007), '"I count myself as being in a different world": African gay and bisexual men living with HIV in London', London, Homerton University Hospital NHS Foundation Trust.

Doyal, L. and Anderson, J. (2005), '"My fear is to fall in love again ...": How HIV-positive African women survive in London', *Soc Sci Med*, 60(8): 1729–38.

Doyal, L., Anderson, J. and Paparini, S. (2009), '"You are not yourself": exploring masculinities among heterosexual African men living with HIV in London', *Soc Sci Med*, 68(10): 1901–7.

Doyal, L., Paparini, S. and Anderson, J. (2008), '"Elvis Died and I was Born": Black African Men Negotiating Same-Sex Desire in London', *Sexualities*, 11(1–2): 171–92.

Elford, J., Ibrahim, F., Bukutu, C. and Anderson, J. (2007), 'HIV-Related Discrimination Reported by People Living with HIV in London, UK.' *AIDS and Behavior*, 12(2): 255–64.

Elmahdi, R., Gerver, S.M., Gomez Guillen, G., Fidler, S., Cooke, G. and Ward, H. (2014), 'Low levels of HIV test coverage in clinical settings in the U.K.: a systematic review of adherence to 2008 guidelines', *Sexually Transmitted Infections*, 90(2): 119–24.

Evans, A.R., Hart, G.J., Mole, R., Mercer, C.H., Parutis, V., Gerry, C.J., Imrie, J. and Burns, F.M. (2011). 'Central and East European migrant men who have sex with men in London: a comparison of recruitment methods', *BMC Medical Research Methodology*, 11: 69.

Fidler, S., Anderson, J., Azad, Y., Delpech, V., Evans, C., Fisher, M., Gazzard, B., Gill, N., Lazarus, L., Lowbury, R., Orton, K., Osoro, B., Radcliffe, K., Smith, B., Churchill, D., Rogstad K. and Cairns G. (2013), 'Position statement on the use of antiretroviral therapy to reduce HIV transmission, January 2013: The British HIV Association (BHIVA) and the Expert Advisory Group on AIDS (EAGA)', *HIV Medicine*, 14(5): 259–62.

Glass, D. (2015), 'Why the fight against HIV starts within us', <https://www. opendemocracy.net/transformation/dan-glass/why-fight-against-hiv-starts-within-us> 6 January 2015.

Granada, L. and Paccoud, I. (2014), 'Latin Americans: a case for better access to sexual health services', <http://www.clauk.org.uk/wp-content/uploads/2014/06/CLAUK-and-NAZ-Latin-Americans-a-case-for-better-access.pdf> accessed 6 January 2015.

Haour-Knipe, M., Zalduondo, B., Samuels, F., Molesworth, K. and Sehgal, S. (2014), 'HIV and "people on the move": six strategies to reduce risk and vulnerability during the migration process', *International Migration*, 52(4): 9–25.

Hargreaves, S., Seedat, F., Car, J., Escombe, R., Hasan, S., Eliahoo, J. and Friedland, J.S. (2014), 'Screening for latent TB, HIV, and hepatitis B/C in new migrants in a high prevalence area of London, UK: a cross-sectional study', *BMC Infectious Diseases*, 14(1): 657.

Health and Social Care Act 2012. Available at <http://www.legislation.gov.uk/ukpga/2012/7/contents/enacted/data.htm United Kingdom>

Hué, S., Brown, A.E., Ragonnet-Cronin, M., Lycett, S.J., Dunn, D.T., Fearnhill, E., Dolling, D.I., Pozniak, A., Pillay, D. and Delpech, V.C. (2014), 'Phylogenetic analyses reveal HIV-1 infections between men misclassified as heterosexual transmissions', *AIDS*, 28(13): 1967–75.

Ibrahim, F., Anderson, J., Bukutu, C. and Elford, J. (2008), 'Social and economic hardship among people living with HIV in London', *HIV Medicine*, 9(8): 616–24.

Ingleby, D. (2012), 'Ethnicity, Migration and the "Social Determinants of Health", Agenda Etnicidad, Migración y la Agenda de los "Determinantes Sociales de la Salud"' <http://www.copmadrid.org/webcopm/publicaciones/social/in2012v21n3a9.pdf> accessed 6 January 2015.

Jayaweera, H. (2014), 'Health of Migrants in the UK: What Do We Know?' Migration Observatory Briefing. Oxford, COMPAS, University of Oxford, UK.

Keygnaert, I., Guieu, A., Ooms, G., Vettenburg, N., Temmerman, M. and Roelens, K. (2014), 'Sexual and reproductive health of migrants: does the EU care?', *Health Policy*, 114(2–3): 215–25.

Leber, W.M.H., Marlin, N., Anderson, J., Griffiths, G. (2013), 'Point-of-care HIV testing in primary care and early detection of HIV (RHIVA2): a cluster randomised controlled trial', *The Lancet*, 382: S7.

Lima, V., Fernandes, K., Rachlis, B., Druyts, E., Montaner, J. and Hogg, R. (2009), 'Migration adversely affects antiretroviral adherence in a population-based cohort of HIV/AIDS patients', *Soc Sci Med*, 68(6): 1044–9.

Marks, G., Crepaz, N. and Janssen, R.S. (2006), 'Estimating sexual transmission of HIV from persons aware and unaware that they are infected with the virus in the USA', *AIDS*, 20(10): 1447–50.

Marmot, M. (2010), Fair Society Healthy Lives: the Marmot Report—Executive Summary. 2010, <http://www.instituteofhealthequity.org/projects/fair-society-healthy-lives-the-marmot-review> accessed 6 January 2015.

May, M.T., Gompels, M., Delpech, V., Porter, K., Orkin, C., Kegg, S., Hay, P., Johnson, M., Palfreeman, A., Gilson, R., Chadwick, D., Martin, F., Hill,

T., Walsh, J., Post, F., Fisher, M., Ainsworth, J., Jose, S., Leen, C., Nelson, M., Anderson, J. and Sabin, C. (2014), 'Impact on life expectancy of HIV-1 positive individuals of CD4+ cell count and viral load response to antiretroviral therapy: UK cohort study', *AIDS*, 28(8), 1193–1202.

McGrath-Lone, L., Marsh, K., Hughes, G. and Ward, H. (2014), 'The sexual health of male sex workers in England: analysis of cross-sectional data from genitourinary medicine clinics', *Sexually Transmitted Infections*, 90(1): 38–40.

McIlwaine, C., Cock, J.C., and Linneker, B. (2011), 'No Longer Invisible: the Latin American community in London', Queen Mary University of London.

McKeown, E., Nelson, S., Anderson, J., Low, N. and Elford, J. (2010), 'Disclosure, discrimination and desire: experiences of Black and South Asian gay men in Britain', *Cult Health Sex*, 12(7): 843–56.

Mole, R.C., Parutis, V., Gerry, C.J. and Burns, F.M. (2014), 'The impact of migration on the sexual health, behaviours and attitudes of Central and East European gay/bisexual men in London', *Ethnic Health*, 19(1): 86–99.

National Aids Trust [NAT] (2014), HIV and Black African Communities in the UK. Available at <http://www.nat.org.uk/media/Files/Publications/NAT-African-Communities-Report-June-2014-FINAL.pdf> accessed 6 January 2015.

National Aids Trust [NAT] (2015), HIV prevention in England's high prevalence local authorities: 2013/14 and 2014/15. Examining spending on primary HIV prevention and additional HIV testing. Available at <http://www.nat.org.uk/media/Files/Publications/Prevention_Report_2015-1.pdf> accessed 6 January 2015.

National Health England (2014), Five Year Forward View. London, NHS England. <http://www.england.nhs.uk/wp-content/uploads/2014/10/5yfv-web.pdf> accessed 6 January 2015.

Nellen, J.F., Wit, F., De Wolf, F.W., Jurriaans, S., Lange, J.M. and Prins, J.M. (2004), 'Virologic and immunologic response to highly active antiretroviral therapy in indigenous and nonindigenous HIV-1-infected patients in the Netherlands', *J Acquir Immune Defic Syndr*, 36: 943–50.

NICE (2011), 'Increasing the uptake of HIV testing among black Africans in England. Public Health Guidance', 33.

Office of National Statistics (2012), Census Data: Table KS201EW – Ethnic Group. UK.

Office of National Statistics (2014), 2011 Census Analysis: Social and Economic Characteristics by Length of Residence of Migrant Populations in England and Wales.

Platt, L., Grenfell, P., Bonell, C., Creighton, S., Wellings, K., Parry, J. and Rhodes, T. (2011), 'Risk of sexually transmitted infections and violence among indoor-working female sex workers in London: the effect of migration from Eastern Europe', *Sexually Transmitted Infections*, 87(5): 377–84.

Platt, L., Grenfell, P., Fletcher, A., Sorhaindo, A., Jolley, E., Rhodes, T. and Bonell, C. (2013), 'Systematic review examining differences in HIV, sexually transmitted infections and health-related harms between migrant and non-migrant female sex workers', *Sexually Transmitted Infections*, 89(4): 311–19.

Public Health England (2014), *Addressing Late HIV Diagnosis through Screening and Testing: An Evidence Summary*. London: Public Health England.

Public Health England (2014), HIV in the United Kingdom: 2014 Report. Health Protection. London: Public Health England.

Public Health England (2014), *Making it Work: A guide to whole system commissioning for sexual health, reproductive health and HIV*. London: Public Health England.

Public Health England (2015), *Annual Epidemiological Spotlight on HIV in London. 2013 Data*. London: Public Health England.

Punyacharoensin, N., Edmunds, W.J., De Angelis, D., Delpech, V., Hart, G., Elford, J., Brown, A., Gill, N. and White, R.G. (2015), 'Modelling the HIV epidemic among MSM in the United Kingdom: quantifying the contributions to HIV transmission to better inform prevention initiatives', *AIDS*, 29(3): 339–49.

Rashbrook, E (2013), 'HIV Prevention Assessment Needs for London', ADPH, Public Health England and London Councils.

Rayment, M., Asboe, D. and Sullivan, A.K. (2014), 'HIV testing and management of newly diagnosed HIV', *British Medical Journal*, 349: g4275.

Rice, B.D., Elford, J., Yin, Z., Croxford, S., Brown, A. and Delpech, V. (2014), 'Trends in HIV Diagnoses, HIV Care, and Uptake of Antiretroviral Therapy Among Heterosexual Adults in England, Wales, and Northern Ireland', *Sexually Transmitted Diseases*, 41(4): 257–65.

Rice, B.D., Elford, J., Yin, Z. and Delpech, V.C. (2012), 'A new method to assign country of HIV infection among heterosexuals born abroad and diagnosed with HIV', *AIDS*, 26(15): 1961–6.

Seedat, F., Hargreaves, S. and Friedland, J.S. (2014), 'Engaging new migrants in infectious disease screening: a qualitative semi-structured interview study of UK migrant community health-care leads', *PLoS One*, 9(10): e108261.

Shangase, P. and Egbe, C. (2015), 'Barriers to Accessing HIV Services for Black African Communities in Cambridgeshire, the United Kingdom', *Journal of Community Health*, 40(1): 20–26.

Strudwick, P (2015), 'Hunting the silent killer', <http://mosaicscience.com/story/hepC> accessed 17 February 2015.

Stuart, A. (2013), *Double Jeopardy*. Full report available at <Trust for London. org.uk>

Thomas, F. (2013), 'Multiple medicaments: looking beyond structural inequalities in migrant health care', in Thomas, F. (ed.), *Migration Health and Inequality*. London: Zed Books, pp. 137–49.

Thomas, F., Aggleton, P. and Anderson, J. (2010), '"If I cannot access services, then there is no reason for me to test": the impacts of health service charges on HIV testing and treatment amongst migrants in England', *AIDS Care*, 22(4): 526–31.

Thornton, A.C., Delpech, V., Kall, M.M. and Nardone, A. (2012), 'HIV testing in community settings in resource-rich countries: a systematic review of the evidence', *HIV Med*, 13(7): 416–26.

Wagner, K.S., Lawrence, J., Anderson, L., Yin, Z., Delpech, V., Chiodini, P.L., Redman, C. and Jones, J. (2014), 'Migrant health and infectious diseases in the UK: findings from the last 10 years of surveillance', *Journal of Public Health (Oxford)*, 36(1): 28–35.

Whyte, J., Whyte, M.D. and Hires, K. (2015), 'A study of HIV positive undocumented African migrants' access to health services in the UK', *AIDS Care*, 27(6): 703–5.

World Health Organization (2010), 'Health of migrants: the way forward: report of a global consultation', Madrid, Spain, 3–5 March 2010.

Worth, H. (2006), 'Unconditional hospitality: HIV, ethics and the refugee "problem"', *Bioethics*, 20(5): 223–32.

Zimmerman, C., Kiss, L., and Hossain, M. (2011), 'Migration and health: a framework for 21st century policy-making', *PLoS Medicine*, 8(5): e1001034.

Chapter 13

Afterword

Anne J. Kershen

Anyone reading this book can be left in no doubt as to the impact recent immigration has made on the early 21st century landscape of London. The capital has a long tradition of migrant arrival and settlement and the past few decades have seen dramatic changes in the sources, flows, volume and diversity of incomers. Historians writing about the 18th, 19th and 20th centuries, have described the consecutive 'floods' and 'waves' of immigrants that entered the country from Europe and the New Commonwealth, many settling in the capital. However, by the end of the 1980s with the slowdown of immigration from South East Asia and the Caribbean, there were those who believed that large scale migrant entry was becoming a thing of the past; few anticipated the tsunami of immigrants that would arrive in the United Kingdom in the first decades of the 21st century. In addition to those seeking refuge from political and religious persecution and civil wars in the Middle East and Africa and those reuniting with family already settled in the UK, were incomers from Eastern Europe. People living in countries such as Poland, Hungary, Ukraine, Romania and Bulgaria were awakening to the possibilities that life offered in Western Europe and, in particular, the UK. However, the inflow did not just begin with the Accessions of 2004 and 2007, for as Michał Garapich so rightly points out in his chapter, significant numbers of Polish migrants were seeking economic opportunity in the UK's 'promised land' well before 2004. When concerns were raised about what the Accessions might mean in the case of numbers, government forecasters calmed nerves by suggesting that Accession would bring at most, some 15,000 new Eastern Europe EU citizens each year (Migrant Watch, 2015). How wrong they were. Between May 2004 and June 2006 the government approved just over 427,095 work registration applications from new EU Eastern Europeans; more than half of these from Poland, the remainder from the other seven new entrants (BBC News, 2015). And these were only those who formally applied to register for work. In addition there were those intending to be self-employed, others who did not apply for registration, family dependents and students. In all at its highest, the EU Accession migrant population of the Britain was believed to total at least a million, with the majority based in and around London. In 2013 the Labour Force Survey recorded 723,000 A8 citizens as being employed in Britain (Migration Observatory, 2015). Statistics for the same year also showed that the majority of foreign workers were concentrated in London; 45 per cent of all self-employed and one-third of all employed were working in the capital (Migration Observatory, 2015). A more recent report estimated that 1,079 million foreigners were employed in the Greater London area (Salt, 2014: 51), and that, 'At least half of the French, Italians, Dutch, Greeks, Bulgarians, Romanians, Other Europeans, West Indians, Other Americans and Australians are located in London. For several other nationalities, the proportion is over 40 per cent' (Salt, 2014: 52). A health warning – a number of the chapters in this book have incorporated the most recent available data on the migrant presence in London. However, we know that these statistics are not finite.[1] Migrant arrivals and departures are a weekly occurrence and what may be reported at the end of 2014, might/will have changed by the time this volume has been published.

As the previous chapters have so clearly underlined, the composition of the capital's migrant population, and particularly its workforce, is super-diverse, ranging from high-powered, highly paid bankers, lawyers and other professionals, through to cleaners, market stall owners, restaurant and cafe workers, builders and child carers. As Parvati Nair comments in her chapter, without the contribution of migrant workers at all levels of the capital's infra-structure, London would 'fail to progress'; indeed this could be taken further, to the point where if the migrant workforce were suddenly removed from the capital, London would come to a standstill.

Though the annual volume of immigrants to the UK over the past few years has varied, London's magnetism has remained steady, drawing migrants from all around the globe to its 32 boroughs.[2] Some seek security from persecution, others the chance to build up financial resources in order to return home as rich men/women; still others are part of the new caravan of global nomads, moving from country to country, continent to continent until a point at which they are unsure as to where – or when – was home. These people inhabit the London thoroughfares. Yet though all of them are on view, and many have appeared in the preceding chapters, their 'visibility' varies. A report published in 2009 reported that there were at least 442,000 illegal immigrants in London, representing some 70 per cent of the national total (Somerville, Sriskandarajah and Laterre, 2009.) Some of these are Tendayi Bloom's ghosts, others Cathy McIlwaine's Latin American irregulars and/or illegals; others brought out of the shadows by John Eade's ethnic authors who have cast light – not always favourable – on migrants who have become rooted in London's soil. Bronwen Walter has told us of others, members of the long settled Irish community, who have dropped below the parapet, neglected and forgotten by those who should have been, in Ireland and in London, responsible for their wellbeing. Then there are the confidently visible, successful transnational entrepreneurs and wealthy Russians and Chinese investing in high-priced London properties. Finally, there is a third category, those who slip in and out of 'visibility' dependent on time, place and need.

---

1   Nor can they be taken as exact and allowance must be made for those who have not been recorded.

2   Thirty-three if the City of London is included.

Yet, sight is not the only sense by which we recognise the presence of the other. A visit to one of the thriving and expanding ethnic marketplaces as described by Laura Vaughan, to the Latin American festivals that feature in Cathy McIlwaine's chapter, or a walk down Monica Ali's *Brick Lane*, will alert the olfactory and auditory senses to smells and sounds which are at once exotic and alien, and yet which are taking their place in the capital's cultural landscape.

London is a leading commercial, cultural and financial centre and as such it has been, and remains, a beacon for migrants the world over. Current (March 2015) debates amongst the political parties centre on how to accommodate those migrants already here and those intending to come. In the case of the former, as Michael Keating, Veronica White and Jane Anderson all emphasise, there is an urgent need for local and national government to guarantee that the migrant presence is acknowledged and provided for in their policies, and that the variations of *diversity* are understood – the nature of the capital inexorably changes as incomers, old and new, become a part of its landscape.

As this book goes to press the 2015 General Election looms. Immigration is one of the major issues for the electorate, be it overtly in the visibility and audibility of the other, or more covertly as hospitals and homes become more crowded, and job opportunities would seem to lessen. All the political parties accept the need to address the 'immigration issue'; the minor parties putting forward policies ranging from the extreme to the sympathetic whilst the two major parties, when not each blaming the other for the increased migrant presence, have some draconian measures in mind. The Conservatives – not having achieved their promise to reduce immigrant numbers to tens of thousands – are advocating a clamp down across the board on migrant benefits and an extension to four years before in-work benefits could be claimed. The Labour Party promises tighter boarder controls, two year residency before benefit claims and stricter language requirements (*The Telegraph*, 2015). These are the overt policy statements, but the voting public will also want to know how the parties intend to deal with the migrant impact on housing, jobs and the National Health Service. Whatever the promises, whatever the outcomes, one thing is clear: London's migrant landscape will not remain static; immigrants will continue to come and stay and come and go, ensuring that the capital's migrant population will remain super-diverse and a continuing topic for research and debate.

References

<http://news.bbc.co.uk/1/hi/uk_politics/7737490.stm> accessed 9 March 2015.
<http://www.migrationobservatory.ox.ac.uk/briefings/migration-flows-a8-and-other-eu-migrants-and-uk> accessed 10 March 2015.
<http://www.migrationobservatory.ox.ac.uk/briefings/migrants-uk-labour-market-overview> accessed 10 March 2015.
<http://www.migrationwatchuk.org/faq> accessed 17 March 2015.

Salt J. (2014), International Migration and the UK. Annual Report of the UK SOPEMI Correspondent to the OECD. London, Migration Research Unit UCL.

Somerville, W., Sriskadarajah, D. and Laterre, M. (2009), 'UK: A Reluctant Country of Immigration', Migration Policy Institute. <www.migrationpolicy. org/article/united-kingdom-reluctant-country-immigration> accessed 14 March 2015.

The Telegraph <http://www.telegraph.co.uk/news/general-election-2015/11451936/ General-Election-2015-Immigration-policy.html> accessed 16 March 2015.

Index

Universal Declaration of Human Rights
  (UDHR) 88
Upton Park 41
Uruguay 170

Vertovec, S. 2, 3, 6, 13
Vietnamese 4, 28, 30

Waltham Forest, London Borough of 15,
  17, 194
Walworth Road 42, 50
Wandsworth, London Borough of 16–17

Wapping 138
Webb, B. 114
Welfare Reform Taskforce, Enfield 62
Wessendorf, S. 4, 28–30, 40n3, 43, 49
Westminster, London Borough of 2
Whitechapel 21, 69, 127, 189, 198
Wiltshire County Council 72
Willesden 173
Wirth, L. 46
World Health Organisation (WHO) 194

ZUS (Polish Inland Revenue) 158, 159